STRESS DISORDERS AMONG
VIETNAM VETERANS

Brunner/Mazel Psychosocial Stress Series Volume I

Stress Disorders Among Vietnam Veterans

Theory, Research and Treatment

Edited by

CHARLES R. FIGLEY, Ph.D.

Purdue University

BRUNNER/MAZEL, Publishers • New York

Fourth Printing

Library of Congress Cataloging in Publication Data

Main entry until title:
Stress disorders among Vietnam veterans.

Bibliography: p.
1. War neurosis.   2. Vietnamese Conflict, 1961-1975—Psychological aspects.
3. Veterans—Medical care—United States.   I. Figley, Charles R., 1944-
RC550.S75   616.8'521   77-94734
ISBN 0-87630-164-2

Published by
BRUNNER/MAZEL, INC.
19 Union Square, New York, New York 10003

To

MAX CLELAND

*who typifies the enthusiasm,
commitment and unsung courage
of the Vietnam veteran*

FOREWORD

The Vietnam war was unique. There have been unpopular wars before, but never a war in which, despite the opposition and the nightly confrontation with the reality of combat on the television screens of America, a nation has managed to stay so fundamentally detached and so engrossed in maintaining a posture of business as usual. More than two and a half million Americans served in Vietnam; yet in many ways it is as though they never went, because America did not want to notice they had been gone. Young men who felt they had been to the brink of hell, not to mention those who were permanently maimed, returned to this country, at worst to find their sacrifice hostilely repudiated, and at best treated with apathy.

Similarly, the conduct of the war itself was different from that of any previous conflict. Characterized by some as the first "air conditioned war," it juxtaposed brief periods of intense combat with a relaxed, often luxurious existence in the major cities of South Vietnam. It was a guerrilla war with, for the most part, no fixed battle lines. With rare exceptions, there were not the protracted artillery duels or the aerial bombardments of American troops that characterized the two World Wars and Korea. Perhaps most important of all was the predetermined one-year tour of duty in the combat zone. The G.I. in Vietnam knew that if he could merely survive for 12 months his removal from combat was assured. There was not the same sense of hopelessness that prevailed in previous conflicts where death, injury, or peace became the only possible ways in which the soldier could find himself extricated from the battlefront. At the same time, the sophistication of our leadership in preventing combat psychiatric casualties was immeasurably greater than it had been in previous wars. Adequate training, equipment, leadership, and medical evacuation all helped to keep morale high, particularly during the earlier years of the war, and reduced susceptibility to combat stress. In addition, an effort was made to provide immediate

vii

withdrawal to secure areas for rest and physical recuperation for those engaged in episodes of unusually prolonged and intensive combat.

The clear result during the early years of the war was an incidence of psychiatric casualties in Vietnam that was as low as or lower than in a comparable stateside force. What was not immediately apparent was that this relatively low rate of psychiatric casualties in the combat zone was more than offset by an exceptionally high degree of adjustment problems once the veteran returned to the States. The one-year tour proved to be a double-edged sword. It allowed the soldier with problems to hold out for the duration of his year in Vietnam with the hope that, if he could survive and get back to the States, those problems would resolve. Too often they not only were not resolved, but were exacerbated back in this country, and the psychological breakdown that might have occurred in Vietnam had there not been a one-year tour was, instead, deferred to become a post-Vietnam casualty. The one-year tour was paid for in other ways. Men rotating on individual schedules lacked the emotional support they might have received if they had returned with other members of their units. They also did not return victorious at the successful conclusion of a popular war as their fathers had done after World War II, but instead were too often faced with resentment and blame for this unpopular war over which they personally had no control.

In the later years of the war there was a breakdown in many of the elements that had protected the psychic stability of G.I.s in the earlier years. Morale declined and combat increasingly took on a more traditional mold. A steadily increasing percentage of soldiers returned for more than the one-year tour. Not surprisingly, the incidence of psychiatric casualties steadily went up. Disillusionment with the war mushroomed in the United States, while there was a corresponding dissipation of morale in Vietnam which at times came close to mutiny, with increasingly frequent reports of "fragging" of officers by enlisted men. There was also an explosion of heroin use, resulting in addiction levels as high as 100 percent in some units. Even more vocal opposition to the War and increasingly open resentment in the United States made the return more difficult for the G.I. who may have gone to Vietnam reluctantly to begin with. Many employers declined to hire Vietnam veterans, partly because of the unpopular nature of the war they had been involved in and also, as publicity about drug use increased, for fear they would be hiring addicts.

The magnitude of the adjustment problems were extraordinary. Yet, early reports that combat psychiatric casualties in Vietnam were low tended to make health professionals as well as policy makers discount the need for any special services for Vietnam veterans. However, the evidence of their extraordinary problems continued to mount. Not only was a specific clinical picture identified and labeled "the post Vietnam Syndrome," but the incidence of suicide and homicide among veterans climbed dramatically. In time it became clear that Vietnam veterans were grossly overrepresented in unemployment statistics and, eventually, among prison populations.

When they turned for help, the Vietnam veterans found little solace. Most psychiatrists and psychologists had little understanding of combat or the Vietnam experience and in large percentage were hostile to the war. For the most part, these professionals had little empathy. At the Veterans Administration the young Vietnam era veteran found the system still geared to an earlier generation. It was a system that was supposed to take care of them, but rejected them in every possible way. Sometimes the rejection was conscious and deliberate, but mostly it was due to an inability to relate to the special demands and unique needs of this new generation of combat veterans. The V.A. really saw itself as an appendage of World War II. It had barely accommodated to Korea, but the notion that there was a new war and that they had an equal responsibility for these new veterans was almost impossible for this inflexible system to deal with.

This book represents a unique accomplishment in pulling together in one place the broadest collection of material yet published on the psychological problems of veterans of the Vietnam war. It will provide not only an important historical document, but an invaluable resource in detailing many of the issues which I have outlined above. This book should lay to rest many of the misconceptions about the Vietnam Veteran.

The book is dedicated to Max Cleland, himself a Vietnam Veteran, and also the newly appointed Administrator of the Veterans Administration. His appointment marks a new era in the government's acceptance of its responsibility for the Vietnam Veteran. At last there is recognition of the debt owed to the Vietnam era veteran and of the government's obligation to provide him the long overdue help he deserves.

PETER G. BOURNE, M.D.

CONTENTS

xi

INTRODUCTION

The role of overt American intervention in Vietnam was finally terminated March 25, 1973 with the American evacuation from Saigon. Thus ended one of the most costly wars in American history, engaging over eight and one-half million men and women in the armed services during this country's involvement. Over seven million of these men and women returned to civilian life, including almost three million who survived a tour of duty in Southeast Asia. Fifty-six thousand died there. The theme of the present volume is the concept that *the war is not over for thousands of men who served their country during the Vietnam war*. The papers which follow address the human costs of war, not in terms of deaths, but in terms of psychological debilitation resulting from war-related experiences.

OBJECTIVES OF THE VOLUME

This volume is the first comprehensive report of the long-term psychosocial effects of Vietnam on those Americans who fought there. Certainly the seminal works of Peter Bourne in his collection, *The Psychology and Physiology of Stress* (1969), and his monograph, *Men, Stress and Vietnam* (1970), served as important starting points. In both books Bourne focused on the soldiers who appeared to cope successfully with combat as well as those who did not. Bourne attempted, at the same time, to serve science through scientific inquiry rather than promoting a particular political or philosophical point of view. Our attempt here is to center on the controversy surrounding the nature of combat stress, particularly the long-term consequences.

The specific objectives of the volume are six-fold: *First,* to define the construct of combat-related stress disorders, particularly as it relates to chronic combat stress reactions among Vietnam veterans. Chapter 1 by

Kormos provides an historical and conceptual groundwork for the explication of combat-related stress disorders which will be developed in more detail throughout Section I.

The *second* objective of the collection is to identify the theoretical and clinical importance of the disorders to mental health professionals, particularly to those working with patients suffering from stressful, catastrophic experiences like combat. Soon the American Psychiatric Association will promulgate the third revision of the *Diagnostic and Statistical Manual* (DSM III). More than any other single reference, the DSM is *the* source for psychiatric nomenclature in this country. The new revision should have profound effects on the entire mental health field. It will reflect the most recent conceptualizations in the diagnosis and treatment of mental illness. Thus, it is particularly important and noteworthy that a separate category on *stress disorders* will be included in DSM III. This new category was developed as a result of the work of many professionals in a variety of disciplines, researchers as well as clinicians. It is our hope that the present volume will provide insight into the theory, research, and treatment of stress disorders by both documenting and supplementing the categories promulgated by the DSM III.

The *third* major objective is to provide a full explication of the central thesis of the volume, that the residue of combat stress transcends time and situation. Beginning with the first section and continuing throughout the volume, we will attempt to specify the conditions under which the original stress occurs, as well as its immediate and long-term effects occurring in concert with a host of psychological, physiological, and sociological factors.

The *fourth* objective of the book centers on the question: Why is so little known about the long-term effects of catastrophic experience like combat? Among the very few studies which have attempted to follow combatants of the Second World War (e.g., Archibald, Long & Miller, 1962; Archibald & Tuddenham, 1965; Brill & Beebe, 1955; Dobbs & Wilson, 1960; Futterman & Pumpian-Mindlin, 1951), findings are both striking and consistent: The war was not over for a significant percentage of the men studied. Part of the reason may be professional territoriality. As will be seen later, combat stress is primarily within the domain of military psychiatry, and the military is clearly not interested in post-service adjustment. In addition, the Veterans Administration appears to be oblivious to the role of combat-related stress since few of their clinics and hospitals routinely screen their patients regarding their combat experiences (see Chapter 12 by Haley). Thus, very few professionals or fields of study have a particular interest in the long-term effects of combat-related stress, a central thrust of this volume.

Fifth, the present volume, beyond the theoretical and empirical explanations, provides specific clinical guidelines for working with veterans, including veterans suffering from combat-related stress disorders. Section III on *Treatment Implications* is devoted entirely to treatment issues. Other chapters throughout the book directly or indirectly discuss clinical diagnosis and treatment. A quick perusal of the background information on the contributors will show that most are clinicians involved in direct services within the mental health professions.

Finally, the volume is devoted to expanding the knowledge-base of combat-related stress disorders in particular and the psychosocial adjustment of veterans in general. Collectively the contributors address all of the major issues associated with military service, the combat milieu, and post-military service adjustment in an attempt to advance the field of veteran studies and to provide useful resources for others to build upon.

THE NATURE OF COMBAT STRESS

Although the major focus of the book is on the long-term consequences of combat-related stress, it is important to view briefly the dynamics of combat and the degree to which combatants were able to cope psychologically. The chapter to follow by Kormos provides a comprehensive review of combat psychopathology. Following is a brief overview.

Early Formulations

Aside from some clinical observations from earlier wars (Hammond, 1883), combat psychiatry in general and the diagnosis of various combat-related stress disorders in particular are of relatively recent origin (Glass, 1969). Prior to the First World War, psychological casualties resulting from war were seen simply as weak, lacking military discipline, or both. One of the earliest psychopathologies related to combat was believed to be a psychological manifestation of artillery fire—both sending and receiving. Soldiers diagnosed as "shell shocked" were believed to be suffering from some kind of brain damage resulting from the air blasts of high explosives which left these men dazed and confused. According to Glass (1969), by 1916 the Allied Medical Services believed that "shell shocked" soldiers were suffering from a psychological disorder. According to a recent review (Freedman, Kaplan, & Sadock, 1972), the "shell shocked" combatant displayed one or more of the following symptoms: paralysis, pseudoconfusion, blindness, hypochondriacal, phobic or anxiety symptoms, freezing, catatonic-like stupor, running amok, irritability, overwhelming depression, startle reaction to noises, somatic symptoms, gross tremors, restlessness, insomnia, nightmares, or repetitive battle dream (Brill & Beebe, 1955; Grinker & Spiegel, 1945; Menninger, 1948; Nefzger, 1970).

Following the First World War large numbers of men were treated for combat-related stress disorders which, no doubt, facilitated more sophisticated and detailed nosology. Thus, chronic residual syndromes associated with combat became known as "war neuroses" or "traumatic neuroses" and were categorized as psychoneurosis (Glass, 1969). According to Glass, however, it was the prevailing opinion that, although precipitated by combat, the disorder was a result of predisposing character or personality defects. Thus, the issue of premorbid personality type, pre-military service factors, and other idiosyncratic terms began to appear in the literature, which had the effect of dismissing the traumatic effects of battle and other catastrophic experiences.

Research, writing and psychiatric categorization associated with war increased sharply as a result of the Second World War. Perhaps partly because of the classifications of combat-related stress disorders, neuropsychiatric admission rates were quite high in the various war theaters (see Chapter 1 for a detailed discussion). According to Appel (1966), for example, annual admission rates for combat divisions serving the European Theater were approximately 25 percent, although for infantry battalions, characteristically exposed to the greatest amounts of combat, rates were 20 percent. These rates appeared to be even higher in the Southwestern Pacific Theater. Menninger (1948) and Craighill (1966) believe that the Pacific Theater was stressful, not only because of the battle conditions, but also because of the location. The heat, lack of recreation, excessive physical demands, tropical diseases, isolation, monotony and other discomforts served as additional sources of stress. Such conditions were quite similar to those in Southeast Asia.

In all wars fought by Americans, predispositional factors were assumed to account for most psychiatric war casualties. The Second World War was no exception. The incidence of these disorders, however, had increased 300 percent over the previous world war, even though the pre-induction psychiatric rejection rate was three to four times higher during the Second as compared to the First World War (Bulletin of the U.S. Army Medical Department, 1943). Various terms were adopted to describe these psychiatric casualties.

Early in World War II, for example, "psycho," short for psychopathology, was used. Later the U.S. Army commander in Tunisia ordered that all psychiatric disorders in the combat zone—regardless of the manifestations—would be known as "exhaustion." This move appeared to be a tactic to disregard the mentally debilitating potential of battle for the sake of parsimony. Hanson (1949), however, felt that the term "exhaustion" more accurately described the disorder, and that physical fatigue played an important role in psychiatric breakdown and recovery.

Glass (1957) has observed that unless the specific circumstances under which psychiatric casualties were diagnosed and evacuated are known, low neuropsychiatric casualty rates in combat should be regarded with skepticism. In the case of the Second World War, for example, the stigma of mental illness in concert with neuropsychiatric ratings being associated with ineffective commanders and low unit morale no doubt substantially lowered the official diagnosis of neuropsychiatric fatigue.

Conceptually, what emerged from the Korean War was the distinction of "combat exhaustion" as separate from exhaustion due to physical fatigue. The Department of the Navy, which served both the Navy and Marine troops, adopted the term "combat fatigue" to designate essentially the same category of symptoms described by the terms it replaced. The lower combat-related psychiatric casualty rates in Korea were credited to the rotation policy of nine-month maximum in combat (Glass, 1957).

During the Korean War, the original Diagnostic and Statistical Manual (DSM I) was developed and promulgated (1952). This new manual delineated an extensive class of "gross stress reactions" defined as "situations in which the individual . . . [had] . . . been exposed to severe physical demands or extreme emotional stress," including combat situations.

Unfortunately, the revised manual (DSM II), promulgated in 1968, dropped the gross stress category, replacing it with a vague category, "(Transient) Adjustment Reactions of Adult Life." Combat-related stress is mentioned in DSM II only in the brief explication and illustration of "Adult Adjustment Reaction": "fear associated with military combat and manifested by trembling, running and hiding" (DSM II, 1968), hardly an adequate description.

It is interesting that no war existed between the promulgation of the DSM I and the formative stages of development of DSM II (1964-1965), although the Vietnam conflict was beginning to heat up. It is not unreasonable to assume that combat-related stress reactions were ignored as war veterans of the Korean and the two World Wars were assimilated into mainstream America. In contrast, the development of the DSM III has apparently incorporated the recent research and clinical findings related to the Vietnam veterans' post-combat adjustment.

Current Status of Stress Disorders

As noted earlier, the DSM III will be promulgated soon and will include a separate category on stress disorders (Section XI). To date the special task force of the American Psychiatric Association (Task Force on Nomenclature and Statistics, 1976, p. 56) has proposed the following classification of stress disorders within Section XI:

298.1   Brief Situational Psychotic Disorder
308.30 Brief Situational Nonpsychotic Disorder
308.31 Acute Catastrophic Stress Disorder
308.32 Chronic Catastrophic Stress Disorder

The latter two disorders are particularly relevant to combat-related stress reactions and will be discussed in some detail later. Brief situational psychosis, most often referred to as an hysterical psychosis, is generally a floridly psychotic reaction of rather brief duration. The illness begins quite suddenly, without prodromal symptoms, as a result of some event the patient found extremely upsetting (e.g., death of a loved one, auto accident). Similarly, brief situational nonpsychotic disorder is operative within the same situation, but the patient's behavior is not as acute and is well within the normal range of reactions (non-hysterical).

No one is certain about the specific subcategories and associative discussions which will be included in the DSM III at the time of this writing. At the 1977 annual meeting of the American Psychiatric Association, however, a paper was presented (Shatan, Haley, & Smith, 1977) which made several specific recommendations to the special DSM III Task Force regarding combat-related stress disorder categorization within the new manual. The paper represented over seven years of work by the Vietnam Veterans Working Group (VVWG) beginning with their contact with veterans through the Vietnam Vet Rap Groups (see Chapters 3 and 10) between 1970 and 1974. It appears that the Special Task Force will adopt their recommendations.

The VVWG has proposed the following text within the Stress Disorders section of DSM III (Shatan *et al.*, 1977, p. 4):

298.1   Brief Situational Psychotic Disorder
308.30 Brief Situational Nonpsychotic Disorder
308.31 Acute Catastrophic Stress Disorder (ACSD). Specify stress

as (a) "natural" disaster (e.g., flood, tidal wave, fire) or (b) "social" catastrophe (e.g., combat, concentration camp (KZ), hijacking)

308.32 Chronic Catastrophic Stress Disorder (CCSD). Specify stress as in 308.31 (a) and (b)

308.33 Delayed Catastrophic Stress Disorder (DCSD). Following symptom-free interval ("incubation period"), specify stress as (a) Acute (e.g., Post-KZ, post-combat, post-hijacking) or (b) Chronic.

Briefly, catastrophic stress disorders denote reactions to events (e.g., tidal waves, flash floods, forest fires, concentration camp internment, combat) affecting a community or group of people including, for example, a family. The flood in Johnstown, Pennsylvania, in the summer of 1977 and the fire at the Beverly Hills Supper Club in Kentucky are illustrations of catastrophic disasters which breed the stress manifested by suicides, alcoholism, drug abuse, family violence and other reactions. Mental health crisis teams have characterized these reactions as the "after-the-deluge blues."

Acute catastrophic stress disorder is the immediate reaction to the disaster and brief in duration. Similarly, chronic catastrophic stress disorder is a reaction to disaster, but over a long period of time.

Delayed catastrophic stress disorder includes an immediate reaction, often rather brief in duration and mild in intensity. After a "latency" or "incubation" period, however, the disaster-associated stress is re-experienced. A more extended explication of this category will be discussed later with regard to Vietnam combat veterans. Because the suggested nosology has not been officially incorporated within the DSM III, detailed discussions of the specifics of the disorders would be meaningless. What is important, however, is the recognition of the occurrence of catastrophic stress in delayed as well as acute and chronic forms and the validation of the observations of a large number of clinicians in the mental health fields who are convinced that traumatic events, including combat, cause stress reactions which transcend time, situation and predisposition. Chapters by Lifton (Chapter 10) and Horowitz and Solomon (Chapter 13) discuss the delayed stress reactions in greater detail.

THE NATURE OF COMBAT IN VIETNAM

There are numerous accounts of the peculiar characteristics of the war in Southeast Asia in both the professional literature (e.g., Bourne, 1969; 1970; Sanford & Comstock, 1971; Helmer, 1974; Starr, 1973; Lifton,

1973a) and popular publications (e.g., Polner, 1971; Levy, 1971a; Linden, 1972). It is not the purpose of this chapter to describe exhaustively the various facets of the war which affected the soldier's reaction to it. The reader is encouraged to seek other sources as noted above for a more detailed discussion, including Chapter 3 of this volume. Following is an attempt to capture the essential dynamics of the war environment to allow the reader to appreciate better the stress disorders which evolved from it.

Based on his observations during the Second World War, Edwin Weinstein suggested that combat-induced neurosis is largely associated with the disruption of the combatant's interpersonal relationships. "The nature of modern warfare," notes Weinstein (1974, p. 309), "is such that in order to survive in combat, the soldier must function as part of a group, and his resistance to the trauma of combat will vary with the ability to integrate himself with the group." This, in concert with the personality make-up of the combatants within the group, appears to account for much of the trauma associated with combat (e.g., Weinstein, 1974; Menninger, 1947; Stouffer, 1949; Grinker & Spiegel, 1945). Further, Weinstein (1974) found that more breakdowns occurred in newly and hastily formed combat units and that replacements, particularly those new to the combat scene, were especially vulnerable. Tischler (1969) found that half of the soldiers referred for neuropsychiatric evaluation/treatment had been in the combat zone for less than four months. Attrition fell off markedly after the third month, but rose again after the ninth month and then slowly subsided again.

In Vietnam, in contrast to the two world wars, unit integrity was scant. After military units had arrived in Vietnam, their reinforcements and replacements arrived individually. After arrival in Vietnam, most often by air, the incoming combatant was viewed as a "new guy," a "boot" who was automatically mistrusted (Bey, 1972) because he might make a mistake that would endanger the lives of the others. Once established in the combat unit, the combatant quickly learned that there were no "front lines" in guerrilla warfare. "Search and destroy" missions meant leaving the garrison to take a specific military objective, perhaps the same hill taken last month, then returning to the base camp. These and other factors jeopardized individual and unit morale.

Another interpersonal element affecting the combat experience was thoughts about home. As will be noted in Chapter 5 by Figley, millions of veteran family members were affected by the war. Many combatants felt guilty and helpless because their families needed them. Certainly

many men received the proverbial "Dear John" letter, which was particularly prevalent during this war (Tanay, 1976) and led to acts of
unestimable violence. Chapter 9 by Hunter stresses the significant impact of the war on the family system.

THE HOMECOMING

Just as he arrived alone in the war zone, the soldier returned home
individually, without his unit, after his year-long tour of duty in Vietnam. This end of one experience and beginning of another for the
Vietnam veteran is cogently captured by Stanton (1970b):

> . . . You might expect that his flight back to the States would be
> a jubilant affair filled with boisterous joking, raucous laughter and
> other forms of tension release. This is frequently not the case, how-
> ever. He is too preoccupied with fears and unknowns to be jovial.
> At some level of consciousness he may be wondering whether he can
> muster up his old defenses in order to make it back in "the world."
> He wonders whether he will still feel the same towards his loved
> ones and how they feel toward him. For some time now he has been
> working through the problems of separation from his buddies, and
> he questions which parts of the past year can he forget and which
> parts should he forget. . . . He may show startle responses to sudden
> loud noises, even to the extent of hitting the dirt when an auto-
> mobile backfires. . . . It is not uncommon for the returnee to want
> to almost completely withdraw from social contacts and become se-
> clusive. He may feel ill at ease with old friends because he no longer
> has common ground on which to relate to them. He has been out of
> touch with stateside life on the one hand and finds it difficult to
> relate or describe his own experiences on the other. In some ways
> he feels older and wiser, and he has learned to take nothing for
> granted (pp. 36-37).

Certainly the unpopularity of the war made the homecoming less than
joyful, and no doubt frustrated and embittered many Vietnam veterans,
making their post-service adjustment even more difficult.

Borus (1976) has observed that several important axioms evolved
from the experiences of other wars regarding strategies for facilitating
the veteran's homecoming and transition from the battle zone. They included the following: (1) helpfulness of gradual rather than precipitous
transition from combat to noncombat status; (2) need to re-orient combatants to different roles and routines stateside; (3) the need for formal
and ceremonious acknowledgment to the soldier and his significant others
of his change in status; (4) the helpfulness of the immediate group or

small unit in sharing experiences and facilitating readjustment; (5) the need to prepare and forewarn the veterans of the new stresses associated with this transition; (6) the need to make the continuing noncombat role meaningful to the veteran. As Borus documents in his research, none of the above was provided for the soldiers he studied (all of whom were still in the military). Also, no semblance of orientation was provided for the thousands who were released from the military immediately upon arrival in the United States.

Checking the list provided by Borus, we find that for the Vietnam veteran, (1) the transition from foxhole to home was abrupt, (2) once returned, veterans were rarely helped to make the adjustments to new roles and routines stateside, (3) as far as "ceremonious acknowledgment" of his service in Vietnam is concerned, it was either nil or negative. As one combatant stated to the author, "The first day home I was called a 'baby killer' by my kid brother and the 'bunch who lost the war' by some drunk down at the VFW." They were often loathed by both the "hawks" and the "doves." (4) The "helpfulness of the immediate group/unit" was not available. Unlike the Second World War veteran who returned in troop ships with his buddies, allowing several weeks in which to help each other by working through their war experiences, the Vietnam veteran left his comrades in the combat zone, flying home alone. (5) Rarely were veterans alerted to the potential post-military stresses they might encounter except for passing mention of their VA benefits. (6) Similarly, the returning combatants were left on their own to salvage some meaning from the war and their involvement in it.

In the chapters to follow, the authors attempt to deal with a wide range of issues and factors affecting the Vietnam veteran's post-military adjustment within the context outlined above. Following Kormos' extensive review (Chapter 1) and DeFazio's original conceptualizations (Chapter 2), Shatan attempts to explicate the parameters of the Vietnam war from the point of view of the individual soldier during and after combat. Particularly important is Shatan's analysis of the sanctions for violence in the combat zone and the inevitable emotional toll that this entails.

Complementing the Shatan paper, Chapter 6 by Spilka, Friedman and Rosenberg deals with this emotional toll in terms of the individual combatant's perceptions of death. They report that the expectations of death and the value of life are affected by experiencing death and life-threatening events within the combat zone.

Chapter 4 by Figley provides an overview of research directly or indirectly related to post-military psychosocial adjustment. The remaining papers in Section II focus on various research questions: for example, drug use and abuse (Chapter 5), psychiatric symptoms (Chapters 7 and 9), anomie (Chapter 8) and other post-service adjustments (Chapters 5, 7, 8 and 9). The final chapter of Section II by Hunter (Chapter 9) conceptualizes the Vietnam prisoner of war as a special Vietnam veteran and summarizes a myriad of research findings in terms of the physical, psychological and social costs of war internment. Overall, the various results of the POW research show that years after returning home, the emotional residue of the war in general and the incarceration experiences in particular are still existent among most POWs.

Following these Sections on Theory and Research, Section III presents five chapters by and for psychotherapists. Chapters 10 by Lifton addresses several important issues related to psychotherapy generally. Lifton describes his unique approach to treating Vietnam veterans through the processes of confrontation, reordering, and renewal. This approach is discussed briefly but extended considerably by Egendorf (Chapter 11) and Haley (Chapter 12). Horowitz and Solomon (Chapter 13) note their concern about large numbers of Vietnam combat veterans who will need mental health treatment in the near future due to the delayed nature of the combat-related syndrome. They describe both the nature and treatment of this syndrome. The final chapter of the Section, Chapter 14 by Stanton and Figley, suggests that symptoms associated with combat-related stress disorders may be both a reaction to more recent events and a manifestation of an ongoing family process.

CONCLUSION

There is no doubt that the Vietnam war is unique in recent history in terms of its duration, the political and philosophical opposition at home, the unconventional nature of the fighting, and the racial, economic and political climate existing in the country when the veteran returned. The final chapter by Seymour Leventman, a sociologist, expands on this social milieu theme. Leventman makes a particularly cogent observation regarding certain clinical reports that have emerged regarding the Vietnam veteran's post-military psychiatric profile. He suggests that these reports have, perhaps, done more harm than good. Prepared to inform professionals and, indirectly, the general public about the psychiatric casualties of the Vietnam war, psychotherapists' reports were interpreted by the media to describe *all* Vietnam veterans.

Leventman's observations should serve as an important caveat for all of us, writers as well as readers. All war veterans are *not* permanently damaged emotionally by their military experiences inside and outside the combat theater. At the same time, however, those who *do* carry the emotional wounds of war must be understood and helped. Veteran specialists—researchers as well as clinicians—are often caught in a difficult and frustrating position. The critical needs of the Vietnam veterans are clearly apparent on the one hand, the widespread disinterest of the country on the other. Those of us who work with veterans learn very quickly that the only way to get action (e.g., legislation, research funding, new programs) is to emphasize the unmet needs and problems of the Vietnam veteran. As observed in Chapter 15, the popular media have consistently presented an unflattering stereotype of the Vietnam veteran (e. g., dope fiend, radical, violent murderer, psycho). Thus, in an attempt to generate more interest in the Vietnam veteran, we often reinforce and perpetuate the very stereotypes which partly account for the problems.

This volume attempts to avoid sensationalism and does not overstate the emotional residue of the Vietnam war. The contributors reject the notion that all or even a large percentage of Vietnam veterans are psychiatric casualties of war. We believe that no one factor accounts for either immediate or long-term effects of combat stress. Likewise, no single agency or branch of government—including the Veterans Administration—should be accused of failing the Vietnam veteran. In many ways all of us, individually and collectively, have failed the Vietnam veteran. At the same time, however, the contributors to this volume are concerned about the lack of attention to the plight of those men who *are* emotionally scarred as a result of serving their country in Vietnam—regardless of their numbers. We are concerned about the paucity of research and theoretical development in the veteran studies field in general and the nature and consequences of combat-related stress in particular. The acute lack of therapists trained to work with victims of catastrophic stress, including, but not limited to, war combatants, is, we feel, a result of this. We are concerned about the lack of interest in Vietnam veterans on the part of the public and on the part of those in government who represent them, resulting in poor, underfunded research and treatment programs for these veterans. We hope that this volume will help correct these deficits without reinforcing unfortunate stereotypes associated with the Vietnam veteran.

ACKNOWLEDGMENTS

So many people have played a part in bringing this volume to fruition that any attempt at formal acknowledgments would be dubious at best and, at worst, hazardous to interpersonal relationships. With some trepidation, however, I will proceed. This book is dedicated to Max Cleland, Administrator of Veterans Affairs, who has been both a personal and a professional inspiration to me. His perceptions of the psychosocial adjustments of the Vietnam veteran are based on his personal experiences as a soldier, as a patient in military and VA hospitals, as a member of the Senate Veterans' Affairs Committee and, now, as Administrator of Veterans Affairs. With the appointment of Max Cleland as Administrator, we have the best possible chance of correcting some of the major problems which have limited the study and treatment of the Vietnam veteran.

Another source of inspiration has been my family—my parents, John and Geneva Figley, and my sister, Sandra Elliott. Thanks to their love, respect, and encouragement, I found the strength to endure and deal with my own experiences in Vietnam. My wife and friend, Vickie, has sustained me through this and other challenges, and her excellent editorial skills and practical advice have been invaluable to me.

Clearly, this book would not have been possible without the devoted efforts of the 24 contributors. In addition, these individuals have been a constant source of inspiration and encouragement to me personally.

Numerous individuals have also played significant roles in facilitating the production of this volume, including several faculty and staff members within the Department of Child Development and Family Studies at Purdue University. Jan Roberts was more than my manuscript typist; she corrected my errors, suggested improvements, and maintained our friendship through many retypings. Both as departmental colleagues and friends, Raymond Coward, Donald Felker, Allan Cohen and Douglas Sprenkle have been constant sources of encouragement. Special appreciation goes to my graduate research assistants, William Southerly, Walter Schumm and Nancy Fuhs, for their excellent work. Phillip Metres and Hamilton McCubbin were very helpful, particularly in the early stages of this project, as were Norma Wikler, Paul Camacho, John Helmer, Charles Moskos, Wayne Eisenhart, Stuart Feldman, Rusty Lindley, Ford Kuramoto, Lee Robins, Paul Starr, Charles Stenger, Herbert Stern, David Mantell, Shad Meshad and Leonard Neff. The Society for the Psychological Study of Social Issues donated the reprint costs of the Horowitz and Solomon chapter (Chapter 13) in recognition that all profits will go to the Consortium on Veteran Studies.

In the latter stages of the project, Guy McMichaels, Timothy Craig, Dean Phillips, Robert Spanogle, Thomas Haynes, Linda Scroggins, Anne Murry, Jack McCloskey, Sandra Mumford, Phillip Caputo, Kay Deaux, and, especially, John P. Wilson and Susan Fogg have contributed in various ways to this volume.

A special thanks must go to all the Vietnam veterans who have given so much—and survived.

C.R.F.

March, 1978

CONTRIBUTORS

R. HARLAN BRIDENBAUGH, M.D.

Director of Psychiatric Research, Department of Psychiatry and Neurology, Walter Reed Army Medical Center, Washington, D.C.

VICTOR J. DeFAZIO, Ph.D.

Director of Counseling Services at Queensboro Community College, New York, and clinical psychologist in private practice.

ARTHUR EGENDORF, Ph.D.

Research associate at the Center for Policy Research in New York City; faculty member, Department of Psychiatry, Mount Sinai School of Medicine, New York, and clinical psychologist in private practice.

CHARLES R. FIGLEY, Ph.D.

Staff member of the Purdue University Marriage and Family Counseling Center and a member of the faculty of the Department of Child Development and Family Studies at Purdue University; founded and current Director of the Consortium on Veterans Studies.

LISA FRIEDMAN

Student in the Department of Psychology at the University of Denver, Denver, Colorado.

SARAH A. HALEY, M.S.W.

Supervisory Social Worker at the Mental Health Clinic, Veterans Administration Outpatient Clinic in Boston; a member of the Vietnam Veterans' Working Group which has assisted in the revision of the current Diagnostic and Statistical Manual of the American Psychiatric Association.

MARDI J. HOROWITZ, M.D.

Professor of Psychiatry in the School of Medicine at the University of California, San Francisco; author of *Stress Response Syndromes.*

EDNA J. HUNTER, PH.D.

Chief of the Family Studies Section in the Center for POW Studies and Assistant Director of the Center which is part of the Naval Health Research Center in San Diego; co-author of *Families in the Military System.*

HARRY R. KORMOS, M.D.

Assistant Clinical Professor of Psychiatry, University of California at San Francisco; former commander in the Navy's Medical Corps serving as Head of the Acute Psychiatric Unit, Oak Knoll Naval Hospital, Oakland, California and Assistant Chief, Department of Psychiatry at the San Francisco VA Hospital.

SEYMOUR LEVENTMAN, PH.D.

Professor of Sociology at Boston College; coordinator of a research consortium sponsored by the American Sociological Association which is approaching veteran studies as a problem area within the discipline of sociology.

ROBERT JAY LIFTON, M.D.

Professor of Psychiatry in the School of Medicine, Yale University; author of *Home from the War* and co-author of *Crimes of War.*

DAVID M. MANTELL, PH.D.

Staff member of the Elmcrest Family Institute in Portland, Connecticut, and clinical psychologist in private practice; author of *True Americanism: Green Berets and War Resisters, a Study of Commitment.*

ANDREW L. MEYERS, M. Ed.

A member of the faculty at the University of Pennsylvania and a staff member at the Philadelphia Veterans Administration Hospital.

JAMES MINTZ, PH.D.

A member of the faculty at the University of Pennsylvania and a staff member at the Philadelphia Veterans Administration Hospital.

EDGAR P. NACE, M.D.

Director of the Strecker Program for the Treatment of Alcoholism, Pennsylvania Hospital; Assistant Professor in the Department of Psychiatry, University of Pennsylvania.

CHARLES P. O'BRIEN, M.D., PH.D.

Assistant Professor in the Department of Psychiatry, University of Pennsylvania, and a member of the V.A. Hospital staff in Philadelphia.

ROBERT F. PANZARELLA, PH.D.

Assistant Professor in the Department of Psychology at John Jay College, City University of New York Graduate Center.

NORMAN REAM, M.D.

Psychiatric research associate at the Walter Reed Army Institute of Research, Washington, D.C.

DAVID ROSENBERG

Student in the Department of Psychology at the University of Denver, Denver, Colorado.

CHAIM F. SHATAN, M.D.

Training analyst and former Co-director of the New York University Postdoctoral Psychoanalytic Training Clinic; founder and coordinator of the Vietnam Veterans Working Group in liaison with the D.S.M. III Task Force.

GEORGE F. SOLOMON, M.D.

Director of Medical Education with the Fresno (California) Department of Health; Chief of Psychiatry at the Valley Medical Center in Fresno; Clinical Professor of Psychiatry at the Medical Schools of the University of California at San Francisco and Los Angeles.

BERNARD SPILKA, PH.D.

Professor of Psychology, Department of Psychology at the University of Denver.

M. DUNCAN STANTON, PH.D.

Assistant Professor of Psychology in the Department of Psychiatry at the University of Pennsylvania School of Medicine; Director of a family treatment program for drug-addicted veterans at the Philadelphia Child Guidance Clinic.

E. ROBERT WORTHINGTON, PH.D.

Chief, Psychology Service, Brooke Army Medical Center, Fort Sam Houston, Texas; Adjunct Professor at the University of Texas Health Science Center, San Antonio, Texas.

Section I

THEORETICAL ISSUES

This section attempts to identify (a) the etiology of combat-related stress disorders, (b) the contributing factors associated with the initial stress experience, (c) the process by which the initial stress disorder is both delayed and prolonged many years after the experience, and (d) the specific symptoms of the disorder and various modalities for treatment.

The first chapter, by Kormos, attempts to bring conceptual clarity to the area of combat-related stress disorders. Kormos outlines the concept of Acute Combat Reaction which he defines as "behavior by a soldier under conditions of combat, invariably interpreted by those around him as signaling that the soldier, although expected to be a combatant, has ceased to function as such." After outlining the essential elements of psychosocial reactions to combat, he applies these principles to the unique features of combat in Vietnam.

Chapter 2 by Victor DeFazio provides an excellent overview of the various theoretical perspectives of stress disorders related to war and combat. DeFazio attempts to develop a "dynamic" perspective focused on the concept of trauma within a psychoanalytic framework. Theoretical and empirical justification for the perspective is presented along with specific case illustrations.

The final chapter in this section, written by Chaim Shatan, is based on seven years work with Vietnam veterans and almost a lifetime devoted to an understanding of traumatic neurosis. The paper first explores the psychodynamics of combat in Vietnam, particularly the sanctions for violence. The latter part of the paper explicates the six themes associated with what Shatan has called the *Post-Combat Syndrome*.

1

1

THE NATURE OF COMBAT STRESS

HARRY R. KORMOS, M.D.

Introduction

It is customary, when discussing a psychiatric "illness," to begin by giving an accurate description of the symptoms or the clinical picture. This usually means an account of observations of human behavior as it occurred under certain specified conditions, for example environment, characteristics of the population under study, methods of observation. Since the intent is to provide the foundation for all further assertions, it is imperative that maximal clarity be achieved in this initial stage. An accepted way of accomplishing this is to keep the observations as pure as possible, i.e., limited to verifiable perceptions uncontaminated by any prior assumptions. Teleological reasoning is especially to be avoided. The dominant approach in contemporary psychopathology thus follows what is customarily called the scientific or inductive method which establishes a hierarchy among the various assertions made in the course of the study of a phenomenon. In this hierarchy, the material labeled "observations" will occupy the highest place.

The descriptive material is elevated to the rank of "observed fact" and will be expected to form an undisputed basis for the inferences, conclusions, theories and speculations which are so scrupulously avoided in the initial stage. Authors tend to be much more tolerant of criticism aimed at these inferential aspects of their work than they are of challenges to what they consider the well established, initial observations. The latter, as mentioned, are usually assigned the role of "fact" and as such are regarded as entitled to protection from attack. This is not the place to specify the objections against the methodology outlined above;

The author wishes to thank Ms. Rosa Housman for her competent and cordial bibliographic assistance.

it should suffice to mention that dissatisfaction with it is increasing and that this criticism appears to be capable of opening up new paths of inquiry.

Temporarily falling back on basic methodological considerations of the type encountered above will, however, be necessary if an attempt is made to evaluate current knowledge about the phenomenon of "combat stress." Why such a tactical retreat, rather than a frontal attack, is advisable will become clearer if we turn toward the accounts of combat stress given in authoritative textbooks of psychiatry (Arieti, 1966; Freedman, Kaplan & Sadock, 1975; Redlich & Freedman, 1966). What we find in these sources adds up to such a variety of symptoms, syndromes and behaviors, linked with such a multiplicity of explanatory concepts and theories, that any attempt to immediately unify this material is unlikely to succeed. The complexity is indeed such that we are obliged to begin by making the following basic terminological stipulation: For the sake of brevity and with heuristic intent, the designation "Acute Combat Reaction" will from here on be used as a neutral generic. Use of any of the existing terms, such as shellshock, traumatic neurosis, battle fatigue, combat exhaustion, and five-day schizophrenia, would inevitably produce a degree of allegiance to one of the competing schools, thereby defeating the purpose of giving a critical overview. "Acute Combat Reaction" will from now on refer to "all psychopathology associated with combat," without prejudice as to the form or origin of that pathology.

Testimonials to the existing diversity of opinion are easy to provide. Kardiner and Spiegel state: "In the domain of psychopathology the confusion is difficult to describe . . ., in most instances there is no psychopathology at all, only circumstantial explanations . . . each investigator . . . makes his own personal classification . . . this chaotic condition is further confused by the official classification" (Kardiner, 1947). Bond, in his discussion of nomenclature, observes that "an important error was the attempt to express many ideas by one word, such as psychoneurosis. . . . There were at least 60 different expressions of a similar nature, all holding different connotations to different men" (in Mullins, 1973, p. 873). The heterogeneity of symptoms can perhaps best be appreciated by a look at the following (incomplete) compilation. Soldiers have, at different times and in different locations, been diagnosed as suffering from Acute Combat Reaction on the basis of any one or any combination of these symptoms: loss of appetite, irritability, jumpiness, disturbed sleep, gross conversion reactions of various types (e.g., paralyses, blindness, aphonia), disorientation, complete disorganization, confusion, panic, apathy, choreiform movements, tics, stammering, syncopal attacks, delirium, stupor.

THE NATURE OF COMBAT STRESS

Toward the end of Word War II, a commission of prestigious representatives of American psychiatry was appointed to "attempt an evaluation of the psychopathology as observed at the forward echelon, for the purpose of correlating it with established treatment methods" (Bartemeier, 1946). The reason for appointing such a commission was made clear in a letter from the Surgeon General: ". . . it is obvious that the psychiatrists in the army, and particularly the group at the combat level, do not have time and are not necessarily professionally equipped to undertake any such research" (Bartemeier, 1946). It is noteworthy that the report of this high-level commission, written after an extensive tour of the European Theater of War, turned out to be quite tentative. The final conclusion concentrates on what battle fatigue was *not:*

> . . . this picture of psychological disorganization does not correspond, either in its moderate or its extreme form, to any recognized or established psychiatric syndrome . . . it certainly is not merely a state of exhaustion . . . it certainly is not a neurosis in the ordinary sense . . . it certainly cannot be adequately described as anxiety or fear . . . it comes closer to a situation psychosis than anything else but its subsequent clinical course is quite different (p. 422).

The affirmative part of the conclusion is modest: "a temporary psychological disorganization out of which . . . various more definite and more familiar syndromes evolve" (p. 422).

So much for the difficulty in organizing the observations. The diversity in explanatory concepts and proposed etiologies is equally impressive. It is particularly important to note that the disagreement in this area is of a special type: Many of the existing theories do not simply contradict each other; rather they adopt concepts which are almost inherently irreconcilable because they make use of different categories and therefore speak different languages. Unless it is realized that such is the case, the unsuspecting reader is apt to find himself frustrated and confused when attempting to arrive at a working concept of combat stress. The more influential paradigms for the development of an Acute Combat Reaction will be briefly mentioned here to illustrate the above; they will be elaborated upon later.

1. *The illness model.* Latent, or potentially present intrapsychic conflict is (re-)activated by combat experiences. There may or may not have been previous neurotic symptoms. Other forms of pathology can be substituted for "intrapsychic conflict," leaving the illness model intact. Traumatic neurosis is the most commonly used term in this model.

2. *The endurance model.* This represents perhaps the most pragmatic view. It is often summarized by the statement that "everyone has his breaking point." Its application can have a strongly exonerating effect, since neither illness nor strength of character are at issue; endurance, at least in principle, resembles such value-free parameters as height or muscular strength. "Circumstances can become such that traumatic neurosis falls within the range of normal behavior" (Cameron, 1963). "Combat exhaustion" and "battle fatigue" convey this notion.

3. *"Voluntaristic factor"* (Kardiner, 1947). This term is used only by Kardiner; it designates for him a large number of more or less conscious motivations. It has perhaps the disadvantage that the issue of free will versus irresistible impulse must be faced.

4. *Environmental or "external induction" theories.* These rest largely on studies identifying discrete factors which, in particular settings, and in various combinations, were judged to have been causally associated with psychopathology. Examples of such "external" factors are: physical exhaustion (Hanson, 1949), quality of leadership and interpersonal relationships (Weinstein, 1947),

> deprivation and danger, dislocation from family and loved ones, intercurrent illness, lack of sleep, monotony of food, inadequate training, continued exposure to climatic extremes or to primitive living conditions . . . improper job assignment, lack of promotion opportunities and problems at home . . . each of these might be as important as personality structure in any given case and in combination frequently more so. . . . (Appel, in Anderson, 1966, p. 387).

5. *Experimental neurosis model.* This way of organizing the data resembles the illness model in that there is an element of conflict. However, the type of that conflict is seen as analogous to the "experimental neurosis," artificially produced in animals by Pavlovian investigators. Victims of Acute Combat Reaction are, in terms of this model, unable to resolve a dilemma consisting of the wish to survive and the wish to perform their duty (Archibald & Tuddenham, 1965; Dobbs & Wilson, 1960).

6. *The judgmental model.* This "old fashioned" approach relies on the moral and ethical notions of duty and patriotism. The question

could be raised whether a category error occurs if such a model is included in this listing of "scientifically" inspired theories. If we, however, limit ourselves to an examination of what a judgmental approach has to say about the treatment of Acute Combat Reaction, then we will be dealing with a list of comparable concepts. *Neuropsychiatry in World War II*, the historiography prepared by the Office of the Surgeon General (Mullins, 1973), supports such a position in that it assigns directly homologous roles to morality and psychiatry (pp. 989-990):

> Only since the early days of World War I has the inability of combat personnel to cope with battle-conditions become accepted as a legitimate reason for classifying such personnel as casualties of war. In prior times, such failure of adaptation was regarded as cowardice, weakness, or other moral lapse, and was usually dealt with punitively. This attitude persisted even in World War II.

Continuity with our thinking is then established as follows: "advances in psychiatry and social sciences . . . facilitated awareness that mental disorders could be situationally induced."

At the end of this list of models explaining combat psychopathology an important caveat should be presented. Although an evolutionary trend away from the moral judgmental set seems apparent, it would be erroneous to conclude that we are dealing with a series of theories in which each, in turn, replaced its predecessor, having proven its superiority. Rather, each point of view mentioned above continues to exert its influence, even after it appears to have been "officially" abandoned. Each theory can be and usually is consequential in various degrees and ways in such different areas as diagnostic classification, therapeutic activity and administrative decision-making.

We have now, without trying for completeness, touched upon six conceptually quite different ways of understanding our subject matter. Each of these perspectives is based on battlefield experience and supported also by later, more contemplative clinical study. Each notion has inspired much writing showing the fascination these phenomena stimulate during war, as well as the suspect speed with which they are abandoned in times of peace. As Baxter noted, "the knowledge gained in World War II . . . had been forgotten" (1970, p. 128). Also, "the contributions of World War I were largely disregarded and forgotten. More than two years elapsed in World War II before the concepts and practices of World War I were relearned and reestablished" (Mullins, 1973). To explain both the fascination these themes evoke and the subsequent rapid suppression they undergo, psychoanalysis and anthropology point toward their evidence for the existence of powerful, deep-seated human reaction patterns connected with war and warriors. Productive though this approach appears to be, it will only be referred to in this context (Adair, 1949; Freud, 1961, 1963, 1963a).

Perhaps the variety of the opinions and the depth of the emotions aroused are related in other ways as well. Maybe all the disagreements and confusion do not simply point toward a regrettable but limited and remediable area of underdevelopment in our scientific knowledge. Instead, it could be that changes in paradigms of Acute Combat Reaction are expressions of development in fundamental structures of thought, themselves reflecting the evolution of the perception of reality. We will now direct our attention to the articulations between theory, therapy and psychopathology as they appear to function at the present time.

THE ESSENTIAL ELEMENT OF ALL COMBAT REACTIONS

The interpretation to be offered here is that a particular definition of Acute Combat Reaction is operative in all of the competing speculations and theories. Such an interpretation can be formulated as follows: *Acute Combat Reaction consists of behavior by a soldier under conditions of combat, invariably interpreted by those around him as signaling that the soldier, although expected to be a combatant, has ceased to function as such.* For completeness, it should be added that the behavior in question is polymorphous and cannot be primarily accounted for by somatic factors.

The definition is offered in this particular "skeletal" form to make it useful in a wide variety of situations. The apparent diagnostic criteria for Acute Combat Reaction are somewhat different in each war and a list of the typical features of the signaling operative in a particular context can be added to the definition, to flesh out the skeleton. *Neuropsychiatry in World War II* expresses this principle as follows: "failure in the battle role had to be manifested by symptoms or behavior acceptable to the combat reference group as representing an inability rather than an unwillingness to function" (Mullins, 1973, p. 990). The essential element of the definition in its general or special versions is, however, that of a message to the environment stating that a particular combatant is no longer functional as such. It should be noted that an important issue is being sidestepped here, namely that of *inability* versus *unwillingness* to continue combat. Little can be gained by an attempt to settle a question of this type, which has so successfully defied so many proposed solutions in the past. Rather, it should be pointed out that one of the pragmatic advantages of the latest form of treatment for combat reaction is precisely its capability of ignoring the dichotomy "inability versus unwillingness" without hindering treatment in any way.

Also, it should be emphasized that the interpretation offered does not represent as radical a departure from other approaches as might seem to be the case. Many observers have recognized an oppositional aspect in the behavior of soldiers diagnosed as suffering from war neuroses; they do not however place this component of the syndrome at the heart of the matter.* Interestingly enough, more awareness of this negativism is apparent in the pragmatic guidelines for treatment than in the explanatory concepts underlying these same guidelines. Accentuating this relatively neglected, but demonstrably omnipresent, dynamism is expected to be ultimately helpful in achieving a better articulation between the "classical" literature on the psychological sequelae of war and the Vietnam experience.

It is necessary at this juncture to refer back to the second element of the proposed thesis, which states that the inductive method would have to be modified in such a way as to render it capable of taking into account the communicative dimensions of human behavior.**

---

* The civilian Bartemeier Commission (Bartemeier, 1946) actually comes closer than most authorities to doing this when it introduces its term "morbid resentment state." This state appears "typically as an aftermath of combat exhaustion but sometimes without that experience." Descriptively, "the disorder is a disgruntled, resentful, embittered, aggressive unamiable state in which the patient is particularly resistant and irritable about what he calls being shoved around . . . distrustful of treatment . . . the condition is different from ordinary resentment in both a qualitative and quantitative way."

** Without such a modification, acceptance of the proposed interpretation of Acute Combat Reaction as constituting in essence a signal would mean a break with customary scientific procedure. It should be admitted that interpretation has crept in where only observation was said to belong, and it could even be claimed that teleological contamination has occurred. Faced with a choice between sacrificing purity of method or giving up what appears to be the most helpful conceptualization of our problem, we do well not to abandon the latter. Two further stipulations need to be made. While several of the most influential existing theories can be shown to immediately confirm the validity of the proposed definition, others lend support to it only in indirect and derivative ways. It will, therefore, be claimed that our thesis can be validated directly, as well as indirectly. An example of the latter form of proof would be a demonstration that a particular viewpoint concerns itself with "refusal to fight" by attempting to discredit such a notion. A second stipulation is that the actual therapeutic activity spawned by a theory should be given more weight than the etiologic and psychodynamic aspects of that theory. "Therapy speaks louder than theory." There is, at any rate, probably a more formal than real separation between causal and therapeutic tenets; the latter tend to make clear, although usually implicit, statements about the former.

We will now proceed to examine the current, official military doctrine concerning the treatment of "combat fatigue." Its principles are usually summarized as follows: "Immediacy, Proximity, Expectancy," meaning the patient should be treated as soon as possible after the onset of symptoms, as close as possible to the location where the symptoms started, and with the expectation that he will shortly return to combat. The rationale for this prescription is explained by Glass (1954): The soldier evacuated with signs of combat exhaustion will, if in contact with other than specially trained personnel, be able to elicit so much support for his unwillingness to resume fighting that it will be impossible to force him to do so. On the other hand, everything in the specialized treatment situation is calculated to exert maximal pressure on the soldier to consider his rapid return to combat as a certainty. Considerable effort is constantly made to prevent the patient from entertaining any thought of alternatives (Strange & Arthur, 1967). To accomplish this, all treatment personnel must be thoroughly convinced that combat exhaustion is indeed a reversible, "normal" reaction in battle. It is interesting to note to what extent such a conviction actually has taken hold: Glass (in Mullins, 1973, p. 994) finds that "a myth has been established that genuine psychiatric casualties *only* include individuals with healthy psychic apparatuses." The development of such a myth is probably a logical response from the treatment personnel; certainly a myth of this type is very helpful in the implementation of the expectant approach.

To round out this sketch of the official treatment doctrine, an investigation of its results would be useful. Unfortunately, however, the existing information is quite limited, as might be expected given the conditions of war. The most authoritative sources of data are probably *Neuropsychiatry in World War II* (Mullins, 1973), Kardiner 1947, and Glass, 1947. We find in these sources percentages of cure, usually defined as return to duty, mostly derived from limited surveys or from personal impressions. Success is frequently claimed and the data at first glance tend to support such claims. On closer inspection, however, so many complications appear that the matter is left far from settled. Consider, for example, Kardiner (1947, p. 41), who gives a return to duty rate of 50 percent. "Of this group 80 percent remained on duty, 55-60 percent of this 80 percent were regarded by their commanding officers as being as good or better than before their break." Arithmetic shows that at this point only 25 percent of the original cohort are judged to be functional as combatants. These reports are silent about the persistence or resolution of symptoms or complaints and they often do not specify a time frame for follow-up. It should also be kept in mind that residual deficit or symptomatology might predispose some of the men returned to duty towards becoming surgical or medical casualties. Noteworthy in this connection is that Glass (1947) elected to count all those returned to duty and subsequently killed or wounded in battle as ipso facto having been effective soldiers.

Other considerations limiting the significance that can be attached to the follow-up data address themselves to the "revolving door" problem (i.e., how many of the admissions were primary, and how many represent readmissions of the same men?). Even more important is the matter of initial classification of casualties. For ". . . as high neuropsychiatric rates for units came to be regarded as evidence of low morale or faulty leadership, there arose individual and group needs to utilize the more acceptable organic diagnoses for psychiatric casualties" (Mullins, 1973, p. 996). How real this issue is can be further underlined by another observation from the same source (p. 1013): "the relatively small incidence of NP [neuropsychiatric] disorders can readily be hidden or absorbed in the much higher disease and injury rates, as well as in such deviant behavior categories regarded as disciplinary problems, as AWOL, desertion or even drug addiction." Finally, maintenance of morale and other similar concerns have traditionally biased the collection of military statistics.

The limitations of the available data make it difficult to view the success rate as the most compelling reason for the adoption of the standard procedure enthroning immediacy, proximity and expectancy. Not even the fact that the alternative, as mentioned earlier, is a zero return rate can change this very much. If we, however, take into account the likely preventive effect of the guidelines, much clarity is gained. It is not difficult to find statements to the effect that "escape" must not be made too available, or else epidemics of combat exhaustion will be provoked, e.g., "Keep tight the evacuation screen" (Anderson, 1966, p. 411). Kardiner clearly addresses the same problem when he uses the term "voluntaristic factor."

In sum, a definition of combat exhaustion as primarily characterized by the previously outlined notion of "refusal to fight" is supported by the content of the recommendations found in the official military doctrine. Also, the preponderant influence of a refusal paradigm is illustrated by the observation that this doctrine is justified more by its preventive than by its curative effect.

Predisposition

How does the proposed definition relate to other theories about Acute Combat Reaction? A number of treatment rationales still remain influential, even though they have been operationally supplanted by the doctrine of immediacy, proximity and expectancy. Perhaps the most prominent among these is the assumption that most, if not all, war neuroses would be prevented if adequate screening were practiced prior to induction in the military. *Neuropsychiatry in World War II*, the governmental historical document referred to earlier, discusses the matter at length, as do many other sources. The official outcome of this discussion can be best summarized by a quote from an Inspector General's report, issued in 1944: "If screening is to weed out all those likely to develop a psychiatric disorder, all should be weeded out" (Anderson, 1966, p. 391). This statement clearly indicates a decisive turning point in the official attitude. A review of the debate leading to this conclusion does not, however, reveal arguments inconsistent with our definition; rather, considerable support for it can be found. Difference in priorities or emphasis appears to distinguish this approach from others. By assuming a predisposition toward decompensation in combat, antedating military service, the importance of combat itself is sharply reduced. Such a reduction then acts to deemphasize the significance of oppositional motivations on the part of combatants; it does not, however, argue against the existence of such motivations. Furthermore, those convinced that a prior neurosis always explains breakdown in combat tend to use the term "neurosis" in a disparaging fashion. This further facilitates discrediting the actions and motivations of those who have broken down.

Organicity?

Extending the scope of our review, we now need to focus on a controversy preceding the debate on predisposition and selection. This is the "organic versus functional" polemic. Fortunately, it is a relatively settled matter. All sources appear nowadays to be in agreement that we are dealing with a functional entity. The arguments formerly offered in favor of brain damage have an empathic quality and rested on the readily appreciable traumatizing potential of intense and long-lasting exposure to explosions. They were nevertheless effectively countered, toward the end of the First World War, by the following considerations (Glass, 1954).

1. Wounded soldiers and prisoners of war, exposed to the same blasts as combatants, rarely developed shellshock.
2. Severe, proven injuries to the central nervous system were not usually accompanied by shellshock-type symptoms, whereas just the opposite would be predicted if one assumed that shellshock was the expression of lesser injuries to the brain.
3. There were resemblances between war neuroses and civilian neuroses not associated with injury.
4. Rapid improvement could occur following brief psychological treatment at forward areas.

Military psychiatrists seem to have had a vital interest in obtaining an unequivocal verdict against the organic shellshock theory. This is understandable since without such a verdict it would be more difficult to adhere strictly to the "expectancy" element of the official treatment doctrine. Aita and Kerman (1946), working as neurologists, conclude that there exists an: "inseparability of organic and personality adjustments . . . in most cases intracranial alteration is minimal and reversible" (p. 393). Finally, "minimal though permanent residual cerebral alteration need not equal any functional deficiency." For practical purposes, it follows that, instead of mitigating the expectant attitude in cases where some brain damage might exist, the expectancy should be stressed all the more "in order to avoid permanent disability."

In summary, if there were good reason to assume an organic origin in most cases of combat exhaustion, this would argue against our thesis. However, such is not the case and, furthermore, in situations where some doubt exists, the functional component is generally seen as the more appropriate target of therapeutic endeavor.

The Judgmental Model

The "organic versus functional" debate directly opposed the frame of reference previously operative, namely that of the morality of patriotism and the ethics of duty, referred to above as the "judgmental model." Use of the language appropriate to this model necessarily precluded placing psychological combat reactions under the jurisdiction of doctors. In fact, medical texts used to, by their silence, imply that no such "disease" existed. However, it is the position taken here that phenomena quite analogous to our war neuroses did indeed take place in the past, and that they were handled without a medical vocabulary. Why, at the beginning of this century, medical terminology began to take precedence is a problem beyond the scope of this chapter.

In considering the question of the relation of the "old-fashioned" ethics to the view under discussion here, we find that emphasis on the conative element of the combat reaction, as in our definition, allows for easy reconciliation with an ethical framework. It is perhaps worthwhile to point out that all of the competing modern theories continue to be unable to fully abandon the older way of viewing reality. A historical inquiry thus yields immediate practical benefits in that countertransferential attitudes, rooted in views prevalent during earlier periods, become easier to recognize and understand.

Another line of inquiry capable of clarifying the nature of the Acute Combat Reaction involves surveying past military policies dealing with the problem. Military psychiatrists are unanimous in criticizing top decision makers for having failed to anticipate and plan for the large numbers of psychiatric casualties in both World Wars and the Korean conflict (Farrell, M.J., in Anderson, 1966).

This unpreparedness may be interpreted as a wish to deny the likelihood of numerous future neuropsychiatric casualties [Drayer & Ransom, 1945] as well as an equally subconscious suspicion that adequate provisions for such casualties might actually stimulate their incidence. Furthermore, there is likewise an abundance of psychiatric testimony to the fact that strained relationships between the command and military psychiatry (as well as medicine) were not rare. These difficulties seemed often intimately linked to the incidence of and the approach to combat exhaustion. The mutual recriminations they gave rise to are reflected in the many discussions about the proper delineation of the responsibility and authority of "command" versus "medical corps." For example, an Inspector-General's report of 1944, addressing itself specifically to combat exhaustion, reads: "The majority of cases are not psychoneurotic conditions, because the medical officers wish to make patients out of them, but because the line officers have been unable to make soldiers out of them" (Anderson, 1966, p. xx). On the basis of the above, we can infer that an element of defensiveness has been present in the collective attitude of military authorities with regard to combat exhaustion. Such defensiveness can best be explained as arising out of a degree of awareness of the communicated protest in the behavior of neuropsychiatric casualties. What often makes for real differences (and sometimes friction) between line officers and psychiatrists are not fundamentally disparate observations, but rather divergences in the conclusions drawn from the primary behavioral data. These conclusions, in turn, determine the subsequent course of action taken with regard to putative victims of combat reaction. The psychiatrists opt for a labeling process which responds to the oppositional tendencies, without confronting them head on. The military authorities, on the other hand, tend to ignore subtle and indirect manifestations of such tendencies as long as possible. When this leads to unmanageable consequences, a choice between medical-psychiatric or administrative-disciplinary dispositions is made.

Our contention that a message, indicating discontinuance by a combatant of his role, represents the essential element in Acute Combat Reaction allows for a unified view, encompassing the several psychiatric theories, as well as the more militarily oriented positions.

REACTIONS TO COMBAT IN VIETNAM

In this section, the views developed so far will be applied to the experience of Vietnam. In order to accomplish this, however, a few general statements about that particular war must first be given.* For practical purposes, we can assume that the Vietnam War was experienced by U.S. military personnel as a singular series of events. It follows that whatever "meaning" a particular occurrence in Vietnam had was to an important degree determined by the way in which that occurrence ran counter to certain expectations. The latter were based primarily on military training (Eisenhart, 1975), events in World War II and Korea, and also on other normative sources, such as television (Gault, 1971). With regard to Acute Combat Reaction, a salient point of difference with previous wars emerged in the initial, preparatory stage of the conflict: Contrary to what happened in the early phases of previous wars, this time dire predictions about the expected number of neuropsychiatric casualties were not only made, but also officially taken note of. The grounds for these warnings ranged from simple projections based on statistics of the past, to more specific concerns, for example the lack of clear front lines,

---

* Of all the characterizations of the Vietnam War, the one most frequently encountered is probably the statement that the war was "unique." To what extent and in what ways this is actually true depend entirely on the comparisons one wishes to make: If the point of reference is World War II, or even the Korean Conflict, then the uniqueness of Vietnam is easily enough established. If, on the other hand, a wider comparison is undertaken, certain resemblances with other military campaigns become readily apparent: There is the "First Indochina War," fought by the French but with U.S. support, the Algerian War and a host of other similar military operations, fought by irregulars against conventionally organized forces. Insofar as we are concerned with the typical American experience, these considerations may not carry much weight, since it is not, traditionally, much influenced by comparisons with historical events, especially such as involve other countries.

resulting in the absence of secure rear areas (Levy, 1974, p. 114), domestic opposition to the war (Bourne, 1970), jungle warfare as such (Mullins, 1973, p. 871), and the hit-and-run tactics of an elusive enemy (Levy, 1974, p. 114).

The old maxim about the generals always fighting the previous war instead of the one on hand proved to be applicable to the turn of psychiatric events. As early in the war as 1966 the ominous forecast of heavy psychiatric casualties began to be replaced by extremely optimistic statistical assessments. It would be interesting to speculate about the extent to which this numerically based psychiatric optimism was due to the general military climate, i.e., the then prevailing strong reliance on statistics as a guide to the proper conduct of the war [Halberstam, 1973; Ellsberg, 1972]. However that might be, there is a triumphant note in the early reports on the psychology of the army: "The mental health of U.S. Army troops in Vietnam remains outstanding" (Mullins, 1973, p. 998). Record low rates for psychiatric evacuations were being established, and other parameters showed similar trends. Bourne (1970), after spending time in Vietnam on an official mission, concluded that the problem of Acute Combat Reaction had been solved, and that no recurrence need be feared if proper policy continued in force. The official figures were in fact so impressive that skepticism had to be expected and needed to be countered, especially since the validity of other military statistics also began to be challenged by the media, as well as by the man in the street. With regard to the incidence of psychiatric casualties, there was furthermore a warning from no less an authority than Colonel Glass: "the reported low rates of neuropsychiatric casualties from Vietnam may be questioned, until all categories of non-combat losses are stated" (Mullins, 1973, p. 998). Clearly, an explanation as to why Vietnam should be producing so little distress was needed before the statistics could find general acceptance.

Bourne (1970) and others (Bloch, 1969) did in fact concern themselves with this question and they were able to clarify certain important issues. There is, first of all, the matter of duration of exposure to combat. This parameter definitely established a difference with previous wars; typical engagements in Vietnam were relatively brief. This is a matter of major importance since the knowledge gained in World War II points with certainty toward a correlation between duration of participation in combat and incidence of psychopathology. Further support for the thesis that the episodic character of the fighting was responsible for the good mental health of the troops could be found in the observation that combat reactions of the type described earlier did increase on occasions when the battles lasted longer (Motis & Neal, 1968). The earlier mentioned correlation between degree of exposure to combat and breakdown is now considered to be a lesson well learned by military decision makers. The consequences of this lesson began to be tentatively drawn late in World War II, and after the first year of the Korean War its full implications were accepted. Thus, a rotation system, limiting overseas tours of duty for each man to a certain specified length of time, was established. In Vietnam, such a policy was immediately instituted and adhered to, except for generals. DEROS (Date Expected to Return from Overseas) became a crucial element in the experience of all military personnel. Other factors in addition to limitation of time in battle are credited with contributing to the low rates of breakdown being recorded for the troops in Vietnam. A conscious effort was made to eliminate, insofar as possible, all conditions previously blamed for breakdowns. In a sense, a large scale verification of the theories of military preventive psychiatry was taking place when physical hardships imposed on the troops were limited insofar as possible, when merchandise of all sorts was made accessible, and when efforts were made to generally reproduce the American way of life. It must be noted, however, that at least some of the policies referred to above had serious noxious side effects. This was particularly true of DEROS. It became obvious that DEROS, while promising the soldier an out other than becoming either a psychological or physical casualty (Bourne, 1970), also significantly undermined unit identification and cohesion (Bourne, 1972). This is particularly ominous since many observations made in the past had led to the conclusion that unit morale is one of the most important protections against breakdown available to the soldier. The same drawback was attached to the relative ease of communication with home; facilitation of maintaining ties with family and friends also diminished emotional investment in the military unit. The strict d-limitation of the tour of overseas duty further decreased the soldier's commitment to a successful outcome of the war: "His war begins the day he arrives, and it ends the day he leaves" (Bourne, 1972). It would seem that a trade-off had occurred and this was probably made easier to accept by the fact that the recorded number of official neuropsychiatric casualties was so gratifyingly low.

What has been said so far applied mostly to the early and the middle phases of the war. In examining the later phases, we will be confronted in various ways with what, from the American point of view, turned out to be the most characteristic feature of the Vietnam War, namely that of failure. At this juncture there is again the temptation to see a clear parallel between the military and the psychiatric situation, as there was when we considered earlier the reliance on numerical data by both the psychiatric and the military leadership. In the later phases of the war, the figures concerning evacuation of soldiers for neuropsychiatric reasons and those giving the incidence of combat fatigue continued to be very reassuring, as did the "bodycount," number of hamlets "pacified," etc. At the same time, observations of a different kind began coming in. These had to do with heightening racial tension, drug use increasing to unprecedented levels, and erosion of discipline, culminating in widespread offenses against the ultimate military taboo—assaulting an officer. The paradox was inescapable; on the one hand the conventional indices pointed toward an entirely satisfactory state of psychiatric affairs, while on the other hand the primary goal of the Medical Corps, "conserving the fighting strength," appeared in serious jeopardy due to the moral state of the troops.

Classically, military psychiatry can be said to have developed methods to deal with two major tasks: (1) treatment and prevention of combat exhaustion; and (2) treatment and disposition of more traditional psychiatric syndromes (a small number of psychoses, many more character disorders). Neither of these methodologies appeared particularly suited for dealing with the widespread and novel problems that existed in the later phases of the war in Vietnam. Only the relatively unorthodox ways of thinking, commonly designated as "community" or "preventive" psychiatry, seemed at least to suggest some potentially helpful innovative approach. Whatever the merits of the newer concepts, the dimensions of the problem were soon perceived as beyond even the theoretical capacity of military psychiatry. Eventually, it was left to the highest levels of the command structure to devise appropriate solutions, and, among these, withdrawal of the troops from the theatre of war was to figure prominently.

Thus, seen from the vantage point of the military psychiatrist, there were two cardinal features to the Vietnam War—the unanticipated low rates of combat exhaustion and the equally unexpected extremely high rates of unconventional psychopathology. "Unconventional" in this context means not having previously occurred in U.S. military history with such frequency and intensity (Heinl, 1971). The term "pathology" will perhaps seem only arguably suitable, especially if it is remembered that the problems thus designated were eventually handled mostly through the intervention of the military command, rather than by way of psychiatric activity. Here, the thesis to be defended is that these phenomena should indeed be termed psychopathology, since it can be shown that they arose on the same substrate, and in response to the same general conditions as more narrowly defined combat reactions. We are, therefore, dealing with behavior homologous to that occurring in combat exhaustion. There are obvious differences in external characteristics of that behavior, but the emotional, subjective structure is the same in both instances. For this structural similarity to become clear, it is first of all necessary to refer back to the argument presented initially, namely that the element common to all theories concerning Acute Combat Reaction is that of rejection of the role of combatant. This is the central consideration and how it relates to the "unexpected, unconventional" psychopathology of the Vietnam War needs to be examined. In order to accomplish this, a few statements must be added about the subjective experience of the rank and file military in Vietnam.

It is, of course, a platitude to observe that there was widespread uncertainty, doubt and suspicion among the G.I.'s about "why we are in Vietnam." Not surprisingly, more data about this disquieting sense of purposelessness can be found in the statements of civilian, rather than of military observers. Evidently, the martial atmosphere, filled with concern to devise "operational" solutions to "behavioral" problems, makes it difficult to attend to less concrete issues. It was in fact slightly undutiful even for psychiatrists, once in uniform, to devote much energy to subjective matters. Nevertheless, there is considerable agreement among most observers about the existence of situationally engendered, intrapsychic conflicts among the troops in Vietnam. A number of likely sources existed for such distress: the perception of dissonance between the requirement of risking one's life, as against finding the war devoid of sense (Lifton, 1973); retaining, in spite of training experiences, some conventional superego strictures, as against participating in slaughter (Falk *et al.*, 1971; Fox, 1974); judging concrete military operations to be inspired by racist motivations, as against official, idealistic policy pronouncements (Parks, 1968; Fiman, 1975). Most probably, each individual would be differently affected by any one of a potentially large series of conflictual configurations. The strength and nature of the resulting distress would of course be determined by continuous interplay between actual events, personality structure, support systems available, etc. The essence of the matter is, however, that we are dealing with a military population exposed to combat stress of a type considered unique and displaying collective behavior never engaged in before by U.S. military personnel.

Our contention that the behavioral constellation described above can best be qualified as a special form of Acute Combat Reaction will first be tested as it applies to drug abuse. While the often given explanations, such as hedonistic impulses, availability and acceptability of drugs, are doubtless correct, they also appear incomplete. It is curious to see how little effort is devoted to specifying the nature and meaning of the pleasure derived from the drugs, or the reasons why precisely that pleasure had come to be so prized. Yet, statements from the soldiers themselves are not hard to find and they are informative: The drug experience, while it lasts, frees the individual from the tension produced by the cognitive dissonance referred to above (Lifton, 1973). In other words, drugs offer a self-administered equivalent of the officially prescribed temporary removal from battle which was practiced so widely in World War II. There are even some indications that the military leadership was not unaware of this phenomenon and at times went so far as to foster it (Levy, 1974). On these grounds, a functional equivalence of drug use with the Acute Combat Reaction can be postulated. Both tend to effect at least a temporary interruption in what is perceived as an intolerable situation.

We now turn to what was referred to above as the ultimate military taboo—assaulting an officer. The difficulty in obtaining adequate documentation, earlier encountered in our effort to assess the outcome of the treatment for combat fatigue, prevails here too (Bond, 1976; Gillooly & Bond, 1976). It would seem, however, that what we do know about this particular "withdrawal symptom," as such assaults are called in a non-professional publication (Linden, 1972), reveals its consanguinity with the Acute Combat Reaction. In many cases, the assaulted officers had shown more zeal and ambition in the pursuit of aggressive action than their men found tolerable. The assaults often took place only after the officers had been warned to limit their offensive ambitions, thus underlining the desire of the "fraggers" (Bond, 1976) to prevent or stop combat. The observation that certain attacks were perpetrated by intoxicated aggressors whose early childhood showed evidence of deprivation does not substantially change this.

Insubordination, or the outright refusal to follow orders, is the last item on our list of unconventional symptoms encountered in Vietnam. It, of course, speaks for itself. A passing note should, however, be made of the observation that one of the most publicized collective refusals to engage in aggressive action took place at a time when the unit in question had been in the field for a considerable period of time. Thus, this refusal by an entire unit to initiate combat showed one of the best established characteristics of Acute Combat Reaction, i.e., its tendency to increase in frequency after exposure to combat had exceeded certain limits.

Colonel Glass's admonition (in Mullins, 1973, p. 998) to examine all sickness as well as non-sickness categories of military discharge before settling on a true neuropsychiatric casualty rate deserves to be taken seriously. Many observers have commented on the large numbers of administrative discharges being given during the war years (Solomon, et al., 1971; Braatz et al., 1971). In fact, the figures appear so high that one could appropriately raise the question as to whether an epidemic of combat reaction had been prevented only at the price of an epidemic of character disorder. Nevertheless, a definitive determination as to whether and how great an increase of such administrative discharges took place appears next to impossible if a strictly statistical method is used. This is due to the difficulty in finding appropriate controls as the Vietnam military population is not immediately comparable to the one that fought in World War II. Sociometric differences include age, education and social class, while the draft board practices added yet other variables. Still, the clinical impression is quite strong that administrative discharges played an important role in the development of the eventually occurring psychopathology. Specifically, administrative discharges most likely prevented the emergence of a certain amount of symptomatology directly. Furthermore, knowledge of the potential availability of such a discharge may have functioned as a safety valve for some, thus indirectly preventing their becoming symptomatic. Finally, how correct the diagnosis of character disorder was, and how often it masked another clinical entity, will only be adequately known when, and to the extent that, accurate follow-up takes place (Solomon et al., 1971; Zarcone et al., 1977).

In conclusion, then, the statement that Vietnam produced a remarkably low psychiatric attrition rate is misleading by its narrowness. Such a statement is tenable only if psychiatric attrition is equated with the psychopathology characteristic of the Second World War. Most likely, because of certain distinguishing features of the strategic situation in Vietnam (DEROS, episodic combat, limitations placed on hardships to be endured by troops), "combat exhaustion" occurred there only sporadically. Especially in the later years of the war, however, other forms of psychopathology (drug abuse, fragging, insubordination) reached levels never before attained by U.S. military personnel. This novel, unconventional psychopathology, in its totality, more than made up for the low attrition rate registered if only combat exhaustion is taken into account. It is ironic that, thus, in the last year of the war, the initial pessimistic predictions of large numbers of neuropsychiatric casualties were proven correct. Finally, we have seen that there are cogent reasons to group all symptoms and syndromes collectively designated as Acute Combat Reactions around a central dynamism, namely that of refusal to fight. If this view is adopted, the unconventional Vietnam pathology is seen to be homologous with Acute Combat Reaction since it fulfills a similar function. In purely descriptive terms, every combat situation appears to produce its own characteristic pathology. However, if we address ourselves to the underlying dynamics, it would seem that very analogous psychic mechanisms can be set off by different wars.

2

DYNAMIC PERSPECTIVES ON THE NATURE AND EFFECTS OF COMBAT STRESS

VICTOR J. DeFAZIO, Ph.D.

In the past several years the issue of psychopathology associated with the psychic trauma of combat and military service has again become a topic of concern because of the United States' protracted war in Southeast Asia. The fledgling literature on this war has resurrected long-standing concerns over, among other issues, the incidence of in-service psychiatric casualties, the problems of diagnosis and nomenclature, the debilitating quality of psychic trauma, its long-term effects, and forensic issues related to compensation and rehabilitation. In 1975 the American Psychiatric Association set up a committee to consider a change in the nomenclature of the current Diagnostic and Statistical Manual of Mental Disorders, as noted by Figley in the Introduction. Among a number of changes under consideration is the addition of a separate category for the diagnosis of trauma. At one time (1952) such a category to be called "gross stress reaction" was proposed but it was deleted and replaced in the 1968 edition of the manual with the more general term "adjustment reaction of adult life" (see Chapter 14) .

In a few places in the world, such as Israel, the subject of combat-related stress disorders has remained visible because of the large number of concentration camp survivors who migrated there after World War II and the relatively frequent but brief wars (Sauna, 1975; Solnit & Priel, 1975; Winnik, 1967). In the United States interest in the subject is cyclical and it seems to be regarded, as Freud (1920) once referred to it, as "the dark and dismal subject."

In his excellent and succinct presentation of the topic of traumatic neurosis, Kardiner (1959) pointed out that "the neurosis incidental to war alternates between being the urgent topic of the times and being completely and utterly neglected. Although there is no such thing as a specific neurosis of war, those of a similar character that occur in peace-time are swallowed up in oblivion" (p. 245).

The study of psychic trauma has far-reaching theoretical implications as well as practical application. In wartime, of course, it is directly related to issues of manpower preservation and productivity. This is true in peacetime as well, although on a smaller scale. Although this chapter is primarily concerned with the effects of such trauma on Viet-nam veterans and their special situation, it has bearing on the treat-ment of what at times seems to be increasingly large numbers of citizens who are exposed to single or multiple incidents of trauma through auto-mobile or industrial accidents, civil disorders, kidnapping and other violent crimes.

THE CONCEPT OF TRAUMA

Serious and systematic investigations of trauma and its psychological effects are traceable at least as far back as the work of Brodie in 1837 (Kaiser, 1968). However, trauma took shape as an etiological component within the framework of a comprehensive theory with the efforts of Sig-mund Freud. Initially, traumatic events in childhood of a sexual nature, including seductions involving genital stimulation as well as rape, were viewed as the causal agents in the development of neurosis. The idea, expounded in *Studies in Hysteria* (Breuer & Freud, 1895), was supple-mented by the notion that the trauma had its effect by occurring during a mental state of particular vulnerability, as, for example, a hypnergogic-like state. Freud modified this view somewhat; he saw the mental state as being relatively unimportant compared to the opposition of the idea (of the real event) to the conscious mental life, leading to its repression and the accompanying affect. The repression of the cathected ideation was then viewed as the mechanism whereby the symptoms developed. Gradually, Freud became aware that the reports of childhood seductions by patients were more fantasied than real and from other observations it seemed to him that these fantasies were a means of deflecting mem-ories of forbidden autoerotic activities. One of the effects of this early observation on the theory was to emphasize the meaning an individual attributed to an experience rather than the experience itself. As psycho-analytic theory continued to evolve, the concept continued to change slightly. Each time the emphasis shifted, a different place in the causal chain of pathological and normal development was implied.

In Freud's *Introductory Lectures* (1917) trauma is defined as an "ex-cessive magnitude of stimuli too powerful to be worked off in a normal way." Prior to that it was viewed as any experience involving uncomfortable affects. With the advent of World War I, the study of trauma received an added impetus. Freud (1919) viewed the "war neurosis" as resulting from an ego conflict between the soldier's former peaceful ego and the newly acquired militaristic one which is life threatening.

The symptoms endemic to the war neurosis (the traumatic dream) presented some contradictions to the then current theory, especially the pleasure principle, and precipitated a further change in the development of the idea of the repetition compulsion. At this time trauma came to be associated with "a disturbance connected with a break in an otherwise efficacious stimulus barrier" (p. 33).

Freud (1920) commented further on those neuroses incidental to war. He noted that "the symptomatic picture presented by traumatic neurosis approaches that of hysteria in the wealth of its similar motor symptoms, but surpasses it as a rule in its strongly marked signs of subjective ailment (in which it resembles hypochondria or melancholia) as well as in the evidence it gives of a far more comprehensive general enfeeblement and disturbance of the mental capacities."

With the development of the structural model, Freud used the expression "traumatic situation" to relate to experiences of non-satisfaction and helplessness where stimulation attained unpleasurable levels which could not be mastered or discharged. This definition, along with the reinterpretation of anxiety (signal anxiety), appeared in *Inhibitions, Symptoms and Anxiety* (1926). Later in *Moses and Monotheism* (1939) Freud reaffirmed his belief in the importance of trauma in the development of neurosis but left open the question as to whether all neuroses have a traumatic origin.

In summary, we may conclude from this brief review of the trauma concept in early psychoanalytic theory that trauma was highly significant in (a) the development, to a larger extent, of the topographic model and, to a lesser extent, of the structural model of the theory of the etiology of neurosis; (b) the development of the concept of the repetition compulsion which came out of the need to explain the special qualities of the traumatic dream and its apparent contradiction of the pleasure principle; and (c) the development and revamping of the concept of anxiety.

CURRENT CONCERNS AND CONCEPTIONS

Perhaps the salient question involved in dealing with the effects of psychic trauma in adults is whether, ultimately, the trauma is intrinsically pathogenic or merely the highlight in a history of an ongoing neurosis, psychosis or character disorder. The issue here is not always so academic. Whenever compensation is considered for a victim, it becomes a hotly disputed point as, for example, when the West German government initially decided to remunerate concentration camp survivors.

Furst (1967) outlines a number of phenomena of trauma which offer an opportunity for the study of issues of basic concern to psychoanalytic theory, including (a) the role of constitutional factors in the development of psychopathology; (b) the extent and significance of variations in tolerance for excitation; (c) the mechanisms of interaction between internal and external stimuli; (d) the development of and mechanisms for action of the ego capacities; and (e) functions which maintain psychic equilibrium as well as the effect of experience on subsequent responses to stress and conflict.

While psychic trauma is currently defined with a number of variations and within the various metapsychological points of view, essentially it is seen by analysts like Furst, Anna Freud and Kris as an experience in which the ego is overwhelmed and the individual forced back to pre-ego mechanisms for dealing with internal and external environments. Furst (1967) put it succinctly when he wrote that "traumatic experience confronts the ego with a 'fait accompli,' so that the ordinary and available defenses and adaptive devices are of little value" (p. 10).

Similarly to Furst (1967), Solnit and Marianne Kris (1967) define trauma as "phenomena that reflect a reaction of the individual to an inner or outer demand or stimulus that is experienced as overwhelming the mediating functions of the ego to a very significant degree" (p. 123). The concept of "overwhelming" characterizes the stimulus as being sudden. With respect to the individual's reaction to the demand, characteristically it "rends the stimulus barrier, is disruptive, renders the individual in some manner helpless while disorganizing feelings, thoughts and behavior and promoting regressive phenomenon" (p. 123).

Ernest Kris (1956) differentiated between what he called "shock" and "strain" trauma. Shock trauma reflects the effects of a single, powerful experience while strain trauma represents the effects of long-lasting situations which may cause traumatic effects by the accumulation of undischargeable or unassimilable frustrating tensions. In the case of combat veterans, however, such distinctions are often too artificial to make. Veterans obviously experience a little of both—or, to be more accurate, they experienced a little too much of both.

GENERAL BACKGROUND ON COMBAT STRESS

A comprehension of the theory of trauma certainly is important but an understanding of the nature of the experience is equally of value. The second Indochina War, as the political scientist and economist Bernard Fall called it (1972), was the longest war in American history. It lasted such a long time that the last casualty was only six years old when the first official death of the war occurred in December, 1962. Altogether some eight and one-half million men and women served in the Armed Forces during that period. Of the approximately three and a half million soldiers who served in Southeast Asia proper, about 46,000 died in combat, about 250,000 more became casualties and one to two thousand remain missing in action or unaccounted for.

A much higher proportion of combat deaths in Indochina were due to small arms fire and to booby traps and mines than in either Korea or World War II where higher proportions were due to artillery and other explosive projectile fragments (Musser & Stenger, 1972). The nature of the combat in Vietnam (frequently at close range), the type of wounds (a high proportion to head, neck and thorax) and especially multiple wounds, combined with the excellent medical care, resulted in a higher incidence of certain complicated disabilities including multiple amputations, paraplegia and hemiplegia. These wounded men would undoubtedly have died in earlier wars.

The psychiatric casualty rate for all branches of service has been reported as being much lower for Vietnam. Overall it was 12 per 1000 in Indochina as compared with 37 per 1000 in the Korean War and 101 per 1000 during World War II (Bourne, 1970). This statistic for Vietnam is a matter of much contention but Armed Forces psychiatrists claimed it was a result of a number of unique factors, both planned and unplanned. These factors include: (a) the limited tour of duty (365 days); (b) frequent period of R and R; (c) the lack of prolonged exposure to shelling and bombardment; and (d) the application of modern military psychiatry. This includes standard technique which keeps an anxious, fatigued soldier near the fighting, gives him a few days rest and relies on group pressure and morale to keep him intact when he is sent back to his unit.

An illustration of the military psychiatry perspective is the paper by Arnold Johnson (1975). In it he noted that, "in a war situation the criterion for return to duty was not the absence of symptoms but rather the ability to perform" on the soldier's part (p. 16). The possibility that a return to duty would only fix the neurosis became a secondary consideration.

A somewhat different view is presented by Glasser (1971) in a rather poignant account of the war called *365 Days*. In it he noted that a large percentage of psychiatric casualties were returned to duty without extensive treatment. However, he wondered if their pathologies did not manifest themselves in more malignant ways.

While no current long-term follow-up studies of veterans done by the Armed Forces exist, there is an extensive follow-up project of 1000 cases done by Brill and Beebe (1955) after World War II. Essentially, they found that five years after the war the only groups in which there was a significant change from pre-service personality difficulties was composed of individuals classified as having personality disorders or acting-out characters. In these it was found that there was a moderate increase in neurotic symptoms or acting-out behavior. Coincidentally, studies of psychiatric admissions for Vietnam era veterans show that between 36 percent and 50 percent are admitted to VA hospitals under a heading of personality disorder (Lumry & Braatz, 1970).

In a recent study (DeFazio *et al.*, 1975) of a college student sample of Vietnam veterans, the combat experiences appeared to be important in predicting psychiatric malady symptoms. Results showed that 67 percent of the combat veterans reported frequent nightmares, 32 percent had difficulty in relaxing, 35 percent had trouble in getting close to people, 35 percent were fearful, 28 percent nervous, 32 percent felt they tired too quickly, 41 percent felt themselves to be short tempered and hotheads and so on. It is significant that the average man had been out of service for about five years, and none of the group had ever been classified as a psychiatric casualty.

Results of the DeFazio *et al.* study were compared with the Gringer, Willerman, Bradley and Fastovsky (1946) study of stress reactions in flying personnel during World War II. Both studies were very similar in terms of the methodological structure and content of the instruments and the sample used. For example, (a) both studies contained subjects who spent a limited tour of duty in action—for flyers it was 25 missions which took a year or less, (b) both groups contained men of about the same age when in combat, (c) both groups were comparable educationally. Similar results were found as well. It was discovered that the mean number of symptoms for the combat group was almost identical for pre- and post-combat periods in the DeFazio study compared with the mean number of symptoms in Gringer's "mild" battle fatigue group.

Gringer's group had almost identical mean symptoms with the DeFazio non-combat group. The most prevalent symptoms were almost identical in each study (i. e., nightmares, restlessness and irritability, sleep difficulties, various signs of depression and psychosomatic difficulties).

Although separated by time, men in similar circumstances develop similar reactions to stress. Kardiner has observed that a war situation can revive preexisting syndromes heretofore dormant, *but* the stress of combat can also create new ones. "No one exposed to war experiences comes away without some of the symptoms of the traumatic syndrome, however temporary they may be" Kardiner (1959, p. 243).

A quite different view had its origin in Germany after World War I which suggested a more cognitive or pragmatic explanation for symptoms of trauma. A much noted observation of the period was a relatively low psychiatric casualty rate among Allied prisoners taken during the battle for Verdun and an alarmingly high one for German soldiers still fighting. Both had been through a similar experience. It was assumed that such a phenomenon resulted from the German soldiers' wish to be withdrawn from action while for the prisoner the battle was over (Kalinowski, 1950). Similar experiences in peacetime railway accidents led to the adoption of the view that pathological symptoms were not caused by the traumatic experiences themselves but rather by secondary gain associated with, for example, the wish to escape from danger and financial compensation for suffering. During the German retreat from Stalingrad, for example, psychiatric casualties were almost unknown. It was reasoned that since "becoming ill" was not useful (no secondary gain) to a soldier (since it would only lead to death from exposure or at best being a Russian prisoner), they did not become ill. It is a concept which places great reliance on conscious wish and "will power" and seems to confuse the issue of secondary gain in symptom persistence with the development of the neurosis. The practical result of this policy was that compensation and rehabilitation were greatly curtailed. Although these skeptical views were modified slightly, the notions of preexisting neurosis and constitutional factors sufficiently undermined the perspective illustrated by Kardiner (1959) and significantly reduced the number of compensation awards to the survivors of concentration camps by German courts (Krystal, 1968).

THE VIETNAM EXPERIENCE

To understand the effects of the war, one must be somewhat familiar with the experience of it. The Vietnam War was not simply a jungle war (like the American experience in the South Pacific during World War II) but a conflict fought against an indigenous revolutionary army (Fall, 1963; 1972). This fact is important because it accounts for the very special character of the war. Its clandestine nature led to considerable brutalization on both sides. It left American troops with a sense of helplessness at not being able to confront the enemy in set-piece battles. The spectre of being shot at and having friends killed and maimed by virtually unseen forces generated considerable rage which came to be displaced on anyone or anything available. The dehumanization of the Vietnamese was aggravated by the striking differences in race, language, culture and the recurrent threat that even the most gentle looking person could, in fact, be the enemy.

The combatants learned to adjust to the dehumanization as a way of survival. A machine gunner on a helicopter describes the process of adjustment in referring to an incident in which he contributed to the death of an innocent 12-year-old boy as their helicopter took off.

> When that happened, my first reaction . . . was . . . I would guess you would consider normal. It would be horror, pain, and then I realized that I caught myself immediately and I said, "No, you can't do that," because you develop a shell while you are in the military. . . . They take all the humanness out of you and you develop a crust that enables you to survive in Vietnam. And if you let that protective shell down for even a second, it could mean—it's the difference between you flipping out or managing to make it through. And I caught myself tearing the shell down and I . . . and
> I . . . tightened up right away and started laughing and joking about it (Vietnam Veterans Against the War, 1972).

Even the language of the war was replete with references and euphemisms which minimized the significance of events, blunted affect, and made everything sufficiently unreal. The average G.I., for example, became a "grunt," a sort of sub-human no longer capable of thought or affect. People were "zapped," not killed. The built-up tension was vented on perimeter guard during "mad-minutes," a sort of sanctioned irrationality when everyone fired aimlessly at the surrounding jungle. According to Lt.Col. A. Herbert (1973):

> Everybody there seemed to have a pseudonym of some sort or another . . . maybe that was some way of escaping any guilt about their work. It was my first contact with the dreamlike quality of the war. Perhaps that is one of the factors contributing to our defeat there. The war was unreal. The SF (Special Forces) people took on as-

sumed names. The enemy became "dinks" and "slopes" and "gooks."
The plane that fired miniguns was called "Puff, the Magic Dragon"
and areas designated for complete destruction were called "free fire
zones." It was like going through the looking glass and, after your
tour was finished, you could step back through the mirror and leave
all the horror and the dread in another, unreal world (p. 40).

Lastly, the war fostered in many men a sense of mistrust. Unable to
distinguish friend from foe, they came to mistrust all Vietnamese. Further, they came to mistrust the official representatives of religion (chaplains) and of mental health (psychiatrists) whom they saw as only interested in supplying "bodies" to fight with (Lifton, 1973). The hazy
moral and political reasons for the war created doubts for almost everyone. Soldiers expected definitive responses from chaplains when they had
no clear-cut guidelines to give. Thus, their authority as moral leaders
was diminished. Veterans even developed a distrust for their own senior
commanders, whom they viewed as being solely concerned with promoting themselves with phoney "body-counts," without regard to the lives
of the average "grunt." Stories of the "fragging" of officers (tossing a
hand grenade under an officer's bunk or in his foxhole) were widespread.
When many returned to the "real world" (the U.S.) they found themselves once again confronted by an official government presence which
they mistrusted.

HOMECOMING

After World War II, Hollywood film makers produced a number of
fine movies which had socially significant ramifications for the veteran
and the milieu to which he returned. In films like *The Man in the Grey
Flannel Suit* and *Pride of the Marines* the killing of other human beings
in combat is justified on grounds of self preservation; thus the returning
soldier is not stigmatized and is relieved of guilt. *The Best Years of Our
Lives* deals entirely with readjustment difficulties, both psychological
and physical, and had the general effect of preparing the civilian audience to be sympathetic and accepting of the returning vet. *Home of the
Brave* which dealt almost entirely with the initial rehabilitation of a
hysterically paralyzed Black veteran gave an audience a sympathetic but
rudimentary understanding of some of the effects of the trauma of
combat. This was especially important when one considers that in 1943-
44 about 45 percent of all medical discharges (or 9,000 of 20,000 men a
month) were for neuropsychiatric reasons (Rennie, 1944). In still other
movies relevant reality issues like the G.I. Bill, friends' reactions to phys-

ical disabilities, employment and the like are openly discussed by various characters.

The contrast between that treatment of veterans and the treatment of Indochina veterans in the media is striking. In movies like *The Stone Killers* and in various episodes of TV dramas like *Police Story* or *Medical Center*, Indochina veterans are portrayed as depraved fiends, mercenaries and psychopathic killers. It is as if the entire social structure had projected every unacceptable and reprehensible impulse onto these men.

Vietnam veterans are frequently described as being a very angry group. It is not really sufficient to say that some of these men are or were merely angry. Their words and the tone of their words are saturated with vindictiveness. In combat it might be asserted that such feelings are a natural outgrowth of helplessness. However, years after the external danger has passed, it seems that the vengefulness tends to have other purposes. As both Horney (1949) and Searles (1956) have pointed out, it can be utilized unconsciously as a defense against the awareness of repressed grief over the death of friends and repressed separation anxiety. It can also represent the hidden awareness of feelings of hopelessness about oneself. Lastly, it can be a way of restoring injured pride.

This latter point becomes particularly salient when one remembers that the Vietnam War was one of the few in which soldiers did not return from an unqualified victory. In a combat situation the vindictiveness is often experienced as a righteous wrath, while in peacetime it is felt as a smoldering resentment directed at institutions and individuals in authority. Minor rebuffs or oversights can be met by the veteran with hints of retaliation and anger which seem all out of proportion to the initial act. Mates or friends are at a loss to understand what they have done to provoke such a response. The end results are frequent rifts between the men and their friends or families. Polner (1971) found that regardless of the veterans' professed view on the war (i.e., whether they were hawks or doves), all had doubt about the morality of the war.

GENERAL CHARACTERISTICS OF TRAUMA CASES

Almost regardless of what nomenclature or category is used to describe the individual combat veteran, there are certain commonalities which the group shares. There are, as well, certain characteristics of the trauma itself about which some general statements can be made.

Unstableness

Rangell (1967) has suggested that "trauma is characteristically an unstable and transient psychoeconomic condition." He believes, how-

conscious wish to undo the traumatic situation. The concomitant anxiety in these dreams is a reaction to the reenacted trauma. Thus, the trauma leaves the ego with an incomplete task which can be handled on many levels, i.e., through reality testing, adaptation, or the re-establishment of ego autonomy. All these require the ability to extend the dominance of secondary process thinking. In the dream where primary process thinking prevails, however, the ego regresses to such mechanisms as undoing. In general, the trauma inhibits the learning of new ego techniques for the gratification of instinctual demands.

According to Shur (1966), the same mechanism also plays a role in many instances of impervious resistance to working through the trauma, that is, in instances of severe traumatization in which "one of the main problems is one of a masochistic character disorder with a tendency to depression; reconstructions and recall result in little change" (p. 189). In these instances the patient expects change to come from the therapist, analyst or other figure in the environment. "What impresses one as clinging dependency and occasional sulky accusations with paranoid undertones can be revealed as a projection of the same magic wish to undo the past" (p. 189).

The political activism which some veterans engaged in during the war frequently resulted in positive change because it represented the ego's attempt to repair the breach in the stimulus barrier on a level of secondary process through action and reality testing which resulted in an adaptation to the consequences of the trauma, physical or psychic.

CATEGORIZATION OF PATHOLOGY

The veterans suffering from the effects of trauma can be categorized into three somewhat overlapping groups. These groups indicate the degree of success with which the veterans' ego autonomy has been reinstituted, their ability to refrain from the institution of more primitive defensive styles and their concomitant ability to neutralize aggressive drives.

Traumatic War Neurosis

By far the most dramatic cases fall into the group of the typical traumatic war neuroses. Although much has been written on this syndrome, only a very small number of individuals seen can be justifiably diagnosed as such.

The traumatic neurosis as described by Kardiner (1959) is characterized by catastrophic dreams, general irritability (in the sense of sensitivity to loud noises, etc.), a proclivity toward aggression and even violence which alternates with extreme tenderness and a general contraction in the level of functioning. In addition, there may be amnesia, memory disturbances, and psychosomatic disorders. The ego structure in such victims seems to suffer from an inability to make symbolic transformation; as a result, the compromise symptoms seen in an ordinary neurosis are conspicuously absent. Using a more liberal definition of traumatic neurosis, combat fatigue or gross stress reaction, other authors (Neff, 1975; Horowitz & Solomon, 1975) tend to classify larger numbers of veterans into this group.

Numerous authors (Van Putten & Emory, 1973; Solomon, 1971) have noted the frequent misdiagnosis of men falling into this category. The contraction of ego functioning often resembles schizophrenic deterioration while the phobic elaboration that the world is a hostile enemy-infested place is often mistaken for a psychotic persecutory delusion. Not infrequently they suffer from compulsive memories of an almost hallucinatory type which may be set off by the sight of one oriental face, a low flying plane, or other stimulus associated with the war. Shatan (1973) has referred to these twilight experiences as "flashbacks."

Recognition of the syndrome is important since it implies a treatment process which includes the recapitulation of the traumatic experience through verbalization rather than the institution of drug therapy, especially the phenothiazines.

Exaggerated Character Pathology

The second group consists of men who suffer some form of character pathology, i.e., higher level borderline conditions, narcissistic personality disorders, character neurosis, etc. without the presence of the more debilitating traumatic syndrome. These men can be described as having more successfully defended against the trauma but would probably have developed difficulties anyway, although in milder proportions. While they characteristically use more primitive defenses like denial, splitting and projective identification, demonstrating strong oral-aggressive conflicts, they often have valuable powers of sublimation (see Kernberg, 1975). Many of the apparently odd behaviors may be viewed as attempts at self-esteem regulation made difficult by the exacerbation of ego-superego conflicts and a further regression in already weak ego functioning.

The case of John may illustrate some of the points made. John's presenting problems included episodic violence, alcohol and drug abuse, occasional nightmares, interpersonal problems, especially marked by the inability to sustain an intimate love relationship with any woman. At the time, he had already fallen into an exploitative interpersonal style. He left home because of a terrible argument with his father and enlisted in a combat branch. The choice of service was partially dictated by a wish to become tough so that he could defeat his father in an open confrontation when he returned home. His first tour of duty in Vietnam was relatively uneventful. When he returned home he continued to feel degraded and abused by his father. John's ambivalence towards him had not changed at all. John became employed but almost as quickly lost the job. In the interim he had run up huge debts which his father was forced to pay in order to prevent his son from being sent to jail. John decided his only way out was to go back into the service. In their final confrontation before John left for his second tour of duty in Vietnam, his father expressed the wish that John would be killed in battle.

During John's second tour of duty in Vietnam a most traumatic incident occurred when he and a small security ambush were caught outside their own wire while the company position was being overrun. He and his men scrambled back through the darkness and were caught in a cross fire between the NVA and their own comrades. For a few seconds he was unsure whom to fire at since both sides presented a threat. When he reached his own position the NVA were already there. They fought their way past; at one point an NVA soldier pointed an AK-47 right at his head at almost point-blank range. John moved his head slightly and when the round went off, his helmet was blown off his head but he was unhurt. At that moment he remembered thinking that his father had wished him dead. He knocked the NVA soldier down but didn't shoot him. In fact during two years in Vietnam he never fired a shot in combat.

When he returned from Vietnam the second time, the same pattern repeated itself. He got a job but lived far beyond his means. Eventually, fearing arrest after his father refused to pay his bills, he left his hometown. For a year or so he wandered across the country getting into numerous scrapes with the law and having frequent short-term sexual liaisons with women who had to be beautiful. He eventually wandered to a large city and entered college. He was obsessed with the idea of becoming successful so he could become wealthy and possess many beautiful women. Sometime after he was asked to leave the first college he enrolled in, he came in for treatment.

John's nightmares always started out with his being back in service, but ended differently. For example, in one, when the issue of his ambivalence towards his father was salient in the treatment, he dreamed he was back in the service but was on the floor crying, insisting that he really loved the service and wanted to stay. In another, when the issue of money was paramount, he dreamed he was back in the service and on his bunk were dimes. The dream ended with him embracing a pillowcase full of dimes. However, the dimes were all in foreign currency.

Without going into the precise dynamics of the case, it becomes apparent that many of the symptoms, the ego system, and dynamics would have been similar regardless of his combat experiences. In some ways his pre-combat history dictated his choice to enter the service he did and to opt for a tour of duty in a combat zone. His experiences while there, apart from those cited, were pretty much interpreted by him in terms of earlier experiences.

One, however, does get the impression that the symptoms might not have developed in such a pronounced fashion had it not been for the stress of overseas duty and combat experience. John would probably have developed, at least, a superficial style of social conformity which might have allowed him some semblance of a normal and stable lifestyle. His rage may have been confined or developed into an intense competitiveness rather than being acted out in a more direct fashion.

Disassociated Symptom Pictures

The last group consists of individuals who are apparently healthy. They do not suffer from the typical syndrome but are referred because of marital problems, sexual difficulties and the like. This group seems to deny, isolate, or disassociate from the traumatic experience.

An example of this is a veteran with sea experience who came to see me because of a minor academic problem. As he came in I noted that he was limping slightly and I inquired about it. The man had been having episodic severe lower back pain since he left the service. The veteran explained that several weeks before he was to be sent home his ship was assigned to shell the North Vietnamese coast.

He went on to say, "The last time we went out I remember I could hear the North Vietnamese firing back. They didn't hit the ship but you could hear the shrapnel hit the hull when their shells exploded in the water. You know . . . those ships have thin hulls . . . really thin hulls. I was sitting below deck there with five other men. It was cramped, hot and uncomfortable sitting that way." I went on to ask where he was sitting He replied, "Oh . . . I was in the powder magazine."

The powder magazine is, of course, where all the high explosives are stored. One piece of shrapnel through that thin hull would have meant instant death. The vet went on to explain that the pains started shortly after that incident and that several orthopedic examinations were all negative. There were no physical explanations for the pain. He failed to make further inquiries.

In defense of the examining physicians it should be added that when they asked when the pains began, he always replied, "after I left the service." He never bothered to mention the incident or the fact that he had been out only a few weeks when it occurred. In fact, the severity of the pain did not begin until after he left the military. This is not an uncommon occurrence. Here we have almost a classic case of a symptom developed directly out of a traumatic episode. In some ways it seems almost too simple to be true. However, the point is that absolutely no connection is made between the symptom and the event on the part of the individual as would be the case in an hysterical personality.

CLOSING COMMENTS

I hope I have been able to convey some sense of the kind of men and experiences one encounters when working with Vietnam combat veterans. As the years pass I am sure these men will present themselves for treatment for a variety of problems which have their origin in military service. While I have seen a number of veterans in psychotherapy, I have yet to treat one in psychoanalysis. In fact, one finds few case reports of recent vintage (Wexler, 1972). I know other practitioners who have also treated veterans and they have had similar experiences. I am familiar with the literature on Holocaust survivors and there one finds a similar kind of picture. While all the data have yet to be gathered on these men, among those Holocaust survivors who encountered the most severe traumas, psychoanalysis seems to be unsuccessful in a high proportion of the cases. Among the survivors for whom the experience occurred during adolescence and who were badly sexually abused, analysis seems most difficult. This relative failure of the analytic process has been attributed to the results of the ensuing regression which reinstitutes traumatic ego adaptive devices, a failure in the synthetic functions of the traumatized ego, and inevitable negative transferential difficulties in which the analyst is viewed as a malignant, even persecutory, figure.

In spite of these difficulties, psychotherapy with veterans has generally met with a reasonable success rate. One must always consider constitutional factors, the pre-morbid personality picture, the extent and severity of the trauma, and subtle interactions between possible neurological-physical and psychological components in viewing such individuals in the treatment setting.

3

STRESS DISORDERS AMONG VIETNAM VETERANS: THE EMOTIONAL CONTEXT OF COMBAT CONTINUES

CHAIM F. SHATAN, M.D.

SANCTIONS AND SYSTEMS OF VIOLENCE IN VIETNAM

Authoritative Sanctions for Killing

The Vietnam war machine fulfilled Sanford and Comstock's (1971) two enabling prerequisites for the creation of mass executioners: the *dehumanization* of victims and *social permission* for collective destructiveness. As Milgram's (1963, 1965, 1967, 1974) studies of obedience suggest, the principle of authoritative sanction functions even in the absence of warfare. Most of Milgram's subjects followed orders unquestioningly—even if it meant harming others—as long as two conditions were met: (1) the instructions came from someone in a position of authority and (2) the setting made the tormentor dependent upon that authority. If the victim could be rendered remote or faceless, the tendency to inflict pain upon command was even greater. A victim can become faceless if his head is tied in a bag; he can become remote if he is 5,000 feet below the warrior. Readiness to commit evil acts goes hand in hand with the temptation to attribute responsibility for the decisions and their results to the experimenter—an option which is built into the experimental design.

In counter-guerrilla combat in Vietnam, terror was so total and the dehumanization of Orientals so pervasive (cf. Leventman & Camacho, 1974; Shatan, 1977) that mass slaughter became almost as automatic as it was in Nazi death camps. The summary punishments for disagreeing with authority, and the rewards bestowed upon and by those in command, facilitated killing even more.

43

Institutional Arrangements for Killing

Another generalization from the Milgram studies cited above is that division of labor, assembly-line fashion, makes it easier for subordinates to carry out violence. Milgram's experiments duplicate the hierarchy of orders and actions characteristic of the modern military. The experimenter in authority is removed from the violent act since he himself does not execute it. The experimental persecutor is separated from responsibility, even though he perpetrates the acts of violence, since he neither prescribes nor enforces them. Both the policies and the rewards come down the chain of command from the top. This handy institutional arrangement helps dilute feelings of personal guilt and accountability. Fritz Redl (1971) has labeled this "putting the superego in uniform." Moreover, the remote control panel of the computer glosses over whatever individualized reactions are left.

When Colonel (now General) and Mrs. George S. Patton III proudly supported the soldiers by mailing full-color Christmas cards of dismembered Viet Cong, it is no wonder that the soldiers tried to give him more bodies. It hardly mattered whether the bodies were VC, as long as the stacks were big enough and were labeled "Merry Christmas, George—from the boys." And when Colonel Patton's chaplain prayed, "Lord, give us the wisdom to find the bastards and the strength to pile on," he was almost invoking the authority of God for such actions (Livingston, 1969). Patton was not the only officer who craved such Christmas gifts: Four days before the 1969 Christmas truce, a Marine commander wrote on the order board, "Four more killing days till Christmas" S. J., 1971). Many a military chaplain reformulated the sixth commandment, "Thou shalt not kill," to "Thou shalt not murder," sanctifying the chain of permission for massacre (Nicholson, 1971).

The process by which My Lai massacres become logical developments can begin slowly. It can start when a G.I. is overcharged for a soda by a "slope broad" but decides not to shoot her after all (Sacks, 1970). He lets her go. Step number two is stopping some peasants, beating up an old man, and releasing the group. Step number three is interrogating the farmers, beating up the old man, and then machine-gunning him. And step four is wiping out the entire village. This progression may be intensified by the ritual of taking trophies after slaughter. This is encouraged by such chants as "Cut off da ear, or you're a queer!" which evoke memories of "fag-baiting" from basic combat training

(Levy, 1971). Such pyramiding of atrocity upon atrocity appeals to men who feel degraded by atrocities heaped on them—by both sides— a process vividly recorded by Seymour Hersh (1970).

Captain Medina ordered a more precise count of My Lai civilian casualties, but General Koster—in his helicopter overhead—immediately countermanded Medina. That a general officer took this responsibility at My Lai is only one of many demonstrations that terror was countenanced throughout all levels of command (Hersh, 1970). My Lai was only one of numerous instances of universal terror—terror designed for its mass psychological impact by the policy-makers at the top. For, as a Marine officer in Vietnam said, "When you've got them by the balls, the hearts and minds will follow" (Opton, 1971).

Sensory Disorientation and Perceptual Dissonance

The atmosphere of terror and counter-terror saturated the lives of the G.I.'s as well—though its impact on them was seldom officially acknowledged. Under the compelling sway of terror, they experienced a type of *sensory dislocation*. Emotionally anesthetized, ethically immunized, without bearings, disconnected from any human reality, our anti-guerrilla warriors existed in a dreamlike sleepwalker's no-man's land.

To adapt and survive in such a setting, the soldier must deform his "self" as radically as concentration camp inmates did in the psychotic reality of the extermination camps (Tanay, 1968). When death (as in an ambush) is the new "reality principle," the paranoid position of combat affords the only hope of staying alive. Styles of affect, action, and cognition are transformed when military reality eclipses civilian reality. As destructiveness—which once appeared remote—becomes the ever present reality, one's old perceptual world seems to vanish "through the membrane of reality" (Kingry, 1972). The perception of outer events, the way they are experienced inwardly, is completely restructured. Acquisition of this new perceptual and experiential frame of reference completes the "*transfiguration* of the personality (Shatan, 1972). The new inner reality again feels synchronous with the new outer reality. In basic training jargon, the G.I. is now "combat-effective" (Shapiro, 1973, p. 119).

An alternative to this adaptation is a clash between the two systems of perceiving reality, a *perceptual dissonance:* The "membrane of reality" has only been gashed or torn but not penetrated. Inner and outer are not in harmony, and the soldier can function neither for battle nor for survival. Clinical "symptoms" may set in, and he becomes a psychiatric casualty. This perceptual dissonance is a major factor in delayed combat trauma (Shatan, 1973; Horowitz & Solomon, Chapter 13). The paranoid hyperalertness and autonomic arousal of the combat stance emerge as manifestations of disturbed functioning. While obviously adaptational in the combat zone, they are maladaptive elsewhere.

HOME FROM THE WAR: POST-COMBAT ADJUSTMENT

My awareness of and encounter with post-combat syndromes arose in the course of my work with Vietnam Veterans' Rap Groups (Lifton, Chapter 10). Even if there had been as few psychiatric casualties within the war zone as the Army boasted (cf, Bourne, 1969), veterans often experience emotional turmoil after they return to civilian life. Under the computerized rotation system of the Vietnam war, vets returned piecemeal, singly, not with their units, not with their buddies, and with no parades to welcome them home.

Public recognition of the so-called "post-Vietnam syndrome" began to emerge after a Medal of Honor winner was killed in a Detroit robbery attempt. Jon Nordheimer's front-page *New York Times* story sensitively described Sgt. Dwight Johnson's apathy and alienation, his demoralization by unemployment, and his suspicion that he was being exploited by the army, even when he was in the hospital. His government's highest martial honor weighed heavily around his neck each time he was praised for slaughter—and thereby forced to recall that he was the sole survivor of his tank crew, buddies during eleven months of warfare. While the army used him in recruiting drives, empty promise piled upon empty promise and his cynicism grew.

Johnson had been placed in restraints and narcotized for 24 hours immediately after his final day of combat—the action for which he received the supreme distinction. Yet, 48 hours later, he was back in the U.S. with a non-psychiatric discharge. His emotional difficulties received no official interest until he became a "hot property." His treatment began more than a year after his return home, at the Valley Forge Army Hospital. There he was diagnosed as suffering from "depression caused by post-Vietnam adjustment problems." (Nordheimer, 1971).

On several occasions, he asked his psychiatrist how society would react if he were to respond to the black dilemma in Detroit with the same uncontrolled ferocity that had earned him the highest recognition in battle. He found his ultimate answer, not in a distant jungle but on the floor of a hometown grocery. There he lived out his haunting fantasies and nightmares of being killed at point-blank range.

Delayed Stress Reactions

Nine to 60 months after demobilization many veterans begin to "go through changes." They notice—often for the first time—growing apathy, alienation, depression, mistrust, cynicism, and expectation of betrayal, as well as difficulty in concentrating, insomnia, restlessness, nightmares, uprootedness, and impatience with almost any situation or relationship.

This very *delay* in clinical manifestations fostered the Nixon administration's claim that the Vietnam war had resulted in fewer psychiatric casualties than any other war in which the U.S. had fought.

In Congressional testimony, however, Army consultant Gerald Caplan (1970) and his associate, Charles Levy, confirmed our own impressions that significant numbers of Vietnam veterans, especially those with *extensive combat experience,* are troubled emotionally. Moreover, the onset of disturbance may not be clinically apparent until some time after discharge. William Niederland (1972), who devoted 25 years to working with concentration camp survivors, noted that the same delay preceded their "survivor syndrome." He suggested that, in both groups, the initial triumph over staying alive prevented immediate symptoms; only as the advanced psychic numbing wore off did symptoms become prominent.

The returns are not yet in on the corollary: How long do post-combat symptoms last? Most combat veterans bear out Audie Murphy's resigned comment to a reporter: "You know, you never get over combat, I don't think you ever do." Until the day he died, our most decorated World War II veteran endured frequent nightmares and kept a loaded German automatic pistol under his pillow. Murphy and a cook were the only ones to escape death, injury, or capture out of an original command group of about 300.

SYMPTOMS OF POST-COMBAT SYNDROME

In our experiences with the Vietnam Veterans Rap Groups, six common themes of post-combat difficulty emerged: (1) guilt feelings and self-punishment; (2) feeling scapegoated; (3) rage and other violent impulses against indiscriminate targets; (4) combat brutalization and its attendant "psychic numbing"; (5) alienation from one's own feelings and from other people; and (6) doubt about continued ability to love and trust others.

Guilt Feelings and Self-Punishment

Easiest to voice are shame, guilt, and disgust about those killed and wounded—on both sides—and preoccupation with the fate of friends. Veterans will often ask, "How do we turn off the guilt? Can we atone? Why didn't we get killed, rather than carry out illegal orders?" Their own answers follow quickly: They speak of "paying their dues" for surviving unscathed when others did not survive. They invite self-punishment by picking self-defeating fights, inviting rejection from near ones, even getting involved in a remarkably high number of single-car, single-occupant accidents. Comparably, epidemiological studies of American POWs from the Korean and Second World Wars show a similar extraordinarily high rate of violent deaths from homicide, suicide or automobile accidents (Nefzger, 1970).

Feeling Scapegoated

Many veterans feel scapegoated and victimized. After they stop complaining about inadequate medical and educational benefits, they begin to focus on society at large. They feel used, deceived and betrayed when senior officers are let go scot-free for war atrocities. Meanwhile, GI's— like the bearers of bad news throughout history—carry the burden of the war's unpopularity. John Kerry, a leader of Vietnam Veterans Against the War, reported that one Midwest American Legion post rejected Vietnam veterans for membership because "they have lost the war." Even pro-war parents fear that their sons, newly returned from "the 'Nam," may terrorize civilians at home. Yet other vets have been repudiated by pacifist college women whether or not the vets themselves espoused anti-war attitudes.

Rage and Other Violent Impulses Against Indiscriminate Targets

Rage follows not only on the heels of such humiliating rebuffs as those described above, but also from the veterans' beliefs that they have been betrayed and manipulated (Bourne, 1970). This is exacerbated when the returnees discover that, as part of the closing of ranks at home, their old status and roles have been given away to others—a development which may be impossible to reverse. The survival skills which they acquired in the military can be a dangerous liability in coping with the ambivalent reception at home, for the automatic, *tactical* nature of counter-guerrilla training encourages the unleashing of rage, sometimes in violent impulses, against indiscriminate targets. When Steve, a medic, found out that his younger brother had become a pacifist, he hurled him down the stairs; this response was so automatic that he didn't know how his brother had come to land in a heap on the floor—he was stunned by his own behavior. Such outbursts are prominent in the "flashback" syndrome (Neff, 1976).

Combat Brutalization and Its Attendant "Psychic Numbing"

"Harassing the troops" in basic combat training promotes obedience through maltreatment and humiliation. In line with the principle, "If you can't beat 'em, join 'em," the trainee learns to ape his persecutors, that is, his officers. *They are* the aggressors with whom he identifies (Freud, 1946) in the course of the psychological regression. During regression, his character is rebuilt, so that he turns into a combat personality. Once again, he learns how expendable he is. This brings us back to our earlier discussion of obedience.

In basic training, according to Ken Campbell of Philadelphia, recruits were ridiculed and punched if they did not understand that they were never to use the term "Vietnamese"; only such epithets as "slope," "gook," "dink," were permitted—for both friend and foe (cf. Eisenhart, 1975 for a similar and more detailed account). As noted earlier in this chapter, a combat zone is an atrocity-producing situation in which dehumanization has no clear-cut boundaries; hate encompasses *any* Oriental, and ultimately any civilian.

Few veterans doubt the appropriatness of their hatred for Orientals until they are discharged. But their quandary is more than an ethical one. Survivors of more traditional warfare may be able to keep their tendencies towards savage behavior relatively compartmentalized and forbidden. In counter-insurgency warfare, the opposite is the case; limits on the expression of violent impulses remain obscure, and are, therefore, not easy to bring under control. Sensitivity and compassion, on the other hand, tend to be inhibited or even suppressed.

Alienation from One's Own Feelings and from Other People

After consistently anesthetizing their empathic reactions and cutting themselves off from ordinary sensory experience under fire, many ex-combatants find it painful and difficult to have humane feelings for other people—difficult because they are frozen in a state of "emotional anesthesia," painful because thawing out their numbed reactions to the evil and death which enveloped them in combat is insupportable. Unable to forget, unable to endow their Vietnam experience with meaning, they relive it endlessly. Frequently, they find inner peace only by devising a "dead space" in their psyches where memories live on, cut off from their enduring emotional impact. The price of this peace—alienation from feelings in general—creates a powerful obstacle to the formation of close relationships. Friends may perceive veterans as perched on the edge of parties like gargoyles, gazing in detachment at humanity far beneath them—the proverbial "thousand-mile" stare. If the war is discussed they may quickly retreat further into their "mental foxholes." Girlfriends say that they find these men to be all but unreachable.

Doubt about Continued Ability to Love and Trust Others

Anguished uncertainty about their continued ability to trust others, let alone love, is one of the most poignant features of the returned soldiers' dilemma. Many fear that their capacity for accepting affection or giving affection has been permanently stunted. As one veteran said, "You paid a high price for trusting other people in the 'Nam. Whenever you acted human, you got screwed." Another veteran lamented that his "sensitivities burned up and died somewhere," that he had been "deprived of my heart." Still another affirmed: "I hope I can learn to love as much as I learned to hate—and I sure learned to hate. But love's a pretty heavy word." Occasionally, soldiers felt reassured by the warmth and tenderness that Vietnamese children awakened in them—but this last shred of humanity could be shattered when they saw comrades blown to pieces by a little girl with grenades around her waist under her dress. While it was dangerous to hate because one could turn this hatred on one's own buddies, it was also perilous to love, because one might love one's enemy, and that might make one totally unable to act. Accordingly, when they come home, they allow little emotion and little intimacy to develop in relationships. Close relations have become charged with great potential for anxiety and hurt. In despair and in hopelessness, they keep their deepest emotional energies in reserve.

"IMPACTED GRIEF"

Rage, torture, and self-recrimination are not a fortuitous collection of symptoms. Clinicians are emphatic in their recognition of these as hallmarks of frustrated grief and submerged mourning. After working intimately with these men, professionals are often unable to avoid being haunted by the subtle resignation which pervades their lives.

In extreme situations—concentration camps, active combat—grief threatens the morale necessary for survival and combat effectiveness. Grief and intimacy are among the emotions which are strenuously discouraged in the modern military. Recruits are cautioned against friendships which are too close lest a buddy should die and provoke mourning, depriving his comrades-in-arms of combat spirit. They cannot afford to be tender and caring with each other lest they relax the constant vigilance demanded by warfare, Vietnam style. However, since combatants remain human, brutalization may often suppress but seldom eradicate normal human bereavement responses.

During World War I, Freud (1912) elucidated the function of grief in helping the mourner let go of a missing part of life and acknowledging that it continues to exist only in the memory. The *"post-Vietnam syndrome"* confronts us with the unconsummated grief of soldiers—"impacted grief" in which an unending, encapsulated past robs the present of meaning. Their sorrow is unspent, the grief of their wounds is untold, their guilt is unexpiated. Much of what civilians view as cynical disillusionment is really the veterans' numbed apathy from an excess of death and bereavement. The welcome with which the soldiers are met is equivocal: They may be regarded as those who "lost the war," as well as trained killers. This absence of social acceptance, this defensive rejection of their needs, aggravates their failure to mourn even more. Experiences whose horror they can barely convey set them apart from the rest of the population.

CONCLUSIONS

The survivor of combat returns home from a world in which military reality eclipsed civilian reality. In an ambush, death is the new "reality principle." In an ambush, a soldier can stay alive only by transfiguring his ego and permitting everyday reality to "slide through a membrane" (in the words of one veteran). His perception of events is completely changed as he takes on the paranoid posture of combat. His styles of feeling, thinking and acting are transformed as he restructures his personality. All that is needed to achieve "reality control" is "doublethink," an "endless series of victories over your own memory" (Orwell, 1948).

When he comes back, the veteran must penetrate through this membrane of reality again. No formal help is available for this task. Once again, outer reality is not congruent with remembered inner reality. As he faces the renewed clash between the two reality-perception systems, the warrior experiences "perceptual dissonance." In due course, "symptoms" arise. "Normally," combat and killing relieved his tension. Now the seething tension must be restrained, locked, held in. The impulse to discharge it presses constantly for expression.

Section II
RELATED RESEARCH

This section presents findings based on empirical investigations of the parameters of veterans' psychosocial adjustment in general and stress disorders among Vietnam veterans in particular. Included is the most significant research in the area, representing a variety of perspectives. For example, in contrast to research efforts which identify combat as a major source of prolonged stress, Worthington contends that predispositional personality and personal background factors account for current veteran psychosocial adjustment. Other contributors, however, present research which confirms significant differences in veteran readjustment when combat experiences are stratified.

The first chapter reviews most of the research to date which focuses on various psychological readjustment parameters of Vietnam-era veterans ranging from mild negative experiences to acute psychosis. Two views of the literature emerge: the notion of stress evaporation, a perspective which suggests that few if any long-term problems are associated with military service, and the concept of *residual-stress,* which suggests that current mental health functioning can be traced to combat-related stress. Conceptual and methodological problems within the veteran studies area are discussed throughout the review. This chapter also introduces the papers that follow in this section.

The second chapter in this section, by Edgar Nace and colleagues, attempts to deal with one facet of the war experience—long-term substance abuse. The paper reports the results of a follow-up study of 200 Vietnam veterans who were interviewed on an average of 28 months after completing a tour of duty in Southeast Asia. Extensive adjustment problems reflected in substance abuse and depression were still present among the veterans surveyed. Thirty-five percent of the veterans, for example, scored within the clinically depressed range of the Beck Depression Inventory. The relationship between pre-service factors, narcotic use in Vietnam and current adjustment is examined in some detail.

Chapter 6, by Bernard Spilka, Lisa Friedman, and David Rosenberg, provides important insights into the nature of death and the combat experience. The first part of the chapter attempts to briefly introduce the reader to the social-psychological literature on death. Based on their interviews with 104 combat veterans of the Vietnam war, the authors attempt to identify both the current death perspectives of the sample and the major parameters which account for the perspective. Among other things, the researchers find that the Vietnam experience has a continuing effect on the value of life and attitudes toward death. One unexpected finding was the minimal role that being wounded in combat played in accounting for present death perspectives.

Chapter 7 by Robert Panzarella, David Mantell and R. Harlan Bridenbaugh addresses the competing speculations about the current, post-combat, mental health of the Vietnam veteran soldiers still in the military. Of particular interest is the incidence of "numbed guilt syndrome" among 143 soldiers who sought treatment at a military mental health clinic. Although the sample was not stratified for combat experience, it was divided between soldiers who served in Vietnam and those who did not. No significant differences were found in terms of various psychiatric symptoms. Implications of the findings for post-military adjustment are discussed.

In Chapter 8 Worthington goes a step further in challenging research which finds long-term stress resulting from combat. After reviewing the literature related to post-military psychological adjustment, Worthington summarizes a series of research projects conducted under his direction. His findings tend to support the predispositional perspective of post-military adjustment—soldiers with a history of poor coping abilities prior to military service exhibit maladaptive behaviors during and after military service. Similarly, pre-service factors tend to account for more of the variance in post-military psychosocial adjustment than various experiences within the military, including exposure to combat.

Chapter 9 by Edna Hunter is, perhaps, the single most important work written about the Vietnam POW experience. She reviews the research addressed to the immediate and long-term stress associated with the incarceration experience. Included in this review is an up-to-date summary of the ongoing longitudinal research project being conducted by the Center for Prisoner of War Studies at the Naval Health Research Center in San Diego, where Dr. Hunter is the Head of the Family Studies Branch and Assistant Director. Most scholars have acknowledged that the project is one of the most comprehensive research programs of its kind to date.

4

PSYCHOLOGICAL ADJUSTMENT AMONG VIETNAM VETERANS: AN OVERVIEW OF THE RESEARCH

CHARLES R. FIGLEY, Ph.D.

Although the focus of this volume is on a rather narrow group of psychiatric disorders among Vietnam veterans, this chapter adopts a broader scope. Here I will attempt to review most of the available research which has addressed, in some way, post-military service adjustment, with particular attention to the broad area of psychosocial adjustment. Psychosocial adjustment, for the purpose of the review, is defined as a state of general emotional well-being, satisfaction, and relative comfort with other people as well as with oneself. Thus, psychosocial adjustment includes both the interpersonal and the intrapersonal parameters.

Prior to a detailed review of the psychosocial adjustment literature, it is important to point out that the Vietnam war directly affected a great number of Americans. Over eight and one-half million men and women were in the armed services during our involvement in the war starting in 1964. By now over seven million of these servicemen and servicewomen have returned to civilian life, including over three million who survived a tour of duty in Southeast Asia. But the numbers affected do not stop with the military personnel.

In his review of official government records, Lieberman (1971a, 1971b) found that by the end of 1970 there were 18,000 widows and 12,000 orphans attributed to Vietnam on the Veterans Administration rolls. By February of 1969, among the enlisted men alone, 40 percent of the Vietnam war casualties were husbands and 20 percent were fathers. By 1970 approximately 250,000 Americans had been bereaved by death of an immediate family member in Vietnam. This figure includes 30,000 widows and orphans, 80,000 parents, and 60,000 grandparents. Another 750,000 had an immediate family member who was seriously injured in Vietnam. Based on 1971 data, living veterans of all eras comprise one-eighth of the U.S. population and their families comprise nearly one-third. "Add to this the 3.6 million survivors of deceased veterans, and we find that almost half the population are potential recipients of veteran benefits—and problems" (Lieberman, 1971a, p. 712).

Although family-related problems of the Vietnam veteran have not been the focus of any investigations, they have been discussed in a number of reports. Polner (1971), for example, in his detailed investigation of the readjustment problems of nine Vietnam combat veterans, included the reactions of family members. In every case, family members perceived significant impairments in the veteran's emotional stability. Unfortunately, Polner did not focus on how the veteran viewed his family and the family's role in facilitating—or frustrating—the psychological readjustment process.

In an analysis of 200 Vietnam veterans receiving treatment at a large midwestern VA hospital, Lumry, Cedarleaf, Wright and Braatz (1970) found that a high percentage of the sample were having various kinds of interpersonal problems. For example: (a) 57 percent of the sample had "family relationship" problems in that the veteran was "still very dependent upon the family (of origin), causing considerable conflict with the family"; (b) 58 percent were experiencing "socialization" problems since the veteran did not "have satisfying interests or hobbies"; and (c) most had problems in "interpersonal adjustment" in that they were "unable to maintain satisfying interpersonal relationships," including their marital relationships.

These findings have been supported recently by Nace, Meyers, O'Brien and Ream (1975). They found that among a group of veterans who served in Vietnam, two years (on average) after their return to their families marital status clearly differentiated between those who were clinically depressed and those who were not. "The problems leading to the separation or divorce were attributed by subjects in the depressed group, as compared with the non-depressed group, to be more frequently related to the use of drugs or factors intrinsic to military service (e.g., prolonged separations)." (p. 5). Unfortunately, since the primary focus of the study was the follow-up testing of previously detected drug users contrasted with a medical control group, sufficient statistical controls were not used in the data analysis and marital and family factors were not selected as criteria variables. Consequently, as with all of the research cited above, findings which confirm or disconfirm family problems among Vietnam veterans have been coincidental and largely anecdotal.

Perhaps the most comprehensive and programatic research efforts focused on the family in relation to the Vietnam veteran have been underway at the Center for Prisoner of War Studies in San Diego at the Naval Health Research Center. In this volume, Edna Hunter (Chapter 9) reports a portion of the findings, illustrating quite clearly the profound impact the Vietnam war has had on the families of prisoners who returned and those who did not.

OVERVIEW OF THE RESEARCH

Although no research to date has focused primarily on the interpersonal and family life of Vietnam veterans, a significant number of studies have explored various issues within the general area of psychosocial readjustment. Opinions vary widely about the severity, prevalence and importance of the prolonged effects of combat stress on veterans' mental health. A dichotomy of opinion about the psychological fate of the Vietnam veteran has emerged. The *stress evaporation perspective* holds that the combat veteran probably does suffer some psychosocial readjustment problems during and immediately following military service, but that any problems disappear after returning home; in other words, time heals all wounds. On the other hand, the *residual stress perspective* holds that combat-related stress reactions among combat veterans are inevitable and that significant numbers of veterans are trying to cope with severe psychosocial readjustment problems originating years ago in Vietnam.

Stress Evaporation Perspective

A significant number of social scientists who have studied the Vietnam veteran have suggested, based on their findings, that few veterans are suffering from readjustment problems compared to nonveterans, and, similarly, that combat veterans today are not significantly different from noncombatants. In effect, the stress evaporation perspective concedes that combat was a stressful event and may have caused temporary emotional distress, but the findings to date suggest that few veterans continue to suffer from psychological maladjustment. If the veterans were adversely affected by combat experiences, any symptoms of maladjustment had disappeared prior to testing.

Carr (1973) attempted to compare Vietnam veterans enrolled in college (n = 75) in terms of self-concept (self-criticism, response bias, self-perception as measured by the Tennessee Self-Concept Scale) and the individual's perception of control elements in life (internal versus external locus of control, measured by the Rotter I-E scale). The results consistently showed that, in general, no significant differences existed between veteran and nonveteran students with regard to the two dependent variables. Unfortunately, differences between combat and noncombat veterans were not assessed. In addition to other shortcomings admitted by the researcher were uncontrolled demand characteristics introduced when the purpose of the study was explained to the veteran sample prior to completing the instruments. The researcher explained ". . . that it was . . . an attempt to gather data concerned with veterans who appear to be *adjusting** and making an effort toward becoming productive members of society" (Carr, 1973, p. 44).

In terms of manifest anxiety level, Enzie, Sawyer and Montgomery (1973) found no significant differences between Vietnam "combat" veterans and a random sample of undergraduate male students. The study assumed, however, that all veterans who were in Vietnam experienced equal amounts of combat, which, of course, is not the case (cf. Bourne, 1969, 1970). Moreover, no measures of response bias were used (e.g., social desirability) which would be highly relevant in this study ("Why should I be anxious now when I went through so much in the 'Nam?").

In the present volume (Chapter 8), Worthington reviews the findings of a number of studies, including his own. In one study (1973, 1977), for example, Worthington found that among 147 male Vietnam veterans who had been released from the Army in the year before he interviewed them (April 1972 through March 1973), there were no significant differences between veterans serving in Vietnam and those who did not serve there with regard to anomie, self-concept and social adjustment. As in most studies in this area, however, differences between combat and non-combat veterans were not assessed. Based on his findings, on the other hand, Worthington suggests that, more than any other factors, pre-service variables account for both in-service and post-service adjustment (also see Chapter 5).

Perhaps more than any other, the research reports by Borus (1973a, 1973b, 1973c, 1974) continue to be the most widely cited in support of the stress evaporation perspective. Borus found that only 23 percent

---

* Author's emphasis.

of the 765 Vietnam veterans interviewed had some record of discipli-nary-legal maladjustment and emotional maladjustment in their first seven months back in the United States, and that the veteran group did not differ, significantly, from a nonveteran comparison group. On closer inspection of the methodology, however, it is clear that the findings can-not be generalized to a veteran population—especially those who ex-perienced combat in Vietnam—for the following reasons: (1) All of the Vietnam "veterans" sampled were still on active duty in the Army. No sample of discharged Vietnam veterans was available to contrast their "reentry readjustment problems" with those of the seemingly well-adjusted active duty soldiers. (2) The comparison group composed of 244 nonveterans were actually military personnel who did not serve in Vietnam. (3) There was no attempt to collect follow-up data on the sample after they were released from military service. Both intuitively and theoretically there is a high probability that primary reentry prob-lems among Vietnam veterans, especially those who were involved in combat, would not be manifested until the soldier was extricated from the military system which sanctioned war involvement. (4) The Viet-nam "veterans" were not separated by level of combat involvement. A number of studies (e.g., DeFazio, Rustin & Diamond, 1975; Figley, 1977; Strayor & Ellenhorn, 1975) have shown that there are significant differences in readjustment between Vietnam veterans who experienced combat and those who did not. (5) Finally, anyone who has ever served in the Armed Forces is aware that release from military duty will be delayed until all pre-release examinations, psychological as well as med-ical, are passed and no need for treatment is indicated. Thus, there is a strong possibility that all or most of the 765 Vietnam "veteran" active duty soldiers were more concerned about responses which would avoid delays in getting out of the Army than those which would shed some light on the "the readjustment problems of the veteran" for a group of Army psychologists.

Segal and Segal (1976) found little support for the notion that vet-erans (n = 113) differed significantly from nonveterans (n = 124) in an analysis of "23 predominant Likert type attitude items covering trust in government and isolationism-interventionism" (p. 5). Veterans and nonveterans differed significantly on only two attitudes. As the researchers noted, "The most striking finding . . . is the absence of dif-ferences between veterans and nonveterans" (p. 5). Unfortunately, the results add little to our knowledge of the adjustment problems of the

Vietnam veterans since (1) a very small percentage of the veteran population was sampled (113/29 million); (2) all veterans were analyzed as a group even though evidence exists that there are basic differences among veterans of different war eras (eg., Braatz, Lumry & Wright, 1971; Dickerman & Pearson, 1972; Lorr, Peck & Stenger, 1975); (3) separate analyses were not computed to compare combat and noncombat veterans; and (4) only 13 Vietnam-era veterans were sampled, *including* an unknown number who actually went to Vietnam and saw combat.

The nature of the Segal and Segal (1976) paper bordered on a diatribe, refuting claims by Lifton (1973) and Helmer (1974) that the Vietnam veterans were, for example, alienated and hostile toward the government. For instance, in an added attempt to challenge the residual stress perspective, the Segals cite "research reporting that middle-aged civilian women are more favorably disposed to violence than Vietnam era enlisted personnel (Brady & Rappoport, 1974)." A closer reading of the Brady and Rappoport article, however, reveals that "those who report heavy combat experience have the highest general violence scores" (p. 735).

Panzarella and his colleagues (see Chapter 7) sampled 143 American soldiers stationed in Germany who sought the services of an Army mental health clinic. Included in the sample were 34 "veterans" (soldiers who served at least one tour of duty in Vietnam). Unlike most studies of Vietnam veterans, this research attempted to focus specifically on the psychiatric fallout among Vietnam veterans. Factor analytic statistical procedures were performed on the responses to a battery of tests (two adjective checklists and a psychiatric symptoms checklist). Their results tend to support the stress evaporation perspective since they were unable to detect any special psychiatric symptomatology unique to those who served in Vietnam, in contrast to the soldiers who did not serve in Vietnam. As with other studies cited thus far, however, methodological limitations of the study render the results inconclusive. For example, as with the study by Borus, cited above, the entire sample was still in the military and subject to its sanctions. The sample of "veterans" was quite small (n = 34) and no attempt was made to differentiate between those who saw combat and those who did not. Moreover, the investigators fail to account for the fact that 14 of the veterans (41 percent) "had some previous contact with a mental health worker or institution" (p. 10).

Residual Stress Perspective

A growing number of scholars and practitioners have reported findings which support the notion that Vietnam veterans are suffering from psychological readjustment problems. They suggest that the nature of the Vietnam combat experience has made a significant and long-lasting impact on the veteran, making the transition back to civilian life difficult.

Among the veterans surveyed in the Yankelovich (1974) study of 2,516 non-college youth, 176 were veterans who served in Vietnam. Yankelovich found significant differences between Vietnam veterans and nonveterans in that veterans (1) had double the unemployment rate, (2) had a lower general morale, (3) were more pessimistic about their future, (4) felt greater estrangement from American society, (5) were less strict in their moral viewpoint, and (6) were less traditional and more liberal regarding social and political questions compared to their nonveteran counterparts (p. 142). Unfortunately, because the results were reported primarily for popular consumption, levels of statistical differences were not reported; thus some of the claimed differences may be due to sampling error and chance.

In an attempt to learn more about Vietnam veteran psychiatric patients, Struen and Solberg (1972) compared a group of 88 psychiatric patients at a VA hospital and a matched-by-age comparison group at a nearby Army base who were in the process of being discharged. Among the factors investigated were (1) the men's relationship with their parents, (2) family mental behavior, (3) family mobility during childhood, (4) dependency needs, (5) sexual identification, (6) socioeconomic status, (7) drug use, (8) ability to cope with transition to civilian life, and (9) conflicts with wife and/or family. Although both groups were experiencing some degree of problems in most areas, the veterans group appeared to differ significantly from the pre-veteran group in that the veterans (1) were lower in coping abilities, (2) had more stressful parental relationships and (3) had a greater incidence of drug and alcohol abuse.

Struen and Solberg failed to control, however, for the pre-military proclivities. They were unable to show that military service was the major factor in veterans' problems because similar problems could have existed prior to military service. It appeared that veterans who had a history of poor interpersonal adjustment would experience difficulty during the transition back to civilian life. Another problem that challenges generalization of the study's findings to all veterans is that all the subjects were VA psychiatric patients.

Strayer and Ellenhorn (1975) randomly selected and interviewed 40 veterans who were discharged from the Army during the Vietnam war (1970-1971). The researchers were attempting to "differentiate between those who experienced adjustment problems (disorientation, violent acting out, bitterness, hopelessness and apathy) and those who appeared to have been able to cope with their war experiences and became reintegrated into civilian life" (p. 4). Results suggested "that depressions, hostility, guilt and over-all maladjustment are experienced by a diverse and large number of Vietnam Army veterans" (p. 9). Further, combat involvement appeared to be associated with a negative attitude toward the war, guilt, depression and feelings of hostility. The severity of adjustment problems in the sample was found to be highly correlated with, among other things, the amount of combat involvement. Further support for the negative effects of combat experience of veterans was reported. Strayer and Ellenhorn found that 60 percent of the veterans involved in moderate to heavy combat "were rated by the three clinical judges and by themselves (veterans) as poorly adjusted and in need of professional help; and over 37 percent indicated that they felt apathetic and had no goals for the future" (1975, p. 88).

In their "uncomfortable conclusion" Strayer and Ellenhorn (1975) suggest that veterans high in authoritarianism, in contrast to those high in intraception (Adorno, Frankel-Brunswick, Levinson & Stanford, 1950), are "able to cope with the most brutal acts of the Vietnam war and to compartmentalize these experiences . . . and express less bitterness toward the military. . . . However, these same men are more likely to feel more conflict over and to be more sensitive to the paradoxes of the Vietnam war and less able to reduce the dissonance created by their own involvement" (p. 19).

Pollock, White and Gold (1975) found that 54 combat veterans attending college differed significantly from their non-combat cohorts in that the combat veterans (1) displayed political attitudes markedly different from those held by non-combat veterans, (2) were more likely to exhibit alienation from the activity of United States military forces in Vietnam, (3) exhibited little confidence in their ability to control their own destiny, and (4) were more likely to view violence as necessary for certain groups to get their way. Similar findings have been reported by other investigators, regarding alienation (Wikler, 1974) and violence (Brady & Rappoport, 1974).

Pollack *et al.* concluded, sadly, that the final "reintegration" or "renewal" phase of the transition back to civilian life for the veteran, as described by Lifton (1973), is more typically replaced by feelings of alienation among the veterans who experienced combat.

> Our study indicates that the political role disintegration of combat veterans is thorough, enduring and cumulative, a civic tragedy of considerable dimension. Unless these veterans are able to locate or force new civic roles appropriate to the experiences they have undergone, the consequences both for them and for the society could be shattering (Pollock *et al.*, 1975).

Findings from a large epidemiological study (Helzer, Robins & Davis, 1974; Robins, Davis & Goodwin, 1974; cited by Egendorf, 1975) involving a large sample (n = 500) of soldiers recently returned from Vietnam (data collected in September 1971) suggest that a sizable minority of veteran soldiers had symptoms of depression eight to twelve months after returning from Vietnam. The researcher also found that depressive syndromes were significantly more frequent both in men who saw combat and in those who lost friends in combat. Again, the combat experience factor was significant in accounting for adjustment problems.

Nace, Meyers, O'Brien and Ream (1975) reported a rather disturbing finding regarding the incidence of depression among Vietnam combat veterans two years after release from active service. The sample of 150 veterans they surveyed was part of a larger study of follow-up evaluations of veterans who were once treated in Vietnam either for drug use (n = 97 in this sample) or other medical reasons (n = 53 in this sample). When data were analyzed from semi-structured interviews and the Beck Depression Inventory (BDI) (Beck, 1967) was completed, over one-third of the sample (35 percent) scored within the "clinically depressed" range, while another 15 percent were within the range of "mild depression." High correlations were found between BDI ratings and self-ratings of depression. Additional analyses revealed, among other things, that a number of social psychological variables statistically discriminate between the two groups: non-judgmental discipline (Article 15 punishment) while in Vietnam, serving with a combat unit, employment status, level of education and marital status. That is, the depressed veterans more often served in a combat unit in Vietnam, were more often disciplined (but not court martialed) while serving in Vietnam, had slightly fewer years of education (x = 11.3 vs. x = 11.8), were more likely to be divorced/separated or single compared to the nondepressed veterans.

The incidence of depression among such a high percentage of Vietnam veterans is particularly disturbing since (1) it was over two years after they had served in Vietnam, (2) none of the veterans were under treatment or seeking treatment for their depression, and (3) negative psychological fall-out among Vietnam veterans has been reported to be significantly lower compared to previous wars.

Further support for the notion that combat veterans are significantly different from noncombat veterans was found by DeFazio, Rustin and Diamond (1975). A total of 914 veterans were mailed a four-page questionnaire (including demographic questions along with questions related to their present status and items related to military service) and a psychological symptom checklist derived from the MMPI and the Mooney Problem Check List. The subjects were asked to indicate the presence or absence of a symptom "before he entered the service, when he left actual duty and at present," (DeFazio *et al.*, 1975, p. 160). An internal consistency measure of reliability (Kuder Richardson #20) was computed for the latter instrument and the results showed good reliability (.81).

Among the 207 veterans who returned the battery of instruments, 144 had some combat experience and 46 veterans experienced heavy combat. Presumably to accommodate a more accurate analysis of variance with repeated measures, an equal number of noncombat veterans were randomly selected from the initial sample of noncombat respondents who returned their completed instruments. Thus, the basic data analysis was a 2 (groups: combat, noncombat) by 3 (time periods: pre-service, at discharge, currently) factorial design with repeated measures.

Results strongly support the notion that both combat experience and the three time periods were significantly associated with psychiatric symptoms. Main effects were found for both the group factor ($F = 5$; $p < .05$) and the time periods factor ($F = 15.78$; $p < .01$). Although interaction effects did not approach statistical significance, multiple comparison tests (using the Tukey formula) showed that the time of discharge accounted for the most acute differences between combat and noncombat groups. Although both groups were very similar prior to military service, combat veterans reported significantly more problems than noncombat veterans with regard to, for example, disturbed sleep, feeling blue, something wrong with one's mind, belief that one is more nervous than others, life is a strain, am a hothead, unable to relax, and find it hard to get close to others. Although all veterans reported fewer numbers of symptoms at the "present time," a sizable percentage of combat veterans reported, for example, frequent nightmares (68 percent), am a hothead (44 percent), hard to relax and hard to get close to other people (35 percent). These "present time" percentages were twice those of the noncombat group on these items.

These findings are particularly striking because, as DeFazio *et al.* (1975) note, the veterans in the sample "represent one of the most fortunate, well motivated, and intelligent groups of veterans" (p. 162) since they were competent enough to seek education (see Chapter 2 for an extended discussion). The authors later pose an important question which must be addressed immediately by mental health service providers: "If such symptoms exist among a large minority of veterans (college students) who have shown their intelligence, coping skills, patience, and perseverance in the face of difficulty, what must the situation be like for the large minority of veterans who are totally unemployed, imprisoned or hospitalized?" (DeFazio *et al.*, 1975).

In a similar study, veterans attending two college campuses in different parts of the country were sent two questionnaires which focused on various aspects of interpersonal adjustment. The purpose of the study was to assess present levels of psychological readjustment of veterans in contrast to earlier life periods and to compare the responses of veterans who were in combat with veterans who were not. In two separate reports, the findings (Figley, 1977, 1978) focused on qualitative interpersonal adjustment (IPA) scores. Results of a two (combatant vs. noncombatant) by four (adult life periods: before, during, immediately after and presently) analysis of variance revealed: (1) that IPA varied as a function of military service experience during the four adult-life periods among combatants but not among noncombatants; (2) except for the premilitary period, noncombatants had significantly higher IPA scores than combatants over the last three adult life periods. Findings were consistent with the predictions.

In another report (Figley & Eisenhart, 1975), data analysis of individual items revealed that noncombatants had fewer physical fights, arguments, conflicts with the law, violent dreams, and violent fantasies than combatants; they had more close friends, got drunk and got high on marijuana less frequently. The conclusions based on both reports tend to support the notion that there are at least dispositional differences between veterans who were exposed to combat and veterans who were not, and that these differences continue long after release from military service. There appeared to be a linear relationship between the length of time since combat and the perceived level of interpersonal and psychological readjustment. As a group, however, the combatants did not appear to be suffering from severe interpersonal maladjustment at the time of testing.

Haley (see Chapter 12) found that, based on the caseload of Vietnam veterans seeking help at the Boston Veterans Administration Outpatient Clinic, over 75 percent of those who saw combat in Vietnam were suffering from some symptom of stress disorder related to their experiences in combat.

Hunter (see Chapter 9) presents the findings from several studies focusing both on the POW veteran and his family, concluding that incarceration has both immediate and long-term effects in terms of psychosocial adjustment. At the same time, however, Hunter observes that psychiatric pathology became more associated with the marital relationship over the years, and by the two-year post-release evaluation, marital maladjustment was more prevalent than any other factor. Also, POW's with predisposing factors in their past histories were four times more likely to have adjustment problems than those without.

At a recent research symposium chaired by the author at the American Psychological Association conference last year, three papers (Egendorf, Kadushin, Rothbart, Sloan, & Fine, 1977; Figley & Southerly, 1977; Wilson & Doyle, 1977) reported the preliminary findings of three separate research studies of the Vietnam-era veteran. These studies not only represent the most recent attempts to assess the mental health status of the veterans of Vietnam, they also are by far the most comprehensive in scope and methodology of any of the studies conducted in this area to date. Egendorf et al. found clear differences between those who went to Vietnam and those who did not on several mental health indices. One of the more interesting findings, however, was that the group of Vietnam veterans who appeared to be experiencing the most acute stress associated with the war were those who were attached to support groups stationed in rear echelon areas in Vietnam. Those who were in infantry units who saw the bulk of the day-to-day combat felt significantly less stress resulting from their experiences in Vietnam than support troops who were close enough to the battle to be shelled from time to time and see the aftermath of combat, but far enough away not to be involved in the actual fighting. Speculation about the significance of the findings, of course, must await further data analysis.

Figley and Southerly (1977) reported that, based on extensive interviews with 906 Vietnam-era veterans, most veterans had achieved a relatively high degree of personal adjustment when viewed as a group. Closer inspection, however, revealed that sleep difficulties (dreams and nightmares) continue to affect combat veterans in contrast to noncombatants. For example, the combatants reported significantly more nightmares (1) related to military service in general, (2) that were recurring, (3) that woke them up, (4) that made them fear or fight sleep, and (5) that are still occurring.

The Wilson and Doyle paper (1977) and a subsequent report (Wilson, 1977) essentially mirror the findings of Egendorf et al. (1977), Figley and Southerly (1977) and other research which support the Residual Stress Perspective. Wilson and Doyle found significant and large percentages of veterans who served in Vietnam who are still suffering from a variety of interpersonal problems (e.g., problems with affection maintenance, divorce), alienation, emotional-developmental problems (e.g., identity), as well as nightmares about combat and Vietnam.

CONCLUSIONS

Based on the review of existing research focusing on the psychosocial adjustment of Vietnam-era veterans, the following conclusions can be made: First, very little attention has been focused on the family readjustment problems of the Vietnam veteran, particularly in contrast to the research interest in the World War II veteran's family (see Hill, 1949, in particular). This deficit is not as great if we incorporate the returning prisoner of war (RPW) veteran. The impressive research program sponsored by the Center for Prisoners of War Studies serves as an excellent model for investigating the returning veteran and how he affects and is affected by the family system (see, for example, McCubbin, Dahl, Metres, Hunter & Plag, 1975, and Chapter 9 of this volume).

Second, pre-service factors including personality, family life and psychosocial variables appear to be related to in-service and post-service adjustment among Vietnam veterans (Worthington, 1973, 1977, Chapter 8; Nace, et al., Chapter 5; Hunter, Chapter 9; Panzarella et al., Chapter 7; Struen & Solberg, 1972).

Third, Vietnam-era veterans in general appear not to be significantly different from nonveterans in most areas of interpersonal and intrapersonal adjustment when either service in Vietnam or combat experiences are not controlled (Carr, 1973; Borus, 1973a, 1973b, 1973c, 1974; Segal

& Segal, 1976; Nace *et al.*, Chapter 5; Panzarella *et al.*, Chapter 7; Worthington, 1973, 1977, Chapter 8).

Fourth, there appears to be considerable evidence which suggests that service in Vietnam is a significant factor in psychological readjustment. There is considerable evidence to suggest that veterans who experienced combat in Vietnam are significantly different from others with regard to (1) general and specific orientations to violence (Brady & Rappoport, 1974), (2) psychological symptoms (DeFazio *et al.*, 1975; Egendorf *et al.*, 1977; Figley & Southerly, 1977; Nace *et al.*, 1975; Wilson & Doyle, 1977; Wilson, 1977), (3) indices of depression (Helzer *et al.*, 1974; Nace *et al.*, 1975); (4) political alienation (Pollock *et al.*, 1975; Wikler, 1974), and (5) adjustment problems (Egendorf *et al.*, 1977; Figley, 1977, 1978; Figley & Eisenhart, 1975; Figley & Southerly, 1977; Haley, Chapter 12; Hunter, Chapter 9; Strayer & Ellenhorn, 1976; Wilson & Doyle, 1977; Wilson, 1977).

Fifth, currently, except for the RPW research project noted above, there have been few published reports of attempts to systematically investigate the psychological readjustment process of the Vietnam veteran. This situation appears to be changing, however. A research symposium chaired and sponsored by the Consortium on Veteran Studies was presented in 1976 and in 1977 at the American Psychological Association's annual convention. The 1977 symposium, *The Residue of War: Vietnam-era Veterans in Mainstream America*, included brief reports from three large, comprehensive research programs which focused on various adjustment problems of the Vietnam veteran (Egendorf *et al.*, 1977; Figley & Southerly, 1977; Wilson & Doyle, 1977). As these and other reports of the studies are published, we may begin to clarify the complexities and processes of veteran adjustments.

5

ADJUSTMENT AMONG VIETNAM VETERAN DRUG USERS TWO YEARS POST SERVICE

EDGAR P. NACE, M.D., CHARLES P. O'BRIEN, M.D., Ph.D.,
JAMES MINTZ, Ph.D., NORMAN REAM, M.D., and
ANDREW L. MEYERS, M.Ed.

INTRODUCTION

A controlled follow-up study of U.S. Army enlisted men who served in Vietnam during a period of peak heroin use (1971-1972) was conducted two years after their discharge from the service. The purpose of the follow-up study was to assess current alcohol and drug use as well as other indices of adjustment.

This study was prompted by the concern that the heroin epidemic in Vietnam might seed a similar epidemic of addiction and, with it, increasing crime and social disorganization in the United States. During 1970, patterns of drug use among U.S. troops in Vietnam underwent changes characterized primarily by increased consumption of heroin. Highly purified, inexpensive heroin became plentiful during 1970 and, subsequently, heroin-related hospital admissions, deaths, and offenses began to escalate (Baker, 1971). A similar epidemic of heroin and other drug abuse was occurring in the United States during roughly the same time period (DuPont & Green, 1973; O'Donnel, 1976).

Robins (1974) found that fears of continuing narcotic use by returning veterans were largely unfounded. Only about two percent of their subjects, interviewed eight to 12 months following their return to the United States, were currently using narcotics. The present study addressed the same issues as the Robins study and placed particular emphasis on current alcohol use, depressive symptomatology, and the relationship of both pre-service variables and degree of narcotic use in Vietnam to post-service adjustment. An earlier study (Nace and Meyers,

71

1974) compared addicted Vietnam returnees with addicted civilian samples on the basis of variables of prognostic significance. From this comparison the prediction was made that the Vietnam returnees had a favorable prognosis in regard to heroin use as they closely resembled those civilian addicts who had achieved abstinence from heroin.

The present study confirmed the minimal continuing use of narcotics by Vietnam veterans. However, small comfort could be derived from that fact alone. Serious problems in other areas were uncovered and will be described below.

Although this study was not designed to investigate evidence of stress disorders (Horowitz, 1976), our data document a legacy of continuing social and psychological problems for a substantial percentage of Vietnam veterans. Our data do not support the idea that the delayed stress syndrome is a quantitatively significant problem among Vietnam veterans. This may be a function of our methodology or it may reflect an insufficient period of time for the emergence of such symptoms. Alternatively, the excessive use of alcohol in our sample may serve to mask other symptoms. We suggest that the results of this study point to areas of maladjustment which are of greater social consequence than the delineated symptoms characteristic of stress disorders addressed in this volume.

METHOD

Sample

The subjects for this follow-up study were obtained from two sources. All available admission face sheets of clinical records ($N = 10,650$) of soldiers admitted to either of the two drug treatment centers in Vietnam during the period of study (June, 1971-December, 1972) were screened. In addition, the medical records ($N = 14,780$), of soldiers admitted to one of four United States Army hospitals in Vietnam in 1971 and 1972 were also screened. From the above screenings, all face sheets which listed an emergency addressee (usually father, mother or wife) as residing in the city of Philadelphia or within a 55-mile radius of Philadelphia in Pennsylvania or New Jersey were pooled and filed ($N = 312$).

Thus, a sample of 312 veterans was potentially available for follow-up evaluation; 188 of these men had been detected by urine screening techniques as drug positive while in Vietnam, and 124 comprised a medical control group (admitted due to a variety of medical problems) who had not been detected as drug users while serving in Vietnam. Seventy-one of the 312 veterans no longer resided in the geographic area which was the focus of the study. Two hundred and forty-three of the veterans were determined to be still residing in the metropolitan Philadelphia area and 203 of these men were found and interviewed. One interview was dropped from the data analysis because of evidence of gross distortion. Of the remaining interviewees, 125 had been detected as drug users and 77 were in the medical control group.

Procedure

The veterans were contacted by either telephone, letter, or field visit. The nature and purpose of the follow-up study were explained and an appointment for an interview was scheduled. The interviewer explained that the purpose of the study was to assess whether or not Vietnam veterans were having problems following their return to civilian life. Each interview was conducted by one of two trained male interviewers who were skilled in interview techniques and capable of establishing rapport with the veterans. In the large majority of cases, they were conducted at the veteran's place of residence. The interview was semi-structured, lasted one and one-half hours, and assessed areas of current adjustment (employment, marital status, drug and alcohol use, etc.), as well as relevant past and current variables. See Appendix 5-A for the copy of the interview schedule. Each veteran was paid $15.00 for his participation. At the close of the interview each veteran was asked to complete the Beck Depression Inventory (BDI) (Beck, 1967) and to provide a urine sample for drug screening. Of the 202 men interviewed one refused to complete the BDI and two refused to provide urine samples.

Instruments

Two instruments were used for the collection of follow-up data: the Beck Depression Inventory and our follow-up questionnaire. The Beck Depression Inventory is a 21-item self-administered questionnaire used to assess current depression. Reliability, validity, and scores of the BDI have been described and documented (Beck, 1967). The follow-up questionnaire (see Appendix 5-A) was developed by our research team. It served as the primary instrument for data collection, and underwent four major revisions prior to its use in this study. Each revision was tested on a sample of Vietnam veterans in treatment at the Drug Dependence Treatment Center of the Philadelphia Veterans Administration Hospital. The questionnaire was structured so that each question or sub-question was amenable to computer coding. Administration required between one to two hours.

CRITERIA VARIABLES

Listed below are the variables utilized in the data analysis and the criteria upon which these variables are based:

(1) *Pre-service adjustment variable:* criminal behavior (e.g., reported auto theft, burglary, shoplifting, etc.), employment history, extent of education, reason for leaving school, family stability, parental relationships, socioeconomic status (Hollingshead and Redlich classification), hospitalizations, alcohol use, narcotic use, marijuana use and other drug use.

Each subject was rated on each variable using a scoring system of one through three with three representing the best adjustment on that variable. The information necessary to score each variable was obtained from the questions in the interview pertinent to that variable. An attempt was made to group the pre-service variables in a smaller number of factors, but they were heterogenous. Therefore, all pre-service variables were examined individually.

(2) *Drug use status in Vietnam:* Based on narcotic use in Vietnam, the veterans were divided into three groups:

A. Heavy users $(N = 98)$—those who reported at least daily use of a narcotic for a minimum period of one month, or reported the presence of withdrawal symptoms, or subjectively felt that they were addicted to narcotics while in Vietnam.

B. Experimental users $(N = 55)$—those who reported occasional use of narcotics but without indications of having been addicted.

C. Non-users $(N = 49)$—those who reported no use of narcotics while in Vietnam.

(3) *Post-service adjustment variables:* Criminal behavior (reported commitment of or arrest for offenses including shoplifting, burglary, assault, drug dealing, robbery, etc.), depression, physical health, employment/school status, heterosexual adjustment (sexual functioning, satisfaction with relationships, etc.), alcohol use, narcotic use, marijuana use, and other drug use.

As with the pre-service variables, a rating system of one to three was derived based on responses to relevant interview questions. Narcotic use, marijuana use and other drug use were scored according to the reported frequency of use (five or more times per week, one-four times/week, less than weekly, and none). "Other drug" use was a composite score of amphetamines, barbiturates, hallucinogens or other substances. With regard to alcohol use, the veterans were divided into problem drinkers (three or more alcohol-related problems), symptomatic drinkers (one or two alcohol related problems, and no problems (no alcoho-related problems). Eight items were used to determine the presence of alcohol problems: binge drinking, morning drinking, blackouts, treatment for an alcohol problem, school or job problems related to alcohol use, automobile accident associated with drinking, arrested for intoxication, and getting drunk three or more times per week.

Depression was rated according to the score obtained on the BDI (range 0-63).

Each subject was rated on each post-service variable and a total adjustment score derived. In addition, the current adjustment variables could be grouped into two factors. One included the criminal behavior and drug use variables ("Drug Use Factor") and the other included the remaining current adjustment variables ("Social adjustment factor") (see Table 1).

RESULTS

Relationship between Pre-service Adjustment, Addiction Status in Vietnam and Post-service Adjustment

One of the major questions this study attempted to answer was the relative importance of pre-service variables and in-service variables on post-service adjustment. That is, are pre-service behaviors and experiences of equal or greater importance as contributing factors to current adjustment problems than the experience of having used narcotics in Vietnam? To answer this question a series of multiple correlations were computed to determine the relationship between the pre-service variables, degree of narcotic use in Vietnam, and current adjustment.

Multiple correlations were computed relating all pre-service variables to each of the nine current adjustment variables, to the drug use and social adjustment factors, and to the total current adjustment score. As shown in Table 1, the highest correlation found was the multiple correlation between the Vietnam drug group and the current drug use factor. However, the multiple correlation of the pre-service variables

TABLE 1

Multiple Correlations between Current Adjustment Variables,
Vietnam Drug Groups and Pre-Service Variables

$(N = 202)$

	Vietnam Drug Group (heavy user, moderate user, or non-user)	Pre-Service Variables	Vietnam Drug Group with Pre-Service Variables Separated
Overall Adjustment	.58*	.58*	.35*
Drug Use Factor	.60*	.59*	.36*
Criminal Behavior	.30*	.40*	.14
Alcohol Use	.42*	.48*	.26*
Narcotic Use	.40*	.43*	.28*
Marijuana Use	.55*	.46*	.38*
"Other Drug" Use	.45*	.46*	.28*
Social Adjustment Factor	.35*	.47*	.21*
Heterosexual Activity	.26*	.27	.20*
Depression	.30*	.44*	.22*
Physical Health	.22*	.41*	.10
Employment/School Status	.22*	.31	.15

* $p < .05$

with the drug use factor and each of the individual variables that make up the "drug use factor" is significant.

The pre-service variables correlate significantly (.47) with the social adjustment factor but individually with only two of the four components: .44 with depression and .41 with physical health. The overall multiple correlation between pre-service adjustment and current adjustment was .58. Correlations were also computed between the Vietnam drug-use group and current adjustment. For each current adjustment variable, the Vietnam drug group correlated significantly.

Therefore, to determine the contribution of both pre-service variables and Vietnam drug use, a partial correlation was computed between Vietnam drug group and current adjustment, separating the contribution of the pre-service variables to the overall correlation. When the pre-service variables were controlled, the Vietnam drug group continued to correlate significantly with current overall adjustment but at a much reduced level. The drug groupings also continued to correlate significantly, but, again, at a much reduced level, with both the "drug use" and "social adjustment" factors. On the other hand, current criminal behavior did not significantly correlate with Vietnam drug group when the pre-service variables were separated. Also, physical health and employment/school status do not result in significant partial correlations with Vietnam drug group. Therefore, the latter variables are more strongly associated with pre-service adjustment factors than with extent of narcotic use in Vietnam.

Finally, Vietnam drug grouping had a significant partial correlation with current narcotic use as well as use of alcohol, marijuana and other non-narcotic drugs. The same was true for ratings of depression and heterosexual adjustment.

Depression

Thirty-two percent of the veterans scored within the clinically depressed range (score of 10 or more) on the BDI. The majority of the depressed veterans had scores within the moderate (16 to 23) and severe (24 or more) range of depression.

The currently depressed Vietnam veteran, in contrast to the non-depressed Vietnam veteran, was significantly more likely to have consumed alcohol ($p < .05$, χ^2) more frequently prior to entering the service, to have used narcotics ($p < .01$, χ^2), barbiturates ($p < .05$, χ^2) and amphetamines ($p < .001$, χ^2) significantly more frequently while in Vietnam, and was significantly ($p < .005$, χ^2) more likely to have used narcotics since returning from Vietnam. In addiction, the depressed veterans had a significantly ($p < .001$, χ^2) higher rate of unemployment, a significantly ($p < .002$, χ^2) greater incidence of marital problems, and were significantly ($p < .05$, χ^2) more likely to have current legal problems. For a more detailed description of depression in this sample of veterans see Nace *et al.* (1977a).

Criminal Behavior

Criminal behavior was rated according to reported arrests or commitment of illegal acts such as burglary, shoplifting, drug dealing, robbery, assault, etc. Thirty-four, 16 and 2 percent of the heavy, moderate, and non-users of narcotics in Vietnam, respectively, report legal problems related to varying types of illegal acts since discharge from the service ($p < .002$, χ^2). Statistically significant relations (Table 1) were found between the pre-service adjustment variables and post-service criminal variables ($r = .40$; $p < .05$) and between Vietnam drug group and post-service criminal behavior ($r = .30$ $p < .05$). When pre-service factors were controlled, however, Vietnam drug use was not predictive of post-service criminal behavior.

Drinking Problems

Sixteen percent of the sample could be classified as problem drinkers (i.e., having had at least three of the eight alcohol-related problems in the period since discharge), and an additional 23 percent were considered symptomatic drinkers (one or two alcohol-related problems in the period since discharge). Thus 39 percent of the sample were drinking heavily enough to be experiencing alcohol-related problems.

In contrast to current alcohol usage, only 21 percent of the sample had used heroin in the period since discharge, even though nearly 50 percent had been addicted to heroin while in Vietnam.

The problem drinkers were significantly ($p < .05$, χ^2) more likely to have had a parent with a history of alcoholism. In addition, they were significantly ($p < .05$, χ^2) more likely to have received treatment for a drug or alcohol problem in the past and to have sought help for emotional problems. Currently, the problem drinkers were as likely to be employed, but not to have held a job as long. They are more likely to have current legal problems and had received a significantly ($p < .05$, χ^2) greater number of Article 15's (non-judicial punishment) while in the Army. The problem drinkers rated their overall health as being lower than the rest of the sample and were significantly ($p < .05$, χ^2) more depressed as measured by the Beck Depression Inventory. There was no current difference in heroin use although those with current drinking problems reported a longer period of heroin addiction in Vietnam and significantly ($p < .05$, χ^2) more often had positive urine screen results while in Vietnam. For a more detailed description of drinking problems among this sample of veterans see Nace et al. (1977).

Narcotic Use

The central concern that soldiers who used narcotics heavily in Vietnam would return to the United States and pursue a "career" of narcotics addiction has not been substantiated by our data. Of those who had been heavy users in Vietnam, 38 percent have used a narcotic, and 24 percent report a period of addiction within the 28-month period post-discharge. The percentage actually addicted at some time in the three months prior to interview was considerably lower (4 percent).

For those who experimented with, but had not become addicted to, narcotics in Vietnam, 11 percent tried a narcotic since discharge and none became addicted. None of the group who abstained from narcotic use in Vietnam has used a narcotic post-discharge.

Of particular interest is the relationship between narcotic use in Vietnam and use since return from the service (Table 1). Our data provide some support for the contention that narcotic use in Vietnam relates to current narcotic use. Narcotic use since discharge correlated .43 with the set of pre-service variables and .40 with Vietnam drug group (heavy user, moderate user, or non-user) in Vietnam. From this one could conclude that pre-service variables contributed about as much to current narcotic use as did drug use in Vietnam. If the effect of pre-service variables is controlled, the Vietnam drug grouping only correlated .28 with current narcotic use (Table 1). The correlation between pre-service narcotic use (one of the 12 variables entering into the multiple correlation of pre-service variables mentioned above) and current narcotic use is .21.

Marijuana and Other Drug Use

As with narcotic use, marijuana and "other drug" use appeared to be equally predicted by pre-service variables and Vietnam drug groupings. Both post-discharge marijuana use and "other drug" use correlate significantly with Vietnam addiction status, however, after pre-service variables are separated. The age at which marijuana or "other drug" use was first begun does not differ among the three drug use groups, but the heavy users and moderate users were significantly ($p < .001$, χ^2) more likely to have initiated use prior to entering the service.

During military service the three drug use groups differed significantly ($p < .001$, χ^2) in the frequency of marijuana use and "other drug" use whether before, during or after the Vietnam tour. Consistently, the heavy users of narcotics in Vietnam used marijuana and other drugs more frequently in other military time periods.

Compared with use in Vietnam the use of marijuana and barbiturates appeared to decline since discharge in all three groups. The percentage using amphetamines or hallucinogens, however, increased in the three groups. The heavy use group, however, had a significantly greater percentage of individuals than the moderate use group who used "speed" ($p < .05$, χ^2) and "mainlined speed" ($p < .01$, χ^2). Similarly, the heavy use group used barbiturates significantly more frequently ($p < .01$, χ^2) since discharge than the moderate use group.

DISCUSSION

Two years following return from Vietnam a substantial number of Vietnam veterans are still having adjustment problems. The most prominent problems were depression (32 percent), alcohol abuse (39 percent) and unemployment (24 percent). It is not possible to attribute current adjustment problems solely to the degree of narcotic use in Vietnam, however, as both pre-service adjustment and drug experiences in Vietnam correlated significantly with current adjustment.

The data are clear in reference to the central concerns of the Vietnam heroin epidemic: Continuing narcotic addiction and criminal behavior on the part of these men are considerably less than had been anticipated, and, in the case of criminal behavior, no greater than what might have been predicted from their behavior prior to entering the service.

Our data can be compared with Robins' (1974) data by comparing the results from her drug-positive sample with the results from our Vietnam narcotic using sample (heavy and moderate users combined). Very close agreement is obtained. Robins reported that 33 percent of the drug positive sample continued narcotic use and 19 percent became addicted after discharge. In our study 28 percent continued to use narcotics, with 18 percent having had a period of addiction since discharge. As 63 percent of our sample who had used a narcotic in Vietnam were addicted in Vietnam, the 18 percent post-discharge rate shows a marked decline since return to the States.

Nevertheless, the heavy user group has continued to use significantly more narcotics than the other two groups post-discharge (although considerably less than when in Vietnam), and has also more extensively used marijuana and "other drugs." The concomitant use of a variety of drugs in association with regular use of heroin has been reported in another sample (Nace et al., 1975).

A subsample of returning Vietnam veterans seems to be at risk for the development of a depressive syndrome. This syndrome was present at least two years post-discharge and can hardly be considered a "re-entry phenomenon." The current depression seemed to be an example of non-effective responses to developmental tasks, rather than an acute reaction to environmental events. The veterans interviewed for this study did not attribute current feelings of depression to the role (combat or support) that they played in the Army. Both depressed and non-depressed veterans reported comparable degrees of general satisfaction with the Vietnam service experience. An item analysis of the Beck Depression Inventory did not reveal any evidence of more extensive guilt, sleep disturbance, or irritability among the veterans who served in combat roles compared to those who were in support assignments. The depressed veteran seems to have remained essentially outside available mental health systems, as the rate of those seeking treatment is very low.

Additional concern must be expressed about the extent of alcohol-related problems in this sample. Calahan's (1969) studies indicate that young men do migrate in and out of periods of heavy drinking without necessarily progressing to chronic alcoholism. At this time it is impossible to specify whether any or how many will develop more advanced complications of alcoholism. Such a risk certainly exists in this sample as those with current alcohol problems manifested variables predictive of alcoholism: history of parental alcoholism (Goodwin, 1971), early age of drinking (Robins et al., 1968) and school problems (Robins et al., 1962).

Clinicians working with Vietnam veterans are in a position to encounter instances of the delayed stress syndrome (Haley, Chapter 12). Our study did not specifically focus on this syndrome and we, therefore, do not have data on the incidence of stress syndromes in this sample. Since our sample was drawn largely from Vietnam drug users, however, and since a substantial percentage of these men are currently using excessive amounts of alcohol and, in some instances, other drugs, it is possible that this form of "self-medication" may mask many of the symptoms being seen in other veteran patient samples.

Our data indicate that the large majority of veterans with current adjustment problems have not utilized available sources of help. For instance, less than three percent with alcoholic symptoms have, since leaving Vietnam, sought help for a drinking problem. It is clear that an outreach approach to Vietnam veterans is indicated based on the depth and breadth of adjustment difficulties found among our sample. At present these veterans remain essentially outside available mental health systems and seem to be either unaware of the existence of help or reluctant to seek it.

SUMMARY

A follow-up study of 202 Army Vietnam veterans from the Philadelphia metropolitan area who served in Vietnam between June 1971 and December 1972 was conducted. The veterans were interviewed at an average of 28 months post-discharge from the Army, and were divided into three groups according to degree of narcotic use in Vietnam: heavy users of heroin in Vietnam, moderate heroin users (but not addicted in Vietnam), and non-users of heroin.

While this study neither investigated nor detected the presence of various symptoms of stress syndromes, it did point to more diverse manifestations of maladjustment: depression, alcohol problems and drug use.

Alcohol related problems in this group of Vietnam veterans were extensive. Thirty-nine percent of the total sample have experienced at least one alcohol related problem since discharge and 16 percent could be categorized as "problem drinkers."

In addition, a high rate of depression as measured by the Beck Depression Inventory was found, with 32 percent of the subjects falling within a clinical range of depression. The current rate of unemployment for this group (24 percent) is considered to be an important factor in their state of depression.

Of particular interest is the finding that post-discharge criminality and narcotic use are accounted for primarily by pre-service experiences rather than by the use of narcotics in Vietnam. Other variables, such as alcohol use, depression and marijuana use, also are related to pre-service variables and to degree of heroin use in Vietnam.

In spite of the high incidence of depression and alcohol use, very few individuals have availed themselves of any health care delivery system.

APPENDIX 5-A

VIETNAM VETERAN FOLLOW-UP QUESTIONNAIRE*

First, I would like to ask you some questions about your time in the service. If you served more than one tour in Vietnam, most of the questions on Vietnam refer to your last tour there.

1. When did you go on active duty?

   Month | Day | Year
   19-20

2. When did you arrive in Vietnam?
   Code Last Tour
   List any other Tours

   Month | Day | Year
   25-26

3. When did you leave Vietnam?
   Code Last Tour

   Month | Day | Year
   31-32

4. When were you discharged from the service?

   Month | Day | Year
   39-40

5. What type of discharge did you receive?

   Honorable 1
   General under Honorable 2
   General less than Honorable 3
   Medical under Honorable 4
   Undesirable 5
   Bad Conduct 6
   Dishonorable 7

   If less than honorable, ask why? Record verbatim response.

6. How many times have you re-enlisted in the Army?

   Number

   If any re-enlistments, ask why did you re-enlist?

   Liked assignment 1
   Security 2
   To stay with friends 3
   No other job 4
   Other (specify) 5
   No re-enlistments 9

* From the University of Pennsylvania and Veterans Administration Hospital, Philadelphia, Pa.

7. What was the total number of months that you ever served
   in Vietnam?

Months
46-47

    If not twelve months, ask, why did you serve more/less
than twelve months?
Record verbatim response and code.

        Med evac for wound 01
        Med evac for illness 02
        Med evac for psych reasons 03
        Med evac for drugs 04
        Tour reduced 05
        Unit deactivated 06
        Shortened for other reason (specify) 07
        Assigned more than once 08
        Extended for early out 09
        Enjoyed assignment 10
        To stay with friends 11
        To stay with girl or wife 12
        Because of availability of drugs 13
        Lengthened for other reason (specify) 14
        Served twelve months 99

49-49

8. What was the highest rank that you held while in the service? E-

50

9. What was your rank at discharge?
   If rank at discharge is lower than highest rank, ask,
   why were you busted? E-

10. Were you promoted or demoted while you were in Vietnam?

        Promoted 1
        Demoted 2
        No change 3
        Both 4

    If rank changed, ask why were you promoted/busted?
Record verbatim response.

11. How did you get into the service?

        Drafted 1
        Volunteered for draft 2
        Enlisted to avoid draft 3
        Enlisted for legal reasons 4
        Activated reservist 6
        Other (specify) 7

    What was the specific event that led to your entering the service?
Record verbatim response.

12. What was your MOS?   Code _____
    Record MOS code and title. Code MOS.   Title _____

    Would you say this was a combat or support position in Vietnam?

        Combat 1
        Support 2   _____

    Did you receive any medals in the Army?

        Yes 1
        No 2   _____

    If yes, ask what medals did you receive?

13. Were you generally satisfied with your job in Vietnam?

        Very much 1
        Most of the time 2
        About half the time 3
        Less than half the time 4
        Rarely 5   _____

    Why did you feel that way?
    What about the rest of your time in the service?
    Use same code as above   _____

- -

That is enough information about the service at this time. Now I would like
to ask some questions about your life before you entered the service and since
you were discharged. This next set of questions concerns your employment experiences since you were discharged and a few questions on your pre-service
employment.

14. Are you currently employed?

        Full time 1
        Part time 2
        Student 3
        Unemployed 4   _____

    If "Student," ask, are you working at all, even part time,
    while in school?

        Yes 1
        No 2
        Working, not in school 3
        Unemployed, not in school 4   _____

    If "No," go to Question 24.
    If "Unemployed," go to Question 21.

15. Where are you working? Code

Private company 1
Government 2
Self-employed 3
Other 4
Not working 9   _____
                                                        60

16. What do you do?
Record specific job description and code.

Professional 1
White collar 2
Skilled 3
Semi-skilled 4
Unskilled 5
Not working 9   _____

17. How long have you been working at this job?
Code 99 if S is not working.   _____

18. Are you satisfied with your present job?

Yes 1
No 2
Not working 9   _____

Ask, why do you feel that way? Record verbatim response.

19. What is your present salary?
Record as weekly rate.   _____
If not employed, code 999.   65 66 67

20. Do you have any other sources of income, either legal or illegal?

Yes 1
No 2   _____

If yes, ask, what is the source of this additional income?

Friend or partner 1
Another job 2
Parental support 3
Public assistance 4
Social security 5
Veteran's benefits 6
Illegal/Hustle 7
Other (specify) 8
No additional income 9   _____

How much additional money do you have per week?   _____
If no additional money code 999.   70-71-72

If "another job," ask, what kind of job? Record verbatim response.
If "illegal/hustle," ask, what kind of hustle?
Record verbatim response. Go to Question 31.

21. How long have you been unemployed? If employed code 99.

Months
73-74

22. Are you collecting unemployment compensation?

        Yes 1
        No 2
        Employed 9

If "No," ask, why not? Record verbatim response.
If "Yes," ask, how much do you collect per week?
If employed code 999.

76-77-78

23. Do you have any other sources of income, either legal or illegal?

        Yes 1
        No 2

If "Yes," ask, what is the source of this additional income?

        Friend or partner 1
        Parental support 2
        Public assistance 3
        Social security 4
        Pension 5
        Veterans benefits 6
        Illegal/Hustle 7
        Other (specify) 8
        No other income 9

80

Card 2
Col. 1-3

How much additional money do you have per week?
If no additional money code 999.

4-5-6

If illegal/hustle, ask, what kind and record verbatim.

24. What was the last job you held? Code

        Private company 1
        Government 2
        Self-employed 3
        Other (specify) 4
        Currently employed 9

26. How many hours per week did you work?

                                      Hours
                                        9-10

27. How long did you have the job?
    If currently working code 99.

                                        Months
                                        11-12

28. Why did you leave the job? Record verbatim response.

        Fired 1
        Quit—did not like work 2
        Quit—too much hassle 3
        Quit—thought had another job 4
        Laid-off 5
        Other (specify) 6
        Currently working 9

29. Did alcohol or other drugs lead to your losing your job?

        Alcohol 1
        Drugs 2
        Some other problem (specify) 3
        Neither 4
        Never lost job 9

    If alcohol or drug problem, ask, how did alcohol/drugs effect
    the loss of your job?

30. Why haven't you gotten another job? Record verbatim response and code.

        Not looking for work 1
        Don't want to work 2
        Can't find work 3
        Believes no work available 4
        Lacks proper training 5
        Wrong age for good work 6
        Ill/disabled 7
        Other (specify) 8
        Employed 9

31. How many other jobs have you had since your discharge?

                                           Number

    If any other jobs, ask, in general what kind of work did you do?
    Record verbatim response.

32. What was the longest period of time that you held a job
    since your discharge?

                                           Months
                                         18-19

    How long after your discharge did you get a job or return
    to school?

                                           Months
                                         20-21

What did you do during that time? Record verbatim response and code.

Unemployed 1
Traveled 2
Other (specify) 3
Work or school 9   _____

33. What is the longest period of time that you have been
unemployed, and not in school, since your discharge?   _____

Months
23-24

34. Were you working full time or part time before entering
the service?

Full time 1
Part time 2
Student—no work 3
Student—plus work 4
Unemployed 5   _____

If S was employed immediately before service, ask,
where did you work? code.

Private company 1
Government 2
Self-employed 3
Other (specify) 4
Not working 9   _____

What did you do? Record specific job description and code.

Professional 1
White collar 2
Skilled 3
Semi-skilled 4
Unskilled 5
Not working 9   _____

How many hours did you work per week?
If not working before service, code 99.

Hours
28-29

Months
30-31

Did you return to the same employer after the service?

Yes 1
No 2
Not working before service 9   _____

If S did not return to same employer, ask, why didn't you return
to the same employer? Record verbatim response and code.

Did not want same job 1
Was not offered the same job 2
Job no longer available 3
Did not think to check old job 4
Was not working immediately before service . 5
Other (specify) 6
Returned to same employer .... 9 _____

35. What was the longest period of time that you held any one
job before entering the service?

_____
Months
34-35

36. How many jobs did you have before entering the service?

_____
Number

Now I would like to ask you about some of your educational experiences, both
before you entered the service and since your discharge. I am interested in the
type of courses you have taken, or plan to take; and some of your future educational goals.

37. How many years of schooling had you completed before
the service?

_____
Years
37-38

38. Did you ever repeat a grade in school?

Yes 1
No .... 2 _____

If yes, ask, what grade did you repeat? Why did you repeat this grade?
Record verbatim response.

39. What was the reason you left school? Record verbatim response and code.

Graduated 1
Family problems 2
Wanted to get a job 3
No interest in school 4
Legal confinement 5
Military 6
Kicked-out 7
Other (specify) .... 8 _____
40

40. What did you do immediately after leaving school? Record verbatim
response and code.

Went to work 1
Entered service 2
Unemployed 3
In jail 4
Traveled 5
Other 6   _____

41. How long was it between the time you left school and
entered the service?   _____
                                                            Months
                                                            42-43

42. Did you receive any training or schooling while in the service?

GED 1
Military training 2
Civilian training 3
Other 4
None 5   _____

If S had additional training, ask, what field was this training in?
Record verbatim response.
Have you used this training in any way since your discharge?

Yes 1
No 2
Did not receive training 9   _____

If yes, ask, how did you use this training?

43. Have you attended any school since your discharge?

Yes 1
No 2   _____

If no, go to Question 44.
If yes, ask, how much schooling or training have you had
since your discharge?   _____
Record number of courses and code level.   Courses
                                                            47-48

High school 1
College 2
Masters 3
Doctorate 4
Trade school 5
Business school 6
Apprenticeship 7
Other (specify) 8
No additional schooling 9   _____

What was your goal or reason for returning to school? Record
verbatim response and code.

Get better employment 1
Improve knowledge 2
Take advantage of VA benefits 3
Have a good time 4
Pressure from others 5
Other (specify) 6
Did not return to school 9

_____
50

Are you presently enrolled in school?

Yes 1
No 2   _____

If no, go to Question 45.
If yes, ask, how many hours per week do you attend class?   _____
Hours
52-53

Who is financing your present education? If more than one source, code primary source and note others.

Personal 1
Family help 2
VA 3
Scholarship 4
Loan 5
Part-time work 6
Other (specify) 7
Not attending school 9   _____

44. Why didn't you return to school?

45. What is the highest grade in school that you have completed up to now?
                                                   _____
                                                   Years
                                                   56-56

What is the highest certificate or degree you have received?

GED 1
H.S. 2
A.A. 3
B.A. 4
M.A. 5
Ph.D. 6
Trade 7
Business 8
No degree 9   _____

Do you plan any additional education or training?

Yes 1
No 2   _____

If no, go to Question 47.
If yes, ask, how much more schooling or training would you like
to complete? Record verbatim response and code.

High school 01
Two year college 02
College 03
Masters 04
Doctorate 05
Trade school 06
Business school 07
Apprenticeship 08
No formal program 09
Other (specify) 10
No further schooling 11

                                                    59-60

47. How would you say you have done in your schooling up to now?
Record verbatim response and code.

Very well 1
Above average 2
Average 3
Below average 4

Now I would like to ask you some questions about your personal life, and in
particular, any marital relationships that you have been involved in.

48. What is your current marital status?

Never married 1
Married, living with wife 2
Common-law marriage 3
Divorced 4
Separated 5
Widowed 6
Other (specify) 7

If S was ever married, go to Question 49.
If S was never married, ask, are you presently engaged or dating
someone regularly?

Engaged 1
Dating regularly 2
Neither 3
Married 9

Do you have any children?
                                                    Number
Go to Question 57.

49. How many times have you been married?
                                                    Number

50. What was the date of your most recent marriage?

                                         Month   Day   Year
                                           66-67   68-69   70-71

       If never married, code 99/99/99.
       Record date and code.

             Before service 1
             In service 2
             Since discharge 3
             Never married 9

51. How many children do you have altogether?
       Record number and specify how many for each marriage
       and/or out of marriage.   Number

       If still married to first wife and still living with her, go to Question 56.

52. When were you

             Divorced 1
             Separated 2
             Widowed 3
             Never married 8
             Still married 9

Code and record date.

                                           Month   Day   Year
                                           75-76   77-78   79-80

       If still married or never married, code 99/99/99.

                               1   2   3
                                       Card 3
                                       Col 1-3

53. What specific problem led to your divorce or separation? Record
       verbatim response and code.

             Drugs 1
             Alcohol 2
             Service 3
             Sexual 4
             Other (specify) 5
             Never married 8
             Never divorced or separated 9

54. Are you supporting your children?

             Yes 1
             No 2
             No children 9

       If yes, ask, how many of your children are you supporting?
       If no, ask, who is supporting them?

Wife 1
Parents 2
In-laws 3
Government 4
Other (specify) 5
No children 8
Is supporting children 9   _____

55. If you are separated, what do you see for the future? Record verbatim
and code.

Divorce 1
Reconciliation 2
No change 3
Don't know 4
Other (specify) 5
Never married 8
Not separated 9   _____

56. If you are presently married, how would you rate your relationship
with your wife? Record verbatim response and code.

Excellent 1
Very good 2
Good 3
Fair 4
Poor 5
Not married 9   _____

Why would you rate it that way?

- -

Now I would like to ask you some questions concerning your life while you were
growing up, before you entered the service. Most of these questions concern
your parents and other members of your family.

57. Did you live with both your real parents until age 16?

Yes 1
No 2   _____
                                                          10

If yes, go to Question 59.
If no, ask, whom did you live with? Record verbatim response and code.

Mother alone 1
Father alone 2
Mother with stepfather 3
Father with stepmother 4
Foster parents 5
Relatives 6
Institution 7
Other (specify) 8
Lived with both real parents 9   _____

Why didn't you live with both parents? Record verbatim response and code. Be sure to include all important details relating to not living with parents.

Death 1
Divorce 2
Separation 3
Illness 4
Other (specify) 5
Lived with parents 9   _____

How old were you at that time?   _____

Years
13-14

Code 99 if parents still living together.
What effect did the separation have on the family?
Has either parent remarried?

Father only 1
Mother only 2
Both 3
Neither 4
Parents never separated 9   _____

58. Are you still living with your parents?

Both 1
Father only 2
Mother only 3
Neither 4   _____

If yes, go to Question 59.
If no, ask, how often do you see your parents?

Daily 1
3-6 per week 2
1-2 per week 3
2-3 per month 4
Once per month 5
Less than once per month 6
Never 7
Live with parents 9   _____

59. How many brothers and sisters do you have?

Older brothers .... _____

Older sisters .... _____

Younger brothers .... _____

20

Younger sisters .... _____

Indicate if they are natural, step, or half brothers or sisters.

60. While you were growing up (until age 16) what did the person who supported you do for a living? Record specific job description and code.

Professional 1
White collar 2
Skilled 3
Semi-skilled 4
Unskilled 5
Other (specify) 6   ———————

61. How much education did that person have?

Graduate degree 1
College degree 2
Part College 3
High School degree 4
Part High School 5
Less than High School 6
Less than eight years 7   ———————
                                                        23

If does not apply, code 9, or don't know, code 8.

62. Did either of your real parents have any of these problems?

Father only 1
Mother only 2
Both 3
Neither 4
Don't know 5

Explain specific problem and effect on family for each problem discussed and code.

Alcohol ....   ———————

Drug ....   ———————

Legal ....   ———————

Financial ....   ———————

Medical Illness ....   ———————

Emotional Illness ....   ———————

Ask specifically what drugs were involved with any drug problem, if treatment was obtained, and the effect of this problem on the family. Emotional problems include any treatment, either in- or outpatient, for any type of psychiatric or psychological problems, any contact with a counselor, social worker, etc., attempted suicide, etc.

63. Did any of your brothers or sisters have any of these problems?

Yes 1
No 2
No brothers or sisters 9   ———————

For each specific problem, record which brother or sister was involved and what the specific problem was. Record specific details and code.

Alcohol .... _____
                                                    30

Drug .... _____

Legal .... _____

Financial .... _____

Medical Illness .... _____

Emotional Illness .... _____

65. While you were growing up, how would you have rated your relationship with your parents? Record verbatim response and code.

         Excellent 1
         Very good 2
         Good 3
         Fair 4
         Poor 5
         Does not apply 9   _____

66. While you were in the service, what place did you consider home? Record name of town or city.

67. Where are you currently living? Record name of town or city. If S is currently living in a town different from that which he considered his home while in the service, ask, why did you move to a new city after getting out of the service? Record verbatim response.

68. How long have you lived at your current address? Number of   _____
    months since discharge.   Months
                                                                       37-38

69. How many places have you lived since your discharge?   _____

70. In what type of setting do you live now?

         No regular place 1
         Boarding house 2
         Hotel 3
         Apartment 4
         Single family house 5
         Institution (specify) 6
         Other (specify) 7   _____
                                                                       40

71. Who lives with you?

Parents 1
Wife 2
Wife and children 3
Parents and wife 4
In-laws and wife 5
Parents, brothers, sisters 6
Friends 7
Other (specify) 8
No one 9   _____

- -

Now, I would like to ask you some questions about your medical history. I am specifically interested in any problem that required hospitalization, or that was the result of alcohol or other drug use. Finally, I am also interested in any problems that might have led you to seek the help of a psychiatrist, psychologist or some other type of counselor.

72. Have you ever been hospitalized for any reason?

Yes 1
No 2   _____

If yes, go to Question 73.
If no, ask, so you have never had an operation or been sick enough to go into the hospital at all?

Hospitalized 1
Never hospitalized 2   _____

If never hospitalized, go to Question 74.

73. How many times were you hospitalized in each time period?

Before service ....   _____

In service/before Vietnam ....   _____

In service/in Vietnam ....   _____

In service/after Vietnam ....   _____

Since discharge ....   _____

Last three months ....   _____

Record specific information concerning each hospitalization. Include information on cause, duration, and outcome of hospitalization.

Do you have a disability that you got while in the Army?

Yes 1
No 2   _____
                                                        50

If yes, ask, what is the disability? How did you become disabled? What percent disability? What effect does this disability have on you today?

74. Have you ever been in a drug treatment program or an alcohol treatment program, either as an inpatient or an outpatient?

> Yes, because of
> Alcohol 1
> Drugs 2
> Both 3
> No 4   _____

If no, go to Question 76.

75. How many times have you been treated as an inpatient? as an outpatient?

	In	Out
Before service	_____	_____
In service/before Vietnam	_____	_____
In service/in Vietnam	_____	_____
In service, after Vietnam	_____	_____
Since discharge	_____	_____
Last three months	_____	_____

Note: Any inpatient treatments should also appear in Question 73. Record specific information concerning each treatment episode. Include information on specific reason for treatment, duration and type of treatment, and outcome of treatment.

76. Have you ever had any type of emotional or psychological problem about which you spoke to a counselor, minister, chaplain, psychologist, or psychiatrist?

> Yes 1
> No 2   _____

If no, go to Question 78. If yes, ask

77. How many times have you spoken to a counselor, etc. for non-drug related problems?

> Before service .... _____
> In service, before Vietnam .... _____
> In service, in Vietnam .... _____
> In service, after Vietnam .... _____
> Since discharge .... _____
> Last three months .... _____

70

Record specific information for each treatment episode. Include information on specific reason for counseling, duration of treatment, type of treatment, and outcome of treatment.

Now I would like to ask you some questions about problems that you might have had with the police or other aspects of the law. I am particularly interested in any crimes that you have been involved in, whether or not you were caught and arrested for that particular crime. I would also like to know about any time you have spent in jail, either before or after the service. Finally, there will be some questions about any activities in the service that might have led to an Article 15 or to a Court-martial.

78. Have you ever been involved in any of these crimes?

	Committed	Arrested	Convicted	When	Disposition	
Shoplifting	___	___	___	___	___	
Burglary	___	___	___	___	___	
					80	___ ___ Card 4
Robbery	___	___	___	___	___	Col 1-3
Auto theft	___	___	___	___	___	
Assault	___	___	___	___	___	
Armed robbery	___	___	___	___	___	
Rape Manslaughter	___	___	___	___	___	
Murder	___	___	___	___	___	
Drug possession*	___	___	___	___	___	
Drug sale	___	___	___	___	___	
Intoxication	___	___	___	___	___	
Other	___	___	___	___	___	

For committed, arrested, and convicted code number of incidents.

* For drug possession code   Yes 1

No 2

"When"

Before service only 1
In service only 2
After service only 3
Before and in service 4
Before and after service 5
In and after service 6
All three times 7
Never 9

"Disposition"

Jail 1
Probation 2
Other institution 3
Charges dropped 4
Acquitted 5
Fine 6
Other (specify) 7
Does not apply 9

For "when" and "disposition" use code above.
Record specific examples of problems with the law. Include specific charges for each arrest.

79. Have you ever been in jail, even if only overnight?

Yes 1
No 2   _____

If no, go to Question 80.
If yes, ask, what was the reason that you were in jail? Record verbatim response. Make sure to include length of confinement and when each confinement occurred.

80. How many articles 15 did you receive while you were in service?   _____
                                                                    Number
                                                                      60

81. How many courts-martial did you receive while you were in service?

For each article 15 and court-martial, record the specific charge and the disposition of the case.

82. Were you ever in a stockade or PCF while in the service?

Stockade 1
PCF 2
Both 3
Neither 4   _____

If ever in a stockade of PCF, ask, what were the specific situations surrounding your confinements? Record verbatim response. Include dates of confinements, durations, and causes.

83. What is your current legal status?

Court case pending 1
On probation 2
In jail or other institution 3
On parole 4
Treatment program 5
No restrictions 6
Other (SPECIFY) 7   _____

- -

Now, I would like to ask you some questions about your leisure time activities. I am interested in what you do when you are not working or in school and what some of your other interest are.

84. How often do you go out with your friends?

    Two or more per week 1
    Once a week 2
    Two or three per month 3
    Once per month 4
    Less than once per month 5
    Never 6
    Has no friends 9   _____

85. What kind of things do you do?

86. Do you ever drink or use drugs with your friends?

    Drink only 1
    Use drugs 2
    Both 3
    Neither 4
    Has no friends 9   _____

87. How many of your friends are involved with drugs?   _____

    How many of your friends fall into any of these groups? 66-67

    Number who are current addicts .... _____

    Number who are former addicts .... _____

    Number who sell drugs .... _____ 70

    Number who are heavy drinkers .... _____

    Number who are convicts or ex-cons ...... _____

    Number who have no drug or legal problem . _____

88. What church did you belong to while growing up?

    Catholic 1
    Protestant (Specify) 2
    Jewish 3
    Other (Specify) 4
    None 5   _____

  What church do you attend now?
  Code as above but add,

    Black Muslim 6   _____

  How often do you attend church?

    Never 1
    One or two per year 2
    3-11 per year 3
    Once per month 4
    2-3 per month 5
    Every week 6
    More than once per week 7   _____

89. What are some of your other interests that you are involved in?
Ask about hobbies, sports watched or played, clubs, organizations, and charitable activities.

90. Are you a registered voter?

Yes 1
No 2   _____

If yes, ask, when was the last time that you voted?   _____
If never voted, code 99.   Year
                                                          78-79

- -

I would like to find out how you have been feeling in the last few months. I am particularly interested in any problems that you have had or are having at the present time.

91. Have you seen a doctor in the last three months?

Yes 1
No 2   _____
                                                          80

If no, go to question 92.
If yes, ask, what was the reason that you went to see a doctor? Include information on when, specific problem, any treatment received, and the outcome of that treatment.

                                                ___ ___ ___
                                                   Card 5
                                                   Col 1-3

92. Overall then, how would you rate your health?

Excellent 1
Very good 2
Average 3
Fair 4
Poor 5   _____

Why would you rate it that way? Record verbatim response.

93. Has there been any time in the last three months that you have felt depressed or blue, anxious, fearful or nervous in any way?

Yes 1
No 2   _____

If no, go to Question 94.
If yes, ask, what was it that was bothering you? Record verbatim response.

94. Have you seen a doctor or counselor of any kind for a nervous problem, depression, anxiety, or any other problems in the last three months?

Yes 1
No 2   _____

If no, go to Question 95.
If yes, ask, what was the specific problem that led to your seeking help? Include information on when, specific problem, any treatment received, who performed treatment, and outcome of treatment.

95. Have you had any problems with your sexual activity in the last three months?

Yes 1
No 2   _____

If subject appears reluctant to answer this question tell S: Questions concerning one's sexual activities are often embarrassing to answer, but it is very important to us to have accurate information in this area. It is needed so we can evaluate the overall adjustment of the individual. Looking back over the past 3 months would you say there has been a change in your sexual activities?

96. Has your interest in sex either increased or decreased?

Increased 1
Decreased 2
No change 3   _____

Have you experienced a change in your amount of sexual activity?

Increased 1
Decreased 2
No Change 3   _____
                                                        10

Have you experienced any episodes of impotence? That is, have you been unable to get a "hard-on"?

Yes 1
No 2   _____

Have you experienced any episodes of premature or retarded ejaculation in the last three months?

Premature 1
Retarded 2
Both 3
Neither 4   _____

In any situation involving a problem, ask S to explain the problem in more detail. Record verbatim response of S.

97. Do you have any other specific problem that you would like to mention at this time?

Family 1
Legal 2
Financial 3
Drug 4
Alcohol 5
Other 6
None 7   _____

Record specific facts concerning problem and code.

- -

Now, I would like to ask you some questions concerning the history of your alcohol and drug use. I would like to trace your use of alcohol and each of the other drugs (marijuana, hallucinogens, amphetamines, barbiturates and narcotics) back to the very first time you used each specific drug. I am going to start with alcohol and then progress through the other drugs.

98. How old were you when you had your first drink?
    If S never drank code 99.

    _____
    Years
    14-15

99. How old were you when you first got drunk?
    If S never got drunk code 99.

    _____
    Years
    16-17

In all questions, ask specifically about each time period. Do not lump time periods together into one question.

100. In each time period, can you recall how often you had a drink, and how often you got drunk?

    Daily 1
    5-6 per week 2
    3-4 per week 3
    1-2 per week 4
    2-3 per month 5
    Once per month 6
    Less than once per month 7
    Never 8

	Drank	Got Drunk
Last three months	_____	_____
Before service	_____	_____
	20	
In service/before Vietnam	_____	_____
In service/after Vietnam	_____	_____
Since discharge	_____	_____

100a. Did you drink any beer during the last three months?

    Yes 1
    No 2   _____
                                                              30

If no, go to Question 100-B.
If yes, ask, how often did you have a beer?

Daily 1
5-6 per week 2
3-4 per week 3
1-2 per week 4
2-3 per month 5
Once per month 6
Less than once per month 7
Never .... 9 _____

On a typical day that you drank beer, how much did you usually drink?

6 quarts or more 1
5 quarts 2
4 quarts 3
3 quarts 4
1-2 quarts 5
1-3 glasses or 1-2 12 oz btls. 6
Never .... 9 _____

100b. Did you drink any wine during the past 3 months?

Yes 1
No 2

If no, go to Question 100c.
If yes, ask, how often did you drink wine?

Daily 1
5-6 per week 2
3-4 per week 3
1-2 per week 4
2-3 per month 5
Once per month 6
Less than once per month 7
Never .... 9 _____

On a typical day that you drank wine, how much wine did you drink?

5 bottles or more 1
4 bottles 2
2-3 bottles 3
1 bottle 4
2-3 water glasses or 4-6 wine glasses ... 5
1 water or 1-3 wine glasses 6
Never .... 9 _____

100c. Did you drink any whiskey, gin or hard liquor in the last 3 months?

Yes 1
No .... 2 _____

If no, go to Question 101.
If yes, ask, how often did you drink whiskey, gin, or hard liquor?

Daily 1
5-6 per week 2
3-4 per week 3
1-2 per week 4
2-3 per month 5
Once per month 6
Less than once per month 7
Never 9   _____

On a typical day that you drank whiskey, gin, or hard liquor, how much did you usually drink?

4 pints or more 1
3 pints 2
2 pints 3
1 pint 4
11-14 shots (or mixed drinks) 5
7-10 shots (or mixed drinks) 6
7-10 shots (or mixed drinks) 6
4-6 shots (or mixed drinks) 7
1-3 shots (or mixed drinks) 8
Never 9   _____

101. Were you ever a morning drinker?

Yes 1
No 2

Last three months .... _____

Before service .... _____ 40

In service/before Vietnam .... _____

In service/in Vietnam .... _____

In service/after Vietnam .... _____

Since discharge .... _____

If yes to any time period, ask, what was the situation surrounding this? Record verbatim response.

102. Have you ever gone on a "binge" or "bender," when you drank for several days in a row without sobering up?

Yes 1
No 2

Last three months .... _____

Before service .... _____

In service/before Vietnam .... _____

In service/in Vietnam .... _____

In service/after Vietnam .... _____

Since discharge .... _____

If yes to any time period, ask, what was the situation surrounding these benders? Record verbatim response.

103. Have you ever had an automobile accident because of drinking?

Yes 1
No 2

Last three months .... ———————

Before service .... ———————

In service/before Vietnam .... ———————

In service/in Vietnam .... ———————

In service/after Vietnam .... ———————

Since discharge .... ———————

If yes to any time period, ask, can you tell me about the accident? Record verbatim response.

104. Have you ever had a problem with your memory while drinking, that is, have you ever awakened in the morning and not been able to remember what you did the night before while drinking?

Yes 1
No 2

Last three months .... ———————

Before service .... ———————

In service/before Vietnam .... ———————

In service/in Vietnam .... ——————— 60

In service/after Vietnam .... ———————

Since discharge .... ———————

If yes to any time period, ask, what were the events surrounding this memory loss? Record verbatim response.

105. Have you ever been treated for an alcohol problem?

Yes 1
No 2

Last three months .... ———————

Before service .... ———————

In service/before Vietnam .... ———————

In service/in Vietnam .... ———————

In service/after Vietnam .... ———————

Since discharge .... ———————

If yes to any time period, ask, what type of treatment was this? Record verbatim response. Additional information should be recorded in 74.

106. Has drinking ever gotten you into trouble at school or on the job?

Yes 1
No 2

Last three months .... _____

Before service .... _____ 70

In service/before Vietnam .... _____

In service/in Vietnam .... _____

In service/after Vietnam .... _____

Since discharge .... _____

If yes to any time period, ask, what type of problem did your drinking cause? Record verbatim response.

107. If you started to use other drugs, what effect did this have on your use of alcohol?

Increased 1
Decreased 2
No change 3
Did not use other drugs 4   _____

Now, I would like to ask you about your use of grass or hash.

109. When was the first time you smoked grass or hash?

Last three months 1
Before service 2
In service/before Vietnam 3
In service/in Vietnam 4
In service/after Vietnam 5
Since discharge 6
Never smoked 9   _____

If "never smoked" ask, so you have never used marijuana or hash at any time, even while you were in Vietnam?

Never used 1
Used 2   _____

If never used, go to Question 117.
If used, code above.

110. How old were you when you first used grass or hash?   _____

Years
78-79

111. In each time period, how often did you use grass or hash?

Daily 1
5-6 per week 2
3-4 per week 3
1-2 per week 4
2-3 per month 5
Once per month 6
Less than once a month 7
Never 8

Card 6
Col 1-3

Last three months ....   _____

Before service ....   _____

In service/before Vietnam ....   _____

In service/in Vietnam ....   _____

In service/after Vietnam ....   _____

Since discharge ....   _____
                                                 20-21

If used more than once per month code 99.

Last three months ....   _____ 10-11

Before service ....   _____

In service/before Vietnam ....   _____

In service/in Vietnam ....   _____

In service/after Vietnam ....   _____

Since discharge ....   _____

112. If less than one time per month, about how many times did you actually use grass or hash?

113. At any time that you used grass or hash more than three times per week, how long did you use at that level?

Less than one month 1
1-3 months 2
4-6 months 3
7-12 months 4
13-24 months 5
More than 24 months 6
Did not use 3 times per week 7

Last three months .... _____

Before service .... _____

In service/before Vietnam .... _____

In service/in Vietnam .... _____

In service/after Vietnam .... _____

Since discharge .... _____

114. How soon after your discharge did you first use grass or hash?   _____
     If did not use since discharge, code 99.   Months
                                                                       28-29

115. Have you ever felt that you were using too much grass or hash?

Yes 1
No   2
Never used 3

Last three months .... _____ 30

Before service .... _____

In service/before Vietnam .... _____

In service/in Vietnam .... _____

In service/after Vietnam .... _____

Since discharge .... _____

116. About what percentage of your friends used grass or hash in each time period?

Almost everyone 1
More than half 2
About half 3
Less than half 4
Only a few 5
None 6
Don't know 7

Last three months .... _____

Before service .... _____

In service/before Vietnam .... _____

In service/in Vietnam .... _____

In service/after Vietnam .... _____ 40

Since discharge .... _____

Now I would like to ask you some questions about your use of hallucinogens, such as LSD, STP, acid, peyote, mescaline, etc.

117. When was the first time that you used a hallucinogen?

Last three months 1
Before service 2
In service/before Vietnam 3
In service/in Vietnam 4
In service/after Vietnam 5
Since discharge 6
Never used 9   ———————

If never used, go to Question 124.

118. How old were you when you first used a hallucinogen?   ———————
If never used, code 99.   Years
43-44

119. In each time period, how often did you use a hallucinogen?

Daily 1
5-6 per week 2
3-4 per week 3
1-2 per week 4
2-3 per month 5
Once a month 6
Less than once per month 7
Never 8

Last three months .... ———————

Before service .... ———————

In service/before Vietnam .... ———————

In service/in Vietnam .... ———————

In service/after Vietnam .... ———————

Since discharge .... ———————
50

120. If less than once per month, about how many times did you actually use hallucinogens?

Last three months .... ——————— 51-52

Before service .... ———————

In service/before Vietnam .... ——————— 55-56

In service/in Vietnam .... ———————

In service/after Vietnam .... ——————— 59-60

Since discharge .... ———————

If used more than once per month, code 99.

121. In each time period in which you used hallucinogens more than three times per week, how long did you use them at that level?

> One week or less 1
> One week-one month 2
> 1-3 months 3
> 4-6 months 4
> 7-12 months 5
> 13-24 months 6
> More than 24 months 7
> Did not use 3 times per week 8

> Last three months .... _____
> Before service .... _____
> In service/before Vietnam .... _____
> In service/in Vietnam .... _____
> In service/after Vietnam .... _____
> Since discharge .... _____

122. How soon after your discharge did you first use a hallucinogen?   _____
     If did not use since discharge, code 99.   **Months**
                                                                          69-70

123. Have you ever had a bad trip on hallucinogens?
     If yes, ask, did this bad trip effect your future use of hallucinogens?

> Yes 1
> No 2
> Never had a bad trip 8
> Never used 9   _____

     If no, go to Question 124.
     If yes, ask, what effect did this bad trip have on you? Record verbatim response.

- -

Now I would like to ask about your use of amphetamines (speed).

124. When was the first time you used an amphetamine?

> Last three months 1
> Before service 2
> In service/before Vietnam 3
> In service/in Vietnam 4
> In service/after Vietnam 5
> Since discharge 6
> Never used 9   _____

     If never used, go to Question 133.

125. How old were you?   _____
     If never used, code 99.   **Years**
                                                     73-74

126. In each of these time periods, how often did you use amphetamines?

                Daily 1
                5-6 per week 2
                3-4 per week 3
                1-2 per week 4
                2-3 per month 5
                Once per month 6
                Less than once per month 7
                Never used 8

          Last three months ....   ——————————

          Before service ....   ——————————

          In service/before Vietnam ....   ——————————

          In service/in Vietnam ....   ——————————

          In service/after Vietnam ....   ——————————

          Since discharge ....   ——————————
                                                            80

                                            —————— —————— ——————
                                                  Card 7
                                                  1-3

127. If less than once per month, about how many times did you use amphetamines?

          Last three months ....   ——————————— 4-5

          Before service ....   ——————————

          In service/before Vietnam ....   ——————————

          In service/in Vietnam ....   ——————————— 10-11

          In service/after Vietnam ....   ——————————

          Since discharge ....   ——————————

     If used more than once per month, code 99.

128. In each time period in which you used amphetamines more than three times per week, for how long did you use them?

                One week or less 1
                One week-one month 2
                1-3 months 3
                4-6 months 4
                7-12 months 6
                13-24 months 6
                More than 24 months 7
                Did not use 3 times per week 8

Last three months .... _____

Before service .... _____

In service/before Vietnam .... _____

In service/in Vietnam .... _____

In service/after Vietnam .... _____ 20

Since discharge .... _____

129. How soon after your discharge did you first use amphetamine? _____
If did not use since discharge, code 99.   **Months**
                                                              22-23

130. Did you ever spend several days in a row high on amphetamines?

        Yes 1
        No 2
        Never used amphetamine 3

If yes, ask, tell me more about this speed run. Record verbatim response.

131. Did you ever mainline speed?

        Yes 1
        No 2
        Never used amphetamine 9   _____

If yes, ask, when did you do that? What did you shoot up? Record verbatim response.

132. Did you ever feel that you needed more speed to get the same effect?

        Yes 1
        No 2
        Never used amphetamine 9   _____

If yes, ask, when was that? Record verbatim response.

- -

Now I would like to ask you about your use of downers?

133. When was the first time that you used a downer?

        Last three months 1
        Before service 2
        In service/before Vietnam 3
        In service/in Vietnam 4
        In service/after Vietnam 5
        Since discharge 6
        Never used 9   _____

If never used, go to Question 143.

134. How old were you?

                                                        Years
                                                        28-29

135. In each of these time periods, how often did you use a downer?

          Daily 1
          5-6 per week 2
          3-4 per week 3
          1-2 per week 4
          2-3 per month 5
          Once per month 6
          Less than once per month 7
          Never used 8

              Last three months .... ——————— 30

              Before service .... ———————

              In service/before Vietnam .... ———————

              In service/in Vietnam .... ———————

              In service/after Vietnam .... ———————

              Since discharge .... ———————

136. If less than once per month, about hew many times did you actually use downers?

              Last three months .... ——————— 36-37

              Before service .... ———————

              In service/before Vietnam .... ——————— 40-41

              In service/in Vietnam .... ———————

              In service/after Vietnam .... ———————

              Since discharge .... ———————

     If more than once a month, code 99.

137. In each time period in which you used downers more than three times per week, for how long did you use them at that level?

          One week or less 1
          One week-one month 2
          1-3 months 3
          4-6 months 4
          7-12 months 5
          13-24 months 6
          More than 24 months 7
          Did not use 3 times per week 8

Last three months .... ⎯⎯⎯⎯⎯

Before service .... ⎯⎯⎯⎯⎯

In service/before Vietnam .... ⎯⎯⎯⎯⎯

In service/in Vietnam .... ⎯⎯⎯⎯⎯ 50

In service/after Vietnam .... ⎯⎯⎯⎯⎯

Since discharge .... ⎯⎯⎯⎯⎯

138. How soon after your discharge did you first use a downer? ⎯⎯⎯⎯⎯
If did not use since discharge code 99.   Months
    54-55

139. Did you ever have an accident while using downers?

Yes 1
No 2
Never used downers 3   ⎯⎯⎯⎯⎯

If yes, ask, what happenned? Record verbatim response.

140. Did you ever mainline any downers?

Yes 1
No 2
Never used downers 3   ⎯⎯⎯⎯⎯

If yes, ask, what did you shoot up? When did you shoot up? Record verbatim
response.

141. Did you ever feel that you were addicted to downers?

Yes 1
No 2
Never used downers 3   ⎯⎯⎯⎯⎯

If yes, ask, what drug were you using? When was that? Why do you feel you
were addicted? Record verbatim response.

142. Did you ever overdose on a downer?

Yes 1
No 2
Never used downers 3   ⎯⎯⎯⎯⎯

If yes, what happened that you overdosed? Record verbatim response. Be
sure to determine if overdose was accidental or intentional.

Finally, I would like to ask you some questions about your experiences with different types of narcotics such as heroin, opium, morphine, methadone, etc.

143. When was the first time that you used any narcotic?

Last three months 1
Before service 2
In service/before Vietnam 3
In service/in Vietnam 4
In service/after Vietnam 5
Since discharge 6
Never used 9

_____
60

If never used, ask, so, you have never smoked an OJ or used any opium or heroin in Vietnam or since your return?

Never used 1
Used 2   _____

If used, code Question 143.
If never used, go to Question 159.

144. What was the specific drug?

Heroin 1
Opium 2
Morphine 3
OJ 4
Dilaudid 5
Codeine 6
Methadone 7
Other (Specify) 8   _____

145. How old were you?   _____
If never used, code 99.   Years
                                                 63-64

146. In each time period, can you tell me how often you used a narcotic. Be specific about the narcotic used.

Daily 1
5-6 per week 2
3-4 per week 3
1-2 per week 4
2-3 per month 5
Once per month 6
Less than once per month 7
Never 8

	Heroin	Demerol	Opium	Morphine	Codeine	Dilaudid	Methadone	OJ
Last three months	___	___	___	___	___	___ 70	___	___
Before service	___	___	___	___	___	___	___	___ 80
Card 8 Col 1-3		___	___	___				
In service/ before Vietnam	___	___	___	___	___	___	___ 10	___
In service/ in Vietnam	___	___	___	___	___	___	___	___
In service/ after Vietnam	___ 20	___	___	___	___	___	___	___
Since discharge	___	___	___ 30	___	___	___	___	___

147. Did you ever mainline a narcotic?

    Yes 1
    No 2
    Never used narcotics 3

        Last three months .... _____

        Before service .... _____

        In service/before Vietnam .... _____

        In service/in Vietnam .... _____

        In service/after Vietnam .... _____ 40

        Since discharge .... _____

148. What was your most common route of administration in each time period?

    Mainline 1
    Skin pop 2
    Snort 3
    Oral 4
    Smoke 5
    Never used narcotics 8

        Last three months .... _____

        Before service .... _____

        In service/before Vietnam .... _____

        In service/in Vietnam .... _____

        In service/after Vietnam .... _____

        Since discharge .... _____

149. In each time period, for what length of time did you use any narcotic more than once a week?

One week or less 1
One week-one month 2
1-3 months 3
4-6 months 4
7-12 months 5
13-24 months 6
more than 24 months 7
Did not use 3 times per week 8

Last three months ....   _____

Before service ....   _____

In service/before Vietnam ....   _____

In service/in Vietnam ....   _____ 50

In service/after Vietnam ....   _____

Since discharge ....   _____

150. For what length of time did you use a narcotic daily or more?
Use same code as in Question 149.

Last three months ....   _____

Before service ....   _____

In service/before Vietnam ....   _____

In service/in Vietnam ....   _____

In service/after Vietnam ....   _____

151. Were you using other drugs in addition to narcotics, while you were using narcotics?

Yes 1
No 2
Never used narcotics 3

Grass or hash ....   _____ 60

Speed ....   _____

Barbiturates ....   _____

Hallucinogens ....   _____

Alcohol ....   _____

Other (specify) ....   _____

152. How long do you feel you were addicted to any narcotic?

> One week or less 1
> One week to one month 2
> 1-3 months 3
> 4-6 months 4
> 7-12 months 5
> More than 12 months 6
> Never addicted 7
> Never used narcotics 8
>
> Last three months .... _____
>
> Before service .... _____
>
> In service/before Vietnam .... _____
>
> In service/in Vietnam .... _____
>
> In service/after Vietnam .... _____ 70
>
> Since discharge .... _____

153. Have you ever sought help in dealing with your addiction?

> Yes 1
> No 2
> Never addicted 9   _____

If no, ask, why not? Record Verbatim response.
If yes, ask, where did you seek help?

> V.A. DDTC 1
> Other methadone program 2
> Drug free therapy 3
> Detoxification program 4
> Other (Specify) 5
> Never sought help 6
> Never addicted 9   _____

Record verbatim name of program and code type of treatment.

154. How many times have you felt sick or had withdrawal symptoms from not being able to get narcotics?

> Number

If never used narcotics, code 9.
If no withdrawals, ask: So you have never been sick because you could not get narcotics?

> Been sick 1
> Never been sick 2
> Never used narcotics 3   _____

If ever experienced symptoms, ask, what were some of the symptoms that you experienced during your withdrawal?

Mentioned spontaneously 1
Mentioned when asked 2
Did not mention 3
Never used narcotics 8
Never withdrew 9

Do not read list. Let subject respond without prompting. After S has mentioned all he can think of, read remaining symptoms.

Running nose and eyes .... _____

Felt flushed and sweaty .... _____

Chills .... _____

Goose bumps .... _____

Nausea and vomiting .... _____

Card 9
1-3

Stomach cramps .... _____

Muscles twitched .... _____

Diarrhea .... _____

Pains in back or legs .... _____

Trouble sleeping .... _____

Restlessness .... _____

Headaches .... _____ 10

Blurred or double vision .... _____

Other (Specify) .... _____

After you stopped using narcotics, what effect did this have on your use of other drugs?

Increased 1
Decreased 2
No change 3
Never used narcotics 9

Alcohol .... _____

Grass or hash .... _____

Barbiturates .... _____

Amphetamines .... _____

Tranquilizers .... _____

Other (specify) .... _____

155. Did you ever overdose while taking a narcotic?

    Yes 1
    No 2
    Never used narcotics 9   _____

If yes, ask, what was the situation surrounding your overdose? Record verbatim response. Make sure to determine if overdose was accidental or intentional.

156. How soon after discharge did you use a narcotic?   _____

                                                        Months
                                                        20-21

157. If you didn't use a narcotic until you were in Vietnam do you feel you would have used narcotics even if you had never gone to Vietnam?

    Yes 1
    No 2
    Used before Vietnam 8
    Never used narcotics 9   _____

What makes you feel that way? Record verbatim response.

158. Where do you feel the blame lies for your addiction?

    On self 1
    On friends 2
    On Army 3
    On government 4
    Other (Specify) 5
    Never addicted 9   _____

Why do you feel that way? Record verbatim response.

159. Did you ever go through a urine screen to detect narcotics?

    Yes 1
    No 2   _____

If yes, ask, when did you have this urine screen?

    In Vietnam 1
    After Vietnam 2
    Both 3
    No urine screen 4

Was this screen a unit sweep or a DEROS test?

    Unit sweep 1
    DEROS 2
    Both 3
    Neither 4
    No urine screen 9   _____

Did any screen ever come up positive?

Yes 1
No 2
No urine screen 9   _____

What were the results of your DEROS urine screen?

Positive for narcotics 1
Positive for other drugs 2
Negative 3
No urine screen 9   _____

If positive for other drugs, ask, what drugs came up positive? What did you expect the results of your DEROS screen to be? Use same code as above.

_____

160. About what percentage of people you knew used narcotics in each time period?

Almost everyone 1
More than half 2
About half 3
Less than half 4
Only a few 5
None 6
Don't know 7

Last three months .... _____ 30

Before service .... _____

In service/before Vietnam .... _____

In service/in Vietnam .... _____

In service/after Vietnam .... _____

Since discharge .... _____

161. After you returned from Vietnam, how soon did you learn of a place where you could obtain narcotics if you desired?   _____
                                                                         Months
                                                                         36-37

162. After your discharge, how soon did you learn of a place where you could obtain narcotics if you desired?   _____
                                                                    Months
                                                                    38-39

Code 99 in above questions in never learned of place to obtain narcotics.

163. Do you know of someone or someplace where you could go right now to buy narcotics?

Yes 1
No 2   _____
                                                        40

If yes, ask, how far would you have to go from where you are now living in order to get a narcotic?

Within a mile 1
1-10 miles 2
10-50 miles 3
More than 50 miles 4
Don't know how far 5
Don't know of any place 6   _____

164. Have you ever used any drug that we have not discussed?

Yes 1
No 2

     Cocaine .... _____

     Tranquilizers .... _____

     Darvon (pain killers) .... _____

     Inhalants .... _____

     Cough syrup .... _____

     Other (specify) .... _____

Record amount of any drug used, duration of use and location of use. Finally, I have two questions about the VA and benefits that are offered.

165. What different veterans benefits have you used since your discharge?

Yes 1
No 2

     Educational benefits .... _____

     Medical benefits .... _____

     Hospitalization benefits .... _____ 50

     Loans .... _____

     Employment counseling .... _____

     Housing assistance .... _____

     Other (specify) .... _____

166. Have you tried to get any benefits that you have not received?

Yes 1
No 2

Educational benefits .... _____

Medical benefits .... _____

Hospitalization benefits .... _____

Loans .... _____

Employment counseling .... _____

Housing assistance .... _____ 60

Other (specify) .... _____

Why didn't you get these benefits?

- -

Although we have covered many areas, there may be some that we did not devote
enough attention to. Is there anything else that you think I should know about
yourself? Record verbatim response.

Time completed: _____ a.m.
                                 p.m.

Length of interview _____
                        Minutes
                        62-63-64

Interviewer's signature: _____

Location of interview: _____

Home 1
S's office 2
I's office 3
Car 4
Restaurant 5
Hospital 6
Jail 7
Other (Specify) 8   _____

Description of subject:

Weight:
Emaciated 1
Thin 2
Average 3
Obese 4   _____

Honesty of response:
High 1
Medium 2
Low 3   _____

Understanding of Questions:
High 1
Medium 2
Low 3   _____

Ability to articulate answers:
    High 1
    Medium 2
    Low 3   _____

Cooperativeness:
    Cooperative 1
    Suspicious 2
    Hostile 3
    Uncommunicative 4   _____
                                                              70
Privacy:
    Yes 1
    No 2
    Most of the time 3   _____

Any sign of:
    Drunkenness ....   _____

    Drug intoxication ....   _____

    Nervous problem ....   _____

    Withdrawal ....   _____

Code above.
    Yes 1
    No 2

Explain observations.

Ethnic group:
    Black 1
    White 2
    Oriental 3
    Indian 4
    Spanish 5
    Other 6
    Can't tell 7   _____

Urine results:
    Positive 1
    Negative 2

                                        ___ ___ ___
                                        Card 10
                                        1-3

            Methadone ....   _____

            Quinine ....   _____

            Morphine ....   _____

            Codeine ....   _____

            Cocaine ....   _____

            Amphetamine ....   _____

            Barbiturate ....   _____ 10

            Other ....   _____

6

DEATH AND VIETNAM: SOME COMBAT VETERAN EXPERIENCES AND PERSPECTIVES

BERNARD SPILKA, Ph.D., LISA FRIEDMAN
and DAVID ROSENBERG

The Problem

About 15 years ago death was referred to as a taboo topic in psychology (Feifel, 1963). Writing in this area was extremely sparse, highly clinical, speculative and theoretical. Actual research was virtually unknown. The last decade, however, has witnessed a complete reversal of emphasis. Since Kubler-Ross' initial work (1969), there has been an outpouring of popular and technical literature on death and dying that speaks to the deep concern of people with these issues. Motives for this heightened interest in death are probably many and varied, but the fact that the current interest in death appears to have begun at the height of the Vietnam war, which kept death before us daily, suggests the possibility of more than a chance relationship between the two.

Unhappily, the recent development of the psychology of death has given us very little information on the effects of war on death perspectives or how encounters with death in such a setting influence death anxiety, personality and adjustment (Kastenbaum & Aisenberg, 1972). The pre-Vietnam era taboo on discussing death (Dumont & Foss, 1972) may partially account for the paucity of writing on death effects relative to the Second World War or the Korean conflict. Changes in the social-scientific climate relative to the Vietnam war appear to be more supportive of research to understand the psychology of those involved in this war.*

Among the many significant experiences the soldier in Vietnam en-

---

* A few recent attempts to afford this area constructive attention have been undertaken as noted by Figley in Chapter 4.

countered, none appears to have been more profound than his confrontation with death. Lifton (1973) in his classic work, *Home from the War*, leaves no doubt about the role death played in the mind of the combat soldier in terms of death anxiety and death guilt. Despite his explanations, one is still hard put to know in depth how these veterans feel about specific common experiences among combat vets and how their feelings are associated with past and present death perceptions related or unrelated to combat experiences.

Considering the significance of death to the individual soldier in Vietnam, it is surprising how little attention has been afforded it in the research literature. In most instances it is treated almost as if it were a chance occurrence. The concern of the present effort is to correct this deficit in the literature by examining death from the viewpoint of the Vietnam combat veteran and exploring the ramifications of his encounters with death.

THE STUDY OF DEATH: SOME PREDICTIONS

Pre-service Experiences

The research reported on bereavement and the confrontation with death is controversial. In general, one expects the outcome of these experiences to be deleterious as has been extensively documented in the case of childhood loss (Brown, 1961) and the death of spouses and children (Glick, Weiss & Parkes, 1974). In contrast, Carey (1974) indicates that successful coping among adults with one's own inevitable death relates positively to having been close to someone else during their dying process. Although similar work with combat veterans has not been carried out, this research leads to the hypothesis that pre-Vietnam experience with death by combat veterans should mitigate the effects of being present when someone was killed. Indications of less death anxiety on the part of the veteran himself while he was in combat might also be expected.

Religious Background

Religion has been shown to have a strong influence on an individual's death perspectives and anxiety. Again, this is a controversial area (Lester, 1967, 1972), but the weight of evidence suggests that a strong religious background and/or identification seems to act as a defense against death anxiety (Minton & Spilka, 1976; Spilka, Stout, Minton, &

Sizemore, 1977). We might therefore hypothesize that strength of religious background should be inversely associated with evidences of death fear and anxiety while in combat. Value on life, however, should be positively associated with a religious framework.

Life Investments

There is reason to believe that negative orientations and fear of death relate to the investment one makes in life (Spilka, Pellegrini & Dailey, 1968). Such an investment may be inferred from what one has attained and one's degree of involvement with and commitment to others. For example, married individuals with families and those with more education could be expected to demonstrate more distress about death than their single and less educated counterparts. The association of education with class level (Warner, Meeker, & Eels, 1960) further supports this position, as Diggory and Rothman (1961) have shown—middle-class persons who possess more education tend to fear dying more than less educated lower class individuals.

Service Entry Status

Cognitive dissonance theory (Festinger, 1957) points out the effort people make to maintain consistency between their attitudes and behaviors. The military situation offers a unique test of this view since those who enter military service were either drafted or volunteered. Those who enlist express their willingness to serve in combat, so one might, therefore, assume that they would have less concern and fear about death and dying in battle situations, as well as a greater readiness to tolerate the stresses and discomforts of these circumstances. In contrast, drafted veterans would be expected to report more signs of death fear and unhappiness while in combat.

METHOD

Sample

A sample of 104 Vietnam combat veterans participated in this study. Their average age was 30.8 years with a range from 24 to 52 years. Mean number of months in combat was 13.9 with a range from two to 36 months. Although they were vulnerable to enemy attack, most were not actively engaged in combat during their entire tour of duty in Vietnam. Thirty-six of the veterans were wounded or disabled in the military; one refused to answer regarding such a condition.

Tests and Materials

A 28-item questionnaire was constructed with the aid of a number of Vietnam veterans in order to maximize relevance to those sampled. This instrument covered four main areas: (1) background demographic information and early death contacts and feelings; (2) experiences and outlooks relative to the threat of death while in Vietnam; (3) current death perspectives, concerns and expectations; and (4) information on disablement. This questionnaire may be found in Appendix 6-A.

Procedures

The respondents were sampled from many sources: veterans offices in three colleges and universities, two federal hospitals and via personal contact by the authors. In some instances, veterans were solicited from large university classes. The voluntary nature of the investigation was always stressed and in many instances there was reluctance to participate in the study. Where there was personal contact virtually every veteran completed the questionnaire. Considerable variation did occur in rate of return from other sources and because of various problems it is not possible to definitively state the actual proportion of questionnaires filled out. Best estimates place the rate of return and attempted return at two-thirds to three-quarters of those sampled.*

In keeping with the opening statement on the questionnaire, all potential participants were fully informed that the purpose of the study was to understand their death-related experiences both prior to and during combat in Vietnam. Those who coordinated data collection where the investigators were not present were instructed to be open and frank regarding this purpose of the study. Interested or questioning veterans often contacted the first author who further reinforced the above aim of the investigation. A number of veterans desired the results of this work and were provided with them upon its completion.

RESULTS AND DISCUSSION

Background Factors

At the time these men entered combat 34 percent were married, 60 percent were single and 6 percent were divorced. In the latter part of

---

* It is difficult to know how many veterans refused to answer as a number of completed forms were lost by one office and others failed to get to the investigators though obviously mailed by a concerned secretary.

1975 and during 1976 when the data were gathered, these percentages had reversed with 60 percent being married, 27 percent remaining single and 11 percent divorced. About 2 percent were separated from their wives at this later time. Of those who had children when they entered combat (23 percent), the average number was two per veteran.

In terms of pre-combat education, almost half (48 percent) graduated from high school or had some high school instruction. Another 35 percent had some college experience with 7 percent attaining a college degree. Almost 5 percent had some postgraduate training. These percentages suggest a more educated sample than studied by Moskos (1970) and Helmer (1974). Eighty percent or more of their veterans had either completed high school or had not yet attained this educational level. Since approximately half of the present veterans were located through college and university offices, higher levels of education would be expected.

In terms of religious background, 29 percent of the veterans came from conservative to strict orthodox families, while 58 percent grew up with either little or no religious influence in their home. Our veterans' religiosity appears to be almost identical to that reported by Helmer (1974) relative to involvement in church or religious organizations.

It is likely that the manner of one's entry into service might reflect both background factors and later perspectives on death and combat. Most of the sample (70 percent) were enlistees. This falls between the percentage of enlistees for the Helmer (1974) study (85 percent) and Moskos (1970) group (41 percent). The reason for such variations from study to study is unclear, but may be a function of the relatively small sizes of the samples obtained thus far, hence sampling error.

Pre-service Death Experiences

Prior to military service most of the veterans (66 percent) had some contact with death. The majority thought of death rarely or not at all (54 percent) while a small group (5 percent) speculated often about death.

Current Conceptions of Death

The veterans are currently inclined to regard death as the "natural conclusion to life" (30 percent). An equal number introduce religious considerations such as an afterlife or "continuation of the spirit" after bodily death. Another 23 percent think of death as an unknown or simply feel they are unable to define its nature. Since these observations are in line with what has been found elsewhere (Hooper & Spilka, 1970; Kastenbaum & Aisenberg, 1972), our sample is probably representative of young American adults in terms of their conceptions of death.

Personal Confrontation: The Sight of Death

From the time one entered a combat zone, death was a more or less constant companion, both in the arousal of emotion in relation to it and in its physical presence. Central in such experiences was the sight of bodies, both enemy and Americans. Differences in response to the two over time were clearly present. Eighty-six percent of the veterans reported extreme discomfort to the point of sickness when they saw their first American body. A significantly lower level of sensitivity was manifested with regard to the corpses of the enemy as 64 percent reported the same degree of distress. Desensitization took place over time and this was far greater relative to the enemy than to one's own countrymen. When the last American fatality was seen, 76 percent reported great upset while a like response occurred in 39 percent for the last enemy body seen. Such reduced sensitivity has been referred to elsewhere both in the professional and popular literature. Mantell's (1974, pp. 156-169) case studies amply testify to a surprising callousness regarding death. As might have been expected, this seems to be a function of the time spent in combat. The rather considerable lessening of reactivity here is correlated with combat time ($r = -.29$, $p < .01$).

Death Sensitivity in Combat

Sensitivity to death and killing among these veterans seems to reflect a more basic and possibly general disposition. If a veteran was upset at the *first* sight of an American body, he manifested similar discomfort with the initial viewing of an enemy body ($r = .27$, $p < .01$), and the last sight of a dead American ($r = .33$, $p < .01$). Distress at seeing the *last* dead American and a dead enemy did relate fairly substantially ($r = .56$, $p < .01$). A coefficient of .44 ($p < .01$) associated the *first* sight of a dead enemy and the last view of a dead American. Of six possibly significant correlations among these items, four surpassed the .01 level and the remaining two were near the five percent cutoff.

Some hints of factors influencing this sensitivity may be inferred from items that suggest anxiety, particularly concerning death. For example, frequency of thoughts about death is commonly regarded as a sign of death fear, and requests for such information are found on virtually every measure of death anxiety (Dickstein, 1972; Templer, 1970).

Reference was made earlier to a question dealing with thinking about death prior to entering the service. The pattern of responses to that query and one dealing with such thoughts during combat is quite similar. Prior to entering the service 54 percent of the respondents thought of death rarely or not at all and 5 percent reported frequent thoughts of death. In combat the comparable percentages are 56 and 12 percent. It is surprising that thoughts about death increased so little under the stress of combat and potential death. It may be that in combat the soldier is too preoccupied with accomplishing his mission and staying alive to spend much time thinking about death. This appears to support the notions of "delayed stress" discussed in Section I of this volume. In addition, despite the fairly parallel patterns of response to these questions, no significant correlation exists between them, suggesting a similar pattern under such radically different circumstances need not result in persons' holding the same relative position in the response distributions.

Examining the associations of thinking about death during combat along with the other aspects of combat action, we observe that *frequent* death thoughts at this time affiliate positively with disturbance at the *first* sight of a dead American ($r = .30$, $p < .01$), a dead enemy ($r = .20$, $p < .05$), and *last* view of a dead American ($r = .21$, $p < .05$). Generalized anxiety is also suggested by the report that the more the veteran was bothered by the initial sight of an American body, the more he entertained thoughts of being wounded or disabled in Vietnam ($r = .23$, $p < .05$).

Thinking about the likelihood one would be killed in Vietnam was also a significant element in this overall pattern of concerns and feelings about combat experiences. If a veteran regarded his chances of being killed as high, he tended to be more upset at his last viewing of a dead enemy ($r = .25$, $p < .05$). Thus there appears to be a range of sensitivity-insensitivity, among the veterans sampled, to death in the combat situation. Such a range of sensitivity to stress has been found in the general population (Dickstein, 1972; Durlak, 1972).

Death Sensitivity: Disposing Factors

Early death contact. It was hypothesized that contact with death early in life might mitigate later sensitivity and concern about death and dying. Some support for this expectation comes from the finding that the more pre-service contact a veteran had with death, the less distress he reported on viewing his first dead American ($r = -.32$, $p < .01$). In addition, further corroboration may be inferred by noting that early death contact associates with fewer early life fears of one's own death ($r = -.36$, $p < .01$) and low expectations of becoming disabled as a result of combat ($r = -.31$, $p < .01$). Interestingly, such pre-service death experience ties to placing less value on one's life specifically as a function of combat experience ($r = -.31$, $p < .01$). This last finding is unexpected and may mean that what appears to be reduced death anxiety resulting from early death contact may be a thoroughgoing use of the mechanism of denial as a means of coping with such an eventuality; death fear is simply not expressed.

Religion. Our single religious item failed to correlate significantly with any of the attitudinal or death experience measures. No support may be adduced for the hypothesis advanced earlier regarding the possible role of religion. Considering the nature of the item and the fact that only one question reflecting this complex domain was asked, too much was probably expected.

Life investment. The point was made that investment in life in terms of marriage, children and education at the time of combat might stimulate death fear and anxiety. Our few findings relative to this hypothesis are not consistent.

The more children one had when in Vietnam, the more thoughts of death were entertained while in combat ($r = .20$, $p < .05$). This potential support for the hypothesis is negated when education is considered. Those with more schooling appear to have been less anxious about their chances of being killed ($r = -.25$, $p < .01$). They also did less thinking about death in general during combat ($r = -.21$, $p < .05$).

Service entry status. The hypothesis was advanced in line with cognitive dissonance theory that those who volunteered for military service would show less sensitivity to and concern about death than veterans who were drafted. Some support for this expectation was found. Those who enlisted felt prior to combat that their chances of being killed were significantly less than did draftees ($r = -.25$, $p < .01$). In like manner, the former also reported they thought less about death when they were actually in combat ($r = -.21, p < .05$).

Predicting death sensitivity. The findings reported above, particularly with regard to distress at the sight of American and enemy bodies, and pre-combat death expectations, suggest a generalized death concern, the possible causes of which may be found in the veteran's early life and/or experiences in Vietnam. To determine the relative significance of these factors, all variables which were possible precedents of these feelings were further analyzed using a stepwise multiple regression approach.

Only those items which related in a statistically significant manner to the dependent criterion in the univariate analysis were chosen as possible predictors. It was not possible to find any independent variables which predicted in a stepwise manner the distress reported at the first sight of a dead enemy soldier or at the last sight of a dead American. The first viewing of a dead American was predicted significantly by four of the items. The resulting multiple correlation was .41 ($p < .01$) and in order of their contribution to this coefficient were the following: (1) having no or little preservice contact with death, (2) being among those with children when in combat, (3) low educational achievement, and (4) having engaged in much thinking about death when young.

Three variables resulted in a multiple correlation of .39 when the dependent item was distress experienced at the last sight of a dead enemy. In order of their entrance into the stepwise equation, these are: (1) being drafted, (2) shortness of time in combat, and (3) coming from a non-religious background.

When the criterion item was what the veteran felt his chances were of being killed in Vietnam prior to entering combat, four of the items combined to yield a multiple correlation of .43. These are: (1) being drafted, (2) having little education, (3) thinking much about death when young, and (4) shortness of combat time in Vietnam.

In most instances the majority of these independent variables appear supportive of the hypotheses advanced earlier. Though more potential predictors were submitted to the multiple regression analysis, statistically significant contributions could only be justified with those presented here.

Thus, death sensitivity and concern on the part of the Vietnam veteran as reported retrospectively appear to be broad based phenomena. Major determinants are early life experiences and the immediate situation when entering the Vietnam theater. Within the limitations of this work, pre-service contact with death, the presence of children, being drafted rather than enlisting, and brevity of time in combat seem to be the main predictors of death fear.

Combat and the Immediacy of Death

A meaningful factor relating to concern with personal death in combat was being present when someone known to the veteran was killed in action ($r = -.20$, $p < .05$). Eighty-five percent of our sample stated that they were present in combat when someone they knew died. Sixty-nine percent of those in Helmer's (1974) groups report close friends killed in Vietnam. The difference in his and our samples probably hinges on the phrases "close friends" and being "present" when death occurred.

Similarly, thinking about dying in combat tied to like thoughts of becoming wounded and disabled ($r = .24$, $p < .05$). It is interesting to observe that the more one thought about dying while in combat, the more ideas of disability occurred ($r = .27$, $p < .01$). At the same time, the more the person thought about death and was subsequently wounded, the percent of disablement tended to be low ($r = -.21$, $p < .05$). Thus, one can speculate that the greater the soldier's anxiety under combat conditions, the more careful he was, hence chances of survival or incurring less serious wounds were also greater.

The burden of surviving. Being present when someone you knew from your own unit was killed must have had a profound effect on the survivors. Subjective accounts of atrocities and the feelings of men in these situations, as cited by Mantell (1974), suggest that considerable dehumanization does take place.

In an attempt to comprehend the emotional state at this time, the veterans studied here were asked whether they felt hate, sick, anger, fear, pain or just nothing. Forty-eight percent reacted with anger and 14 percent with hate. Pain elicited a 15 percent response with the remaining choices garnering only 6 to 11 percent each.

Shifting from the level of feeling to that of behavior, the veterans were allowed five choices reflecting possible outcomes of losing a man from their unit. Although the dominant reaction was to be "revengeful" (21 percent), no single alternative prevailed. Twenty percent said they were "more committed," 18 percent claimed to be more aggressive, a choice not unlike revengeful. Similar degrees of assent were afforded the other possibilities. On this verbal plane, the basis for a violent and ill-considered response seems evident.

Survivor responses: disposing factors. A search for factors that might distinguish among those who claimed to show an anger-aggressive or an anger-revengeful potential on the two items just mentioned was not very fruitful. Some interesting observations on the possible role of religion are, however, in order and may be worthy of further examination. Religiously conservative and orthodox home backgrounds are almost equally affiliated percentage-wise with aggressive, revengeful and committed stances (21, 18 and 23 percent respectively). Those whose backgrounds were not religious in nature tended to be low in aggression (10 percent) and commitment (6 percent), but higher in revengeful attitude (25 percent) or likely to evidence no reaction when a buddy was killed (33 percent). We would speculate that religious and aggressive soldiers might better maintain their self-control if the likelihood of participating in atrocities were to occur. The extreme revengeful or non-reaction of those who might lack religious controls on their behavior could imply a greater readiness to engage in possible violence against the defenseless. This is, of course, highly speculative, but religion has been known to function as an agency of social constraint in many situations; of course, in some situations religion has spurred on those who participate in violent acts in service to their religious beliefs (e.g., the Ulster and Israeli-Arab fighting).

Another dimension of feeling when someone known was killed derives from being a survivor. The dominant responses reported were feelings of guilt (44 percent) or simply no response (44 percent). These feelings relate significantly to educational level with those up to college level reacting with relief (45 percent) or guilt (20 percent). In contrast, the veterans who entered service with college and above training largely claim no response (27 percent) and few feelings of relief (11 percent) or guilt (4 percent). Education either relates to more denial or simply less sensitivity, further negating the hypothesis advanced earlier. Insensitivity could be a possible function of using intellectualization as a defense. No pattern relative to religious background was found.

The element of possible desensitization due to pre-service contact with death must be considered as 54 percent of those who showed no reaction to being a survivor had much prior death contact while only 20 percent of those lacking such experience felt this way. The main response of the latter relative to the former was relief (38 to 18 percent). This finding may be considered in line with our hypothesis on pre-service death contact.

Desensitization as a manifestation of denial must be considered hypothetically, for those who felt nothing when surviving tended to be the same veterans who reported either feeling pain (33 percent) or also having no reaction (38 percent) when they were present and their buddy died. Needless to say, denial of emotional awareness under war conditions may be adaptive.

Thus, the immediacy of death in combat must have a profound effect on those present in this situation. All are constantly under the threat of sudden annihilation. The overwhelming majority of our sample often had to act under such stress. That death anxiety was present could not be doubted. Survivors often claimed to feel anger and hate. The desire was to act revengeful and aggressive although a wide variety of alternatives could be chosen. The potential for engaging in atrocities would seem an everpresent reality. Religious background might serve as a restraint while education could support a defensive intellectualization with elements of denial of the seriousness of the situation. Preservice contact with death also might function similarly.

The Value of Life

Theoretically, the confrontation with death can be conceptualized as having a profound effect on the value one places on life. Depending on a variety of factors, life may be perceived as tenuous at best and thus to be developed and lived to its fullest. On the other hand it may, with its fragility, come to be seen as essentially worthless. When these veterans were asked if their combat experience had influenced the value they place on their own lives, the majority (53 percent) said it did. Only 10 percent felt that they now place less value on their lives as a result of combat. The other 37 percent apparently felt that combat experiences had little or no effect on how much they valued life.

Among possible influences affecting this change of life valuation present marital status seems significant. Of those who see their lives as being of greater significance today as a result of being in combat, 60 percent are married. Life's worth may therefore be a result of greater investment in it and, as theorized, marriage, and family probably represent such a commitment.

A similar view can be entertained with regard to education, for only 22 percent of those with the least schooling showed a gain in life valuation. This response fairly regularly increases until it reaches 66 percent at the highest educational levels. Again, this is seen as investment in life.

The earlier hypothesized pre-service contact with death as a desensitizing experience may continue its influence relative to life value. Of those with much early death involvement only 28 percent claim an increased significance of life for themselves. Those with little pre-military death contact show the reverse with 73 percent now affirming increased life worth. If research on early life experience with death can be shown to have these somewhat negative effects, educators may have to consider how this can be countered. Unfortunately, little is currently known about the long-range effects of death on young children. The prevalent literature tends to emphasize the negative (Cook, Renshaw, & Jackson, 1973).

Apparently this growth in the value of life relates to the kind of response one made when seeing the first dead American. Forty-four percent of those for whom life now means more were greatly upset by this occurrence, while only 6 percent of the veterans who claimed no feeling revealed an increase in life value. The possible desensitization to dead bodies noted earlier may account for the lack of further similar relationships between life worth and the other queries about the corpses of Americans and the enemy. It is, however, noteworthy that of those present when a buddy was killed, 83 percent claim the value of life has increased for them, suggesting a truly intense effect here.

The death-to-come. Death in combat may, of course, be swift or lingering and painful. Most young adults desire that their own death be quick and occur while they are asleep (Vernon, 1968). Considering the involvement with death of the veterans studied here, and the probability that their experiences might influence perceptions of their own eventual death, they were asked to imagine how this might come about and whether it would be sudden, slow and due to lingering illness, painful or violent. The majority, like students, selected a sudden death (57 percent). The remaining choices received from 2 to 22 percent each, with the lowest options being violent and painful. It is likely that aspiration and expectation may be mixed together.

Once more we see the role of pre-service death contact in this prediction, with 73 percent of those with much early experience expecting a sudden death; 54 percent of those with no prior death involvement foresee a similar outcome to their lives. Personal presence when someone known was killed in combat operates similarly. Of those expecting a sudden demise, 87 percent were present when a member of their unit was killed. Of those not present, only 12 percent chose this likelihood. It is possible the personal horror experienced at such a time creates the expectation (desire) of a sudden death for themselves.*

Predicting the value of life. There is probably no more significant long-range effect for the veteran than what his war experiences portend for his future life. Basic to that future is whether life value has changed. We have seen that a number of different variables relate to such an outcome. To establish what the significant predictive variables for life's value might be, the stepwise multiple regression approach was employed. Eight different independent variables made significant contributions to explaining the variance in the item on life value. The resulting multiple correlation was .45 ($p < .01$). The predictive variables in order of their contribution are: (1) low pre-service death contact, (2) high education, (3) having enlisted, (4) if disabled, having a high percentage disability, (5) not being disabled, (6) not being bothered when last seeing a dead American, (7) not being distressed when last seeing a dead enemy soldier, and (8) brevity of time in combat. It is difficult to summarize, this picture or to comprehend it in a composite sense. Clearly, more research is necessary to clarify the role of these different factors in understanding the value the Vietnam veteran places on his life.

CONCLUSIONS

Death was clearly a central and profound experience for those who fought in Vietnam. Reactions to the death of others and the potential of being killed seem to represent many pre-service life happenings and circumstances. Among these, early home religious atmosphere and contact with death stand out. The influence of personal investment in education and one's own family is definitely suggested. Further efforts beyond those made here are merited, and guidance from some of Mantell's (1974) work is warranted.

Personality components, particularly with regard to anxiety and the potential use of denial and desensitizing mechanisms, continually seem to enter this picture of adjustment to the combat situation. Additional

---

* One wonders if a rather sensitive spot is being touched here, but unfortunately the data gathered in this study do not permit further development of this theme. Also unhappily, this must be viewed as a general difficulty of this investigation. Many suggestive avenues have been opened leading to the recognition of the necessity of more in-depth research in this domain.

direction for deeper treatment of themes will have to be sought in the clinical literature.

Finally, there are signs that the Vietnam experience has continuing effects on the value one places on life and also probably on how one sees one's own death coming about. Helmer (1974), Mantell (1974), a number of authors included in Mantell and Pilisuk (1975), as well as numerous chapters in this volume, offer evidence of the lasting and pervasive influence Vietnam had on those involved directly and indirectly with this war.

As extensive as the findings reported here are, much that was expected to be important was not observed. The manner of entry into the armed services, whether by enlistment or draft, did not appear to be of very great significance. Also surprising was the minimal role that being wounded or disabled in combat seemed to play.

In general, more questions for future research seemed to have evolved than have been answered. The apparent recent upsurge in serious work in this area does suggest that increased efforts to find the necessary answers may be forthcoming.

APPENDIX 6-A

Death Perspectives of War Veterans

This is a questionnaire dealing with the death perspectives of war veterans. Please answer the questions based on your experiences and according to your own feelings. Do not put your name on this survey.

1. What is your present age? _____

2. When were you in combat in Vietnam? (list the number of years and months)

    _____ yrs. and _____months.

3. What was your marital status at the time of combat?

    a. married
    b. single
    c. divorced
    d. other (please write in) _____ _____

4. What is your present marital status?

    a. married
    b. single
    c. divorced
    d. other (please write in) _____

5. How many children did you have at the time of combat?

    a. none
    b. one
    c. two
    d. three or more

6. How did you enter the service?

    a. enlistment
    b. drafted

7. How far did you go in school before entering combat?

    a. up to the eighth grade
    b. some high school
    c. high school graduate
    d. vocational training
    e. undergraduate college
    f. college graduate
    g. graduate school training

8. What kind of religious background did you have when you were young?

  a. strict and orthodox
  b. conservative
  c. liberal
  d. not much
  e. none

9. What job did you hold in the service? i.e. guard, fighter pilot, etc. (please specify)

  _____

10. Before entering the service, I

  a. had no contact with death
  b. had some contact with death
  c. had a lot of contact with death

11. Before I entered the service, I thought of death:

  a. often
  b. occasionally
  c. rarely
  d. not at all

12. I feel death is:

  a. a natural conclusion to life
  b. the unknown
  c. the beginning to an afterlife
  d. the ending of the physical being; the spirit lives on
  e. the final stage in life processes
  f. don't know

13. The initial sight of a dead body of an American:

  a. upset me greatly
  b. made me feel uncomfortable
  c. didn't bother me
  d. I had no feeling

14. The initial sight of a dead body of the enemy:

  a. upset me
  b. made me feel uncomfortable
  c. didn't bother me
  d. made me sick

15. The last sight of a dead body of an American:

  a. upset me
  b. made me uncomfortable

    c. made me sick

    d. didn't bother me

    e. made me feel a sense of relief

16. The last sight of a dead body of an enemy:

    a. upset me

    b. made me feel uncomfortable

    c. made me sick

    d. made me feel a sense of relief

    e. didn't bother me

17. When you entered combat, what did you think your chances were of being killed in combat?

    a. great

    b. about average

    c. didn't think that I would be killed

18. Were you present in combat when people you knew died?

    _____ yes

    _____ no

19. If so how did you feel? (check only one)

    a. hate

    b. sick

    c. anger

    d. fear

    e. pain

    f. nothing

20. When you lost a man from your unit, how did it affect you in combat?

    a. made me more aggressive

    b. made me more committed

    c. made me feel more revengeful

    d. no reaction

    e. made me more fearful

    f. other _____

21. In actual combat how often did you think about your death?

    a. constantly

    b. often

    c. seldom

    d. not at all

22. What were your feelings about surviving when others died?

    a. guilty

    b. relief

    c. nothing

    d. other _____

23. Since your experience in combat, has the value you placed on your life

    a. increased
    b. stayed about the same
    c. decreased

24. How do you imagine your death will come about?

    a. suddenly
    b. slowly, lingering illness
    c. painfully
    d. violently
    e. other _____

_____

1. Are you disabled?

    a. yes
    b. no

2. What per cent is your disability?_____ _____

3. What is your disability? _____

4. Before going overseas what were your thoughts on the possibility of returning disabled?

    a. I was afraid of becoming disabled
    b. I would have preferred to be killed in combat.
    c. I was not afraid of becoming disabled
    d. I never thought about it

7

PSYCHIATRIC SYNDROMES, SELF-CONCEPTS, AND VIETNAM VETERANS

ROBERT F. PANZARELLA, Ph.D., DAVID M. MANTELL, Ph.D.,
and R. HARLAN BRIDENBAUGH, M.D.

STRESS DISORDERS IN VIETNAM

Reports of the incidence of psychiatric problems among U.S. military personnel in Vietnam indicated that there were far fewer psychiatric casualties in Vietnam than there had been in World War II (Jones & Johnson, 1975). Of the cases reported in Vietnam, many seemed to be unrelated to the specific stresses of war. The bulk of cases seemed to come from support units rather than from units engaged in combat. Not even physiological indicators of stress were altered by assignment to combat duty, although physiological stress was evident in young officers assigned to leadership roles (Bourne, 1970). Factors cited by Bourne to explain the low incidence of psychiatric problems were better physical care of soldiers, availability of rapid medical treatment, a type of combat that was sporadic rather than continuous, and, most of all, the definite limitation of a soldier's tour of duty to one year.

Other, more ambiguous factors also seemed to be involved. One was the particular kind of therapeutic role played by military psychiatrists. There apparently was an attempt to redefine reality for the combat soldier. An ideology of psychiatric breakdown which minimized the stresses of war was constructed (Daniels, 1970). The soldier was given a more functional perspective, helping him to accept the belief that much which is abnormal in a civilian setting is normal in a combat setting. Moreover, the soldier was taught that one or a few incidents,

---

The opinions and assertions contained herein are the private views of the authors and are not to be construed as official or as reflecting the views of the Department of the Army or the Department of Defense.

no matter how stressful, could not produce any lasting psychiatric problem. Only very sustained stress of a duration that rarely occurred in Vietnam could cause breakdown. Even then, "normal breakdown" due to sustained combat stresses was expected to be followed by "normal recovery"—rapid recovery through temporary removal from the combat setting followed by quick return to active duty. The soldier who reported for psychiatric care was urged to reexamine his situation in light of this ideology.

Two other factors also may have contributed to the low incidence of psychiatric problems: widespread use of drugs in Vietnam and expeditious administrative discharges. Using drugs may have enabled the soldier to cope with his problems temporarily and delay their emergence (Solomon, 1971). Finally, given the continued difficulties surrounding diagnostic issues, administrative discharges from the armed forces may have been used in many cases to sidestep dealing with psychiatric problems (Daniels, 1970).

PSYCHIATRIC SYNDROMES AFTER DISCHARGE

Toward the end of the war dramatic accounts of psychiatric problems among veterans appeared (Bourne, 1972; Fox, 1972; Levy, 1971; Lifton, 1969, 1970, 1973; Solomon, 1971; Solomon, Zarcone, Yoerg, Scott, & Maurer, 1971). It was proposed that Vietnam-related experiences had resulted in numerous psychiatric problems but that the emergence of these problems had been delayed until after removal from the combat setting or even until after return to the civilian environment. The problems themselves were viewed essentially as defensive adaptations to the combat setting which were inappropriate in noncombat or civilian settings. The origins of the problems were not limited to combat situations. They were also traced to psychological techniques used in basic training, ideological disillusionment with the American ethic when confronted with the actuality of U.S. military action in Vietnam, and shame and guilt fermented by public sentiment against the war in its last few years. Combat neuroses, moral crises, and readjustment problems such as drug addiction and unemployment seemed to flare up, sometimes separately, sometimes together, among Vietnam veterans.

Two kinds of psychiatric syndromes among veterans have been described. One is a "numbed guilt" reaction (Lifton, 1969, 1970, 1973), which consists of an unarticulated guilt generated by "atrocity" experiences and manifested in psychic numbing, a need to victimize others, touchiness, suspiciousness, and withdrawal. Numbed guilt was traced to the combat situation itself, and was said to appear while the soldier was still on duty in Vietnam. The veteran experiencing numbed guilt did not want to talk about the war after his return. Numbed guilt was said to be the usual condition of the Vietnam veteran, at least upon the point of his reentry to civilian life.

The second kind of syndrome described is a full-blown "post-Vietnam syndrome" which occurs after discharge from the military or at least after removal from the combat setting when the numbing begins to "thaw" and the veteran must face the civilian environment with its ethical code, attitude against the war, and restricted opportunities. Fox (1972) has reported spontaneous remission of defensive mechanisms developed in combat situations soon after removal from the combat setting but Lifton has reported that it is extremely difficult to undo the numbing effects of war, although confrontation in veterans' rap groups can apparently achieve this.

The Vietnam literature variously describes the post-Vietnam syndrome as a group of symptoms large and small, specific and vague, and with affective, attitudinal, and adjustment components. There is guilt for atrocities performed in Vietnam, guilt over transgressions of traditional morality in Vietnam (particularly in reference to sex, drugs, and violence), guilt for having failed buddies, survivor guilt, rage, feelings of betrayal by the country which sent the soldier to war, self- and societal alienation, apathy, depression, anxiety, obsessive tormenting memories, nightmares, insomnia, sensory hyperacuity, extensive use of the ego defense mechanisms of denial and suppression, confusion, nihilism, ideological disillusionment, uncontrollable hostility, wanton violence, flashback experiences, drug addiction, unemployment, lack of goal-oriented motivation, reentry shock, inability to adapt to the banality of civilian life after the excitement of war (Bourne, 1972; Fox, 1972; Levy, 1971; Lifton, 1973; Solomon, 1971; Solomon et al., 1971).

The incidence of psychiatric syndromes among veterans is difficult to determine. Some veterans with emotional problems received discharges which preclude treatment services from the Veterans Administration. There have been no resocialization programs for veterans where such problems might surface. The numbed guilt syndrome is liable to escape serious notice as long as it leads to no overt disruptive behaviors. The full-blown syndrome tends not to occur until after return to a civilian environment. Also, even qualified veterans may have a distrust of government agencies and thus not seek help from them. The number of cases actually reported has been small, but much, particularly of the earlier Vietnam veteran literature, has tended to imply that the incidence of such syndromes is rampant. A notable exception has been Fox (1972) who reported that only about one percent of combat veterans stationed at a U.S. military post after return from Vietnam came to the post's mental health clinic with symptoms related to war experiences. Of course, reasons have already been given why not all veterans with such problems would seek help from the military mental health clinic.

There is some evidence that not all Vietnam veterans with intensive combat experience were disturbed by their experience. In a study of the life histories and personality characteristics of Green Berets, inductees, and war opponents, Mantell (1974) found that none of the twenty-six Green Berets in his sample showed evidence of negative reactions to their Vietnam experience. Interviews and extensive questionnaires showed no signs of guilt or grief reactions among them. Their MMPI profiles showed no significant depression, anxiety, oversensitivity, alienation, or self-devaluation. Lifton (1973) has offered the opinion that Vietnam experience has been perceived as a negative, self-demoralizing experience by a small group of veterans; as a positive, self-enhancing experience by another small group; and as a neutral experience with no lasting psychological consequences by the great majority of veterans. It is apparently possible for at least some soldiers to experience and perpetrate violence in combat without manifesting any consequent perception or evidence of psychiatric disturbance. Gault (1971) has outlined some psychological mechanisms, such as dehumanization of the enemy, and technological mechanisms, such as weapons with effects not precisely perceptible to the user, whereby the average soldier was made capable of violence.

FOCUS OF THE PRESENT STUDY

In the above-mentioned literature the veterans who suffered from combat-related disorders appear to have been younger men with high intelligence, high levels of education, considerable verbal ability, middle-class urban background, who may have either volunteered or been drafted but who had achieved no high rank and who already had been discharged from the military. Are such disorders also characteristic of older veterans with lower levels of education and rural background?

To what extent are post-Vietnam symptoms present among veterans of the Vietnam War who are still in the military?

This study investigated whether military service in Vietnam was related to psychiatric syndromes or self-concepts among military personnel reporting to a military mental health clinic. Although there were some disagreements in the existing literature (see Figley, Chapter 4), it was hypothesized (1) that a numbed guilt syndrome would appear among the syndromes of this clinical population and (2) that the numbed guilt syndrome would be related to having served in Vietnam. A syndrome resembling the full-blown post-Vietnam syndrome could not be expected to appear since it was said to be latent until discharge from military service. However, Vietnam experience was also hypothesized (3) to be related to actual and ideal self-concepts reflecting these Vietnam syndromes.

METHOD

This study was carried out among U.S. military personnel on active duty in West Germany in 1973-1974. It was a time of transition from the essentially conscripted military of the Vietnam era to the volunteer military of the post-Vietnam era. The military population was very heterogeneous, containing draftees, enlistees, "short-timers" awaiting discharges, career-oriented personnel, first-term personnel, re-enlisted personnel, personnel who had been in Vietnam and personnel who had not.

Subjects

The subjects were 143 male military personnel who reported to a military mental health clinic between October 1973 and May 1974. Their average age was 22.98 years old with a standard deviation of 4.86 years. Average rank was nearly equivalent to Specialist Fourth Class (E-3.87, with a standard deviation of 1.67). The mean number of years of formal education completed was 12.3 with a standard deviation of 1.52. Fifty-five of them were married. Thirty-three had some prior contact with a mental health worker or institution. Among these 143 personnel, 34 had served in Vietnam. Compared to the others, the Vietnam veterans were older (average age, 27.88) and higher ranking (average rank E-5.35); a greater proportion of them were married (24), and a greater proportion (14) had some previous contact with a mental health worker or institution.

Questionnaire

A questionnaire was developed specifically for this study. It existed in two forms: one for personnel who had served in Vietnam, and one for those who had not. The latter form was identical with the first except that it omitted all the Vietnam related questions. Appendix 7-A includes the complete questionnaire as given to the Vietnam veterans. Some of the items in the questionnaire are not discussed in this report because they turned out to be pertinent in only a few cases.

Procedures

The questionnaires were self-completed as part of a routine clinic intake procedure when male military personnel reported. Nearly all personnel who reported to the clinic were able and willing to respond to the questionnaire. Subjects were told that the questionnaire was part of "a study to learn more about the effects of military life on one's personality." They were told that the questionnaire was not part of the clinic's diagnostic or treatment procedure and that it would not become part of the clinic's records. They were asked simply to help out in a research project while waiting for an appointment. The questionnaire was anonymous. Clinical interviews followed after the questionnaire had been filled out.

Scoring

Items on the "Current Feelings" checklist were scored from 1 (very rarely) to 4 (very often). Unmarried subjects were given scores of zero on items dealing with marital problems; a zero was also given for the item concerning girlfriends if a subject indicated he had no girlfriend. Besides item scores, each subject was given a total score, which was the sum of his scores on the individual items minus a constant of 33, resulting in a range of scores in which only a few reported symptoms would yield a total score near zero.

Items on the actual and ideal personality checklists were scored from 1 (not at all) to 4 (very). In addition, each subject was given a "difference score" consisting of the sum of the differences between the two responses (actual versus ideal) for each item.

Items on the "Family Experiences" questions were scored from 1 (very bad) to 5 (very good). Then item scores were summed to give each subject a single total score on family relationships. If an item did not apply to a subject (e.g., no siblings), his total score was adjusted proportionately to make it comparable to other subjects' scores (e.g., 24/30 became 28/35).

RESULTS

Since the purpose of the study was to derive symptom clusters and related personality variables in combination with them, the data were analyzed by means of principal component analyses with varimax rotations. Three such analyses were done: one for the symptom checklist (labeled "Current Feelings" in the questionnaire), one for the actual personality checklist, and one for the ideal personality checklist.

Symptom Checklist Analysis

The average total score on the symptom checklist was 38.36 and the standard deviation was 18.99. Results of the factor analysis appear in Table 1. There were seven factors which had eigenvalues greater than 1; altogether they accounted for 84.5% of the variance.

The variables identified by numbers in the table are as follows in the order of their appearance: (34) I have difficulty forming any deep, personal relationship; (14) I am frustrated sexually; (22) I am unable to make decisions; (23) I am confused, unable to concentrate or think clearly; (24) I become violently angry; (9) I don't feel anything strongly, I don't care about anything; (26) I daydream of doing violent things, of injuring people; (11) I am unable to express myself to someone else; (48) actual versus ideal personality difference score; (5) I am nervous, touchy, irritable; (8) I feel lonely, cut off from other people; (25) I become violently angry; (36) I have difficulty with other soldiers; (44) marital status; (31) I am having difficulty getting along with my wife; (32) I am having difficulty getting along with my children; (33) I am having difficulty getting along with my girlfriend; (2) I am bored; (3) I feel that I am wasting valuable time in my life; (21) I feel my situation needs to be changed; (4) I feel discouraged, depressed; (18) I feel I am being controlled by other people; (13) I feel that other people are treating me badly; (35) I have difficulty with superior officers; (10) I feel I'm to blame for my problems; (6) I feel I need to change myself; (19) I feel angry at myself; (7) I feel guilty about something; (12) I cannot make sense out of my life; (17) I have nightmares; (16) I cannot sleep at night; (20) I have painful memories; (15) I have headaches or backaches or stomach trouble; (46) previous history of psychiatric treat-

Table 1

Factors Derived from the Symptom Checklist

Variable	Factor: Variance:	1 40.3%	2 16.9%	3 7.4%	4 6.0%	5 5.0%	6 4.6%	7 4.2%
34	Loadings:	0.65	—0.16	0.06	0.09	0.12	0.06	0.06
14		0.59	—0.01	0.25	—0.16	0.12	—0.04	
22		0.58	0.02	—0.03	0.25	0.25	0.09	0.12
23		0.57	—0.01	0.08	0.21	0.20	0.15	0.16
24		0.56	—0.05	0.20	0.21	0.06	0.25	0.05
9		0.54	0.03	0.06	0.21	0.10	0.10	—0.11
26		0.53	0.00	0.09	0.11	0.06	0.19	0.11
11		0.53	—0.03	—0.03	0.25	0.19	0.09	0.07
48		0.52	0.07	—0.01	0.18	0.32	0.01	0.06
5		0.50	0.11	0.29	0.12	0.15	0.20	0.39
8		0.49	—0.10	0.25	—0.08	0.19	0.05	0.13
25		0.43	0.24	—0.01	0.26	0.04	0.05	0.15
36		0.41	—0.13	0.15	0.13	—0.05	0.04	0.40
44		—0.15	0.90	—0.09	—0.02	—0.01	0.03	0.06
31		0.00	0.86	0.01	—0.06	0.06	0.07	0.10
32		—0.01	0.71	—0.07	—0.06	0.11	—0.03	—0.11
33		—0.11	—0.48	—0.05	0.21	0.16	0.02	—0.24
2		0.14	—0.07	0.70	0.07	—0.04	0.12	—0.09
3		0.18	—0.05	0.68	0.24	0.03	0.06	0.05
21		0.09	—0.08	0.57	0.20	0.21	0.07	0.33
4		0.35	0.01	0.51	0.22	0.14	0.14	0.23
18		0.27	—0.11	0.23	0.60	0.05	0.15	—0.01
13		0.21	—0.14	0.20	0.56	—0.05	0.06	0.14
35		0.24	—0.21	0.22	0.51	—0.17	0.14	0.17
10		0.20	0.05	—0.02	—0.15	0.64	—0.01	0.01
6		0.18	0.04	0.23	0.32	0.27	—0.01	0.33
19		0.24	0.18	—0.01	0.12	0.54	0.38	0.24
7		0.36	—0.02	0.16	—0.17	0.51	0.30	0.11
12		0.40	—0.03	0.12	0.28	0.45	0.08	0.17
17		0.11	0.10	0.03	0.14	0.08	0.73	—0.01
16		0.28	—0.04	0.21	0.09	0.02	0.53	0.29
20		0.30	—0.09	0.15	0.08	0.28	0.48	0.02
15		0.20	0.12	0.09	0.30	0.15	0.20	0.52
46		0.03	0.07	0.01	0.02	0.10	0.05	0.50
1		0.07	—0.06	0.25	0.04	—0.01	0.03	—0.09
27		0.07	—0.11	0.13	0.00	0.04	0.22	0.09
28		0.29	—0.21	0.13	0.19	—0.02	0.15	0.06
29		0.10	0.02	0.10	—0.07	0.00	0.15	0.03
30		0.10	—0.04	0.10	0.10	0.22	0.12	0.07
41		—0.14	0.38	—0.14	—0.18	0.03	—0.03	0.12
42		—0.03	0.36	—0.13	—0.19	0.17	—0.08	0.06
43		—0.07	0.02	0.09	—0.10	—0.03	—0.03	—0.04
45		—0.01	0.33	—0.33	0.04	—0.08	0.06	0.00
47		—0.33	0.01	0.04	0.04	—0.24	—0.03	—0.36

ment; (1) I worry about my family or parents back home; (27) I am upset by so much drugs around me; (28) I feel that I need drugs of some kind; (29) I drink too much alcohol; (30) I feel that I could not fit into American society back home at the present time; (41) age; (42) rank in the military; (43) education; (45) served in Vietnam; (47) total score on family relationships.

For the family relationships variable, the mean was 27.95 and the standard deviation was 5.00. The mean difference between actual and ideal self-descriptions was 22.15; the standard deviation of the difference scores was 11.88.

The factors identified in Table 1 were quite consistent and easy to label, with the exception of Factor 1. It included alienation from other people, cognitive disturbances, apathy, anxiety, and violent fantasies and behavior. The label which seemed most appropriate was Personal and Social Alienation. The other factors were labeled as follows: Factor 2, Family Conflicts; Factor 3, Frustration; Factor 4, Victimization; Factor 5, Self-recrimination; Factor 6, Hauntedness; Factor 7, Somatic Complaints.

Although some of these factors represent symptoms which appear regularly in accounts of psychological problems among Vietnam veterans, being a Vietnam veteran (variable 45) did not load notably on any of these factors. Such symptom clusters as Self-recrimination and Hauntedness are no more characteristic of Vietnam veterans than of other people.

Self-concepts

The results of the analyses of actual and ideal self-concepts are presented in Tables 2 and 3. The variables in these analyses, which are identified in the tables by numbers, follow in the order of their appearance in Table 2: (13) intelligent; (16) masculine; (10) humorous; (8) good-looking; (9) healthy (good physical health); (1) active; (49) total score on symptom checklist; (15) excitable, gets angry easily; (17) moody; (18) nervous; (48) difference between actual and ideal self-descriptions; (2) complaining; (41) age; (42) rank in the military; (45) served in Vietnam; (44) marital status; (23) responsible; (3) dependable; (12) industrious, hard-working; (19) practical; (30) worthy of respect; (24) self-confident; (11) independent; (26) strict; (27) stubborn; (4) domineering, bossy; (20) punishing; (43) educated; (5) easygoing; (6) frightening; (7) generous; (14) interested in others; (21)

rational, unemotional; (22) religious; (25) shy; (28) submissive; (29) warm; (46) previous history of psychiatric treatment; (47) total score on family relationships.

Both of these analyses yielded six factors with eigenvalues of 1 or greater. The labels given to the actual self-concept factors were: Factor 1, The Functional Person; Factor 2, The Disturbed Person; Factor 3, The Vietnam Veteran; Factor 4, The Responsible Person; Factor 5, The Authoritarian Person; and Factor 6, The Educated Person.

In the analysis of the ideal self-descriptions only three factors contained items from the self-description checklist; the other three (Factors 3, 4, and 5 below) consisted exclusively of demographic and biographical variables. The first two ideal factors consisted of modifications of the first two factors from the actual self-descriptions. The Vietnam Veteran factor and the Educated Person factor were identical in both analyses. A new biographical factor emerged, which consisted of a positive history of past psychiatric referral and poor family relationships in childhood and adolescence. This factor will be called The Person with a Troubled Past. Another new personality description which emerged in the analysis of ideal self-descriptions consisted of only two traits, *active* and *independent*.

Labels for the ideal self factors depicted in Table 3 are as follows: Factor 1, The Improved Functional Person; Factor 2, The Righteous Disturbed Person; Factor 3, The Vietnam Veteran; Factor 4, The Person with a Troubled Past; Factor 5, The Educated Person; and Factor 6, The Active, Independent Person.

The improvements in the image of the Functional Person consisted of added traits mostly suggesting enriched interpersonal relationships. What has been labeled The Righteous Disturbed Person differs from the image of the Disturbed Person primarily in the reversed direction of the score for the difference between actual and ideal self-concepts. The Disturbed Person manifests a large difference between his actual and ideal self-concepts. The Righteous Disturbed Person manifests nearly all the traits of the disturbed person and even adds some negativism to them, but he is self-confident and describes the ideal personality as very similar to himself. The Righteous Disturbed Person did not score in any consistent direction on the symptom checklist, whereas the Disturbed Person scored high on the total symptom checklist. The Righteous Disturbed Person reported that he is irritable, moody, nervous, etc., but he feels that this is the way a person should be. He may be a person who feels that these characteristics are not only

TABLE 2

Factors Derived from the Actual Self Checklist

Variable	Factor: Variance:	1 31.4%	2 17.2%	3 14.3%	4 7.7%	5 6.5%	6 5.4%
13	Loadings:	0.62	−0.04	−0.03	0.32	0.04	−0.06
16		0.60	−0.01	0.18	0.02	−0.04	0.20
10		0.55	−0.06	−0.18	0.18	−0.00	0.04
8		0.51	0.03	−0.12	0.12	0.01	0.01
9		0.49	−0.32	0.02	0.11	0.07	0.07
1		0.42	−0.22	0.10	0.22	0.16	−0.24
49		−0.13	0.76	−0.22	−0.13	−0.01	−0.07
15		0.10	0.75	0.12	−0.11	0.10	−0.09
17		−0.03	0.71	0.01	−0.25	0.07	0.12
18		−0.20	0.69	−0.08	0.03	0.13	−0.00
48		−0.31	0.52	0.22	−0.27	0.07	−0.14
2		0.15	0.48	−0.22	0.04	0.20	0.19
41		−0.06	−0.08	0.77	0.12	0.06	0.22
42		−0.03	0.04	0.72	0.17	0.10	0.16
45		−0.05	−0.04	0.68	−0.01	0.03	−0.11
44		0.03	−0.03	0.61	0.11	0.13	0.03
23		0.16	−0.13	0.19	0.82	0.00	−0.01
3		0.09	−0.07	0.14	0.73	0.04	0.03
12		0.16	−0.17	0.16	0.65	0.03	−0.11
19		0.11	0.04	0.01	0.56	0.20	0.30
30		0.43	−0.30	−0.10	0.51	−0.14	0.14
24		0.24	−0.42	−0.06	0.46	0.16	0.10
11		0.28	−0.15	−0.06	0.43	0.05	0.03
26		0.01	−0.15	0.39	0.23	0.66	−0.07
27		0.03	0.19	0.01	−0.03	0.60	0.03
4		0.31	0.19	0.22	0.07	0.57	0.00
20		−0.23	0.27	0.11	0.00	0.46	0.07
43		0.21	−0.08	0.17	0.06	−0.03	0.51
5		0.02	−0.05	−0.31	0.00	−0.07	0.02
6		−0.02	0.29	−0.24	−0.04	0.20	−0.11
7		0.15	0.04	−0.15	0.14	0.05	0.00
14		0.32	−0.06	−0.01	0.36	−0.07	−0.38
21		0.01	0.05	0.07	0.17	0.29	0.30
22		0.06	0.01	0.10	0.07	−0.02	−0.09
25		−0.22	0.18	0.07	−0.11	0.06	−0.01
28		0.07	0.19	−0.06	−0.04	0.04	−0.07
29		0.29	0.03	−0.09	0.24	−0.10	−0.20
46		0.03	0.14	0.14	−0.05	0.10	−0.03
47		0.13	−0.28	0.07	0.24	−0.27	0.11

TABLE 3

Factors Derived from the Ideal Self Checklist

Variable	Factor: Variance:	1 38.7%	2 14.1%	3 11.2%	4 9.2%	5 6.9%	6 5.9%
8	Loadings:	0.77	—0.09	—0.11	0.00	0.02	0.02
10		0.65	0.01	—0.01	0.02	0.07	0.20
9		0.60	—0.31	0.18	—0.14	—0.03	0.26
29		0.60	—0.08	0.02	—0.01	0.00	—0.04
16		0.56	—0.08	0.00	0.03	0.21	0.04
13		0.54	—0.24	0.03	0.16	0.15	0.25
30		0.53	—0.36	0.14	—0.11	—0.01	0.19
23		0.42	—0.28	0.08	—0.05	0.04	0.07
7		0.41	0.12	—0.05	0.04	—0.19	—0.10
5		0.40	—0.15	—0.06	—0.15	—0.06	0.05
15		—0.12	0.74	—0.04	0.04	0.01	—0.15
17		—0.07	0.70	—0.18	0.01	—0.03	—0.12
18		—0.24	0.66	—0.08	—0.01	0.02	—0.35
2		—0.08	0.64	—0.18	—0.03	0.16	—0.01
20		—0.15	0.52	—0.04	0.11	—0.28	0.11
27		—0.20	0.51	—0.04	0.22	0.14	0.05
24		0.39	—0.44	0.03	0.10	0.18	0.23
48		0.07	—0.40	0.08	0.23	—0.14	0.22
41		—0.05	—0.19	0.83	0.06	0.14	—0.04
42		—0.02	—0.11	0.72	0.11	0.24	0.11
45		—0.04	—0.13	0.65	0.04	—0.14	0.16
44		0.06	—0.11	0.63	0.06	0.03	—0.31
47		0.17	—0.02	0.11	—0.60	0.05	—0.03
46		0.00	0.00	0.16	0.44	—0.06	—0.02
43		0.14	0.03	0.15	—0.05	0.61	—0.04
1		0.18	—0.12	0.04	0.11	—0.07	0.65
11		0.31	—0.20	—0.10	—0.05	0.08	0.50
3		0.26	—0.14	0.09	0.00	0.01	0.10
4		0.10	0.35	—0.14	0.05	0.26	0.11
6		—0.18	0.39	—0.24	—0.03	0.00	0.13
12		0.18	—0.20	0.12	—0.05	—0.14	0.32
14		0.37	—0.13	0.02	—0.10	—0.31	—0.05
19		0.36	—0.09	0.11	0.36	0.31	—0.03
21		0.17	0.13	0.09	0.38	0.18	0.11
22		0.28	0.03	0.33	—0.15	—0.10	0.01
25		—0.20	0.17	—0.05	—0.02	—0.05	—0.08
26		—0.02	0.06	0.27	0.30	—0.02	—0.06
28		0.03	0.35	0.01	0.04	—0.24	—0.20
49		—0.03	0.18	—0.17	0.30	—0.15	—0.10

justified but commendable responses to certain situations. Soldiers reporting to a mental health clinic often do feel upset but feel that it is justified by the circumstances which brough them there and that they will be fine once their situation is changed.

OTHER FINDINGS ABOUT VIETNAM VETERANS

Interviews with the subjects in this study made it apparent that whether a soldier in Vietnam was assigned to a combat unit or a support unit made no reliable difference in exposure to fear or violence in that war without battle lines. On the whole, both groups reported on the questionnaire about the same amount of physical and psychological stresses. Hence, "combat exposure" was not included as a variable in this study, although the reader can see questions related to it in the questionnaire in Appendix A.

The reader may wonder about some of the other items in the Vietnam veterans questionnaire which were not included in the data analyses of psychiatric syndromes and self-concepts. For statistical purposes there were too few positive responses to some of the items to warrant their inclusion in the analyses. For example, the great majority of Vietnam veterans reported having experienced no notable physical or psychological stresses in Vietnam. By far the greatest cause of psychological stress was concern about one's family. A distant second was concern about death or injury of other Americans, and a weak third (a source of moderate stress to only five subjects and great stress to only three) was fear of being injured or killed.

Of the 34 Vietnam veterans, 23 had discussed their Vietnam experiences seriously with another person, usually a family member. Ten still wanted to talk to someone about their experiences, including one who wanted to talk to Congress and one who wanted to talk to anti-war activists.

All the subjects had been exposed to criticism of U.S. military action in Vietnam, mostly from strangers and the media, least of all from their families. When leaving Vietnam 25 of these subjects had at least a somewhat favorable attitude towards U.S. military action there. The majority had been "somewhat" or "a lot" upset when hearing criticism immediately after returning from Vietnam. But few of them were still upset by criticism at the time of this study.

Although the great majority of subjects had violated traditional sexual mores while in Vietnam, few felt any guilt about it at the time.

and even fewer still felt any guilt at the time of this study. Just under a third of the Vietnam veteran subjects had used some illicit drugs while on duty there, but this violation of traditional mores likewise aroused guilt in only a few subjects, and that guilt was likewise diminished by the time of this study.

Five of the subjects had participated in some kind of injury or destruction which they regarded as unnecessary. Of these, three felt it was unnecessary while still in Vietnam and two came to that conclusion later. All five were still somewhat bothered by this at the time of the study.

Certainty of having personally killed at least one other person in a combat situation was reported by 18 subjects. Most commonly, it was certainty of having killed one or two persons. Only seven subjects were bothered even a little by this at the time of the killing, and only five were still bothered even a little at the time of the study. Twelve reported killing either women or children; seven were bothered at least a little at the time of the event and four were still bothered by it at the time of this study. Five subjects reported having been in situations involving killing of prisoners or suspected enemy sympathizers; three were not bothered by it at that time or later.

Twelve subjects reported having had flashback experiences, usually two or three times. The common cause of flashback experiences was sudden loud noises. The startle reflex itself is not unique to Vietnam veterans. What are unique are the combat fantasy which sometimes flashes in the imagination and a conditioned flight response which often consists of ducking for shelter. Sudden loud noises also startle the non-veteran but he usually has no organized response.

DISCUSSION

The symptoms which previous investigators noted in various inpatient and outpatient clinical populations of Vietnam veterans were found in this study: guilt, withdrawal, suspiciousness, feelings of being abused by others, interpersonal conflicts, tyrannical behavior toward others, apathy, anxiety, irritability, moodiness, depression, confusion, hostile impulses, anger episodes, tormenting memories, nightmares, insomnia, frustration over a banal existence, alienation, flashback experiences, etc. This study suggests that the psychiatric symptoms of disturbed Vietnam veterans do not remain latent until discharge from the military. They are evident even in a military population.

But, unlike most previous studies, this study included non-Vietnam veterans. The result was that the picture of Vietnam veterans who were more or less psychological casualties was not altered in itself but placed in the framework of a broader clinical population. There the Vietnam veterans appeared no different from other persons with psychological problems. Among the symptoms and self-concepts studied, none emerged as especially characteristic of Vietnam veterans, even though the study deliberately focused on symptoms said to be especially characteristic of them.

Official statistics were not available, but unofficial samples and estimates of the male military population served by the mental health clinic at which this study was conducted indicated that the proportion of Vietnam veterans in that population was about the same as the proportion in the sample of those who reported to the clinic during the eight months when this study was being conducted. In other words, the incidence of psychiatric problems among Vietnam veterans appears to have been the same as the incidence among nonveterans in the same population.

The answers to questions concerning guilt experiences at the time of and after Vietnam experiences showed a pattern of diminishing guilt with the passage of time. Removal from the combat zone did not release guilt feelings which were being bottled up while still on duty in Vietnam. There may be cases of individuals with "numbed guilt" at first which later "thaws." But for the subjects in this study guilt feelings were strongest at the beginning and decreased as time passed.

The disillusioning and harrowing experiences of war may indeed have generated psychological problems among some Vietnam veterans, but other kinds of disillusioning and harrowing experiences have generated the same kinds of psychological problems among a comparable proportion of other people. From a therapeutic viewpoint the attribution of the problems of veterans to their Vietnam experiences is as useful as other patients' attributions of their problems to childhood situations or other past experiences. It does not result in a unique symptomatology. Nor does it explain why the same experiences have resulted in psychological disturbances among some people but not among others.

APPENDIX 7-A

MILITARY LIFE QUESTIONNAIRE—VIETNAM VETERANS

This questionnaire is part of a study to learn more about the effects of military life on one's personality. Some of the questions deal with one's present situation, and others deal with past experiences. Both present and past experiences are considered important for understanding one's personality.

Please answer the questions as well as you can, but do not spend too much time on any of them. Nearly all of the questions can be answered with just a check mark or a few words. Your cooperation in this project is greatly appreciated. It will help us to learn more about the problems of soldiers, and especially the problems of Vietnam veterans.

NO NAME, PLEASE!

Today's date: _____

Your age: _____

Are you single or married? Check one: ___ Single   ___ Married

If married, how many children do you have? _____   How old are they? _____

Your rank in the Army? _____

How long have you been in the Army?   _____ years and _____ months.

When you first joined the Army, did you enlist voluntarily? Check one: ___ Yes ___ No

If you enlisted voluntarily, was it because you thought you would be drafted anyway? Check one: ___ Yes ___ No

Have you re-enlisted since first joining the Army?   ___ Yes ___ No

When do you plan to leave military service? (Approximate date:) _____

What is your current job in the Army? _____

What is the highest grade in school that you have completed? _____

Do you identify yourself with any ethnic or cultural group (for example, Italian-American, Spanish-American, Afro-American)? Check one: ___ Yes ___ No

If yes, which group do you identify with? _____

Please give the dates for the time you were in Vietnam. If you were there more than once, give the dates for each time you were there.

Arrived: _____   Left: _____

Arrived: _____   Left: _____

What was your rank (s) when you were in Vietnam? _____

What was your job (s) when you were in Vietnam? _____

_____

Were you primarily in a support or combat unit? Check one: ___ Support ___ **Combat**

Why did you come to the mental health clinic today? Please try to give a very brief but clear statement of your reasons for coming to the clinic.

_____

_____

_____

_____

Have you ever sought professional psychiatric help or been referred to any other clinic or mental health worker in the past? Check one: ___ Yes ___ No

If yes, when? _____ Where? _____

How many times did you go for help? _____

Was it effective? _____

Use the chart below to fill in a picture of your physical health during the time you were in Vietnam. Check whether you had an illness or not, and how serious any illness was. Use the blank space at the end of the list to fill in any other physical health problem you had in Vietnam.

Yes	No		Not Serious	Somewhat Serious	Very Serious
___	___	Skin diseases	___	___	___
___	___	Malaria	___	___	___
___	___	Dysentery	___	___	___
___	___	V.D.	___	___	___
___	___	Combat injury. If yes, please describe below:	___	___	___
___	___	Other injury or disease. Please describe below:	___	___	___

Please use the chart below to check off how much mental stress you personally experienced from different kinds of situations when you were in Vietnam. Some of the situations listed below may have caused you mental stress and others may not have caused you any distress personally. Use the blank spaces at the end of the list to fill in any other important sources of mental stress you felt in Vietnam.

No stress	A little stress	Moderate stress	Great stress	
———	———	———	———	Concern about my family.
———	———	———	———	Boredom.
———	———	———	———	Fear of being injured or killed.
———	———	———	———	Death or injury of other American soldiers.
———	———	———	———	Seeing filth, disease, poverty in Vietnam.
———	———	———	———	Problems with superior officers.
———	———	———	———	Problems with other soldiers in my unit.
———	———	———	———	Public opinion against U.S. action in Vietnam.
———	———	———	———	Personal opposition to U.S. action in Vietnam.
———	———	———	———	Having to kill or destroy as part of my job.
———	———	———	———	Other: _____
———	———	———	———	Other: _____

How much direct criticism of U.S. military action in Vietnam have you heard or seen from each of the following sources, either when you were in Vietnam or since returning?

	None	A little	Somewhat	A lot
Criticism from my family	———	———	———	———
Criticism from friends	———	———	———	———
Criticism from strangers	———	———	———	———
Criticism from veteran groups	———	———	———	———
Criticism from civilian groups	———	———	———	———
Criticism in posters or signs	———	———	———	———
Criticisms on radio or T.V.	———	———	———	———
Criticism in newspapers or magazines	———	———	———	———

After you returned from Vietnam, did it upset you to hear criticism of U.S. military action in Vietnam?

Check one: ___ No ___ A little ___ Somewhat ___ A lot

Does it still upset you now to hear criticism of U.S. military action in Vietnam?

Check one: ___ No ___ A little ___ Somewhat ___ A lot

Have you talked about your experiences in Vietnam in a serious way with anyone since returning?

Check one: ___ No ___ A few times ___ Several times ___ Often

If yes, with whom have you talked? _____

Have you *wanted* to talk (or talk more in a serious way about your experiences in Vietnam?

Check one: ___ No ___ A few times ___ Several times ___ Often

If yes, with whom have you wanted to talk? _____

During your tour of duty in Vietnam, or while on leave from Vietnam, did you ever have sexual contact with Oriental women? Check one: ___ Yes ___ No

If yes, how many times approximately? _____

Did you feel guilty the first time? ___ No ___ A little ___ Somewhat ___ A lot

Did you feel guilty later times? ___ No ___ A little ___ Somewhat ___ A lot

Do you feel guilty about it now? ___ No ___ A little ___ Somewhat ___ A lot

Did you ever smoke pot or hash or use other drugs while in Vietnam?

Check one: ___ Yes ___ No

If yes, how many times approximately? _____

Did you feel guilty the first time? ___ No ___ A little ___ Somewhat ___ A lot

Did you feel guilty later times? ___ No ___ A little ___ Somewhat ___ A lot

Do you feel guilty about it now? ___ No ___ A little ___ Somewhat ___ A lot

Were you ever in a combat situation in Vietnam where you felt that you let your buddies down?

Check one: ___ Yes ___ No

If yes, how much did this bother you? ___ A little ___ Somewhat ___ A lot

Does this still bother you? ___ A little ___ Somewhat ___ A lot

Were you ever in a combat situation in Vietnam where you participated in any kind of injury or destruction that seemed necessary then, but that you would consider unnecessary now?

Check one: ___ Yes ___ No

If so, did you change your mind about it before or after leaving Vietnam?

Check one: ___ Before leaving Vietnam ___ After leaving Vietnam

Does this bother you now? Check one: ___ No ___ A little ___ Somewhat ___ A lot

In Vietnam enemy soldiers were often killed or wounded without any one American soldier being able to say definitely that he fired the shot that did it. But occasionally a soldier did know that he personally fired the shot that killed a particular enemy soldier. Were you ever in a combat situation where you were sure that you personally had killed a particular enemy soldier?

Check one: ___ Yes ___ No

If yes, how many times? _____

Did this bother you the first time?   ___ No ___ A little ___ Somewhat ___ A lot

Did this bother you later times?   ___ No ___ A little ___ Somewhat ___ A lot

Does this bother you now?   ___ No ___ A little ___ Somewhat ___ A lot

In combat situations in Vietnam women and children were sometimes in the role of the enemy. Were you ever in a situation where you either injured or killed any women or children in Vietnam?

Check one: ___ Yes ___ No

If yes, how many times? _____

Did this bother you the first time?   ___ No ___ A little ___ Somewhat ___ A lot

Did this bother you later times?   ___ No ___ A little ___ Somewhat ___ A lot

Does this bother you now?   ___ No ___ A little ___ Somewhat ___ A lot

In combat situations in Vietnam prisoners or civilians were often injured because they were suspected of being enemy sympathizers, or to obtain information, or to avenge the deaths of American soldiers, or for other reasons. Were you ever in a situation where you injured a prisoner or civilian for any reason?

Check one: ___ Yes ___ No

If yes, how many times? _____

Did this bother you the first time?   ___ No ___ A little ___ Somewhat ___ A lot

Did this bother you later times?   ___ No ___ A little ___ Somewhat ___ A lot

Does this bother you now?   ___ No ___ A little ___ Somewhat ___ A lot

If you were ever in a combat situation in Vietnam, did you ever have a "flashback experience" after returning from Vietnam? A "flashback experience" is when a person if fully awake but he imagines that he is back in a combat situation in Vietnam; he imagines it so strongly that he forgets for a minute where he really is and reacts as if the enemy were really present and he were really in the combat situation again.

Check one: ___ Yes, I've had such experiences. ___ No, I haven't had such experiences. If yes, how often? _____

When was the last time you had such an experience (approximate date)? _____

Do any special kinds of situations tend to provoke flashbacks for you?

Check one: ___ No special situations. ___ Yes, special situations do.

If special situations do provoke flashbacks for you, please describe what special situations:

_____

_____

On the last day that you were actually in Vietnam, what was your attitude towards U.S. military action there? Check one:

___ Very favorable

___ Somewhat favorable

___ Somewhat unfavorable

___ Very unfavorable

CURRENT FEELINGS

On the next page is a list of feelings which people have in different degrees. Please use the chart on the next page to check off how often you have the kinds of feelings that are listed there. Use the blank spaces at the end of the list to add any other feelings which you consider particularly important in your present situation.

Current Feelings

Very rarely	Some-times	Often	Very often	
___	___	___	___	I worry about my parents or family back home.
___	___	___	___	I am bored.
___	___	___	___	I feel that I am wasting valuable time in my life.
___	___	___	___	I feel discouraged, depressed.
___	___	___	___	I am nervous, touchy, irritable.
___	___	___	___	I feel I need to change myself.
___	___	___	___	I feel guilty about something.
___	___	___	___	I feel lonely, cut off from other people.
___	___	___	___	I don't feel anything strongly, I don't care about anything.
___	___	___	___	I feel I'm to blame for my problems.
___	___	___	___	I am unable to express myself to someone else.
___	___	___	___	I cannot make sense out of my life.
___	___	___	___	I feel that other people are treating me badly.
___	___	___	___	I am frustrated sexually.
___	___	___	___	I have headaches or backaches or stomach trouble.
___	___	___	___	I cannot sleep at night.

Very rarely	Some-times	Often	Very often	
—	—	—	—	I have nightmares.
—	—	—	—	I feel I am being controlled by other people.
—	—	—	—	I feel angry at myself.
—	—	—	—	I have painful memories.
—	—	—	—	I feel my situation needs to be changed.
—	—	—	—	I am unable to make decisions.
—	—	—	—	I am confused, unable to concentrate or think clearly.
—	—	—	—	I feel that I cannot trust other people.
—	—	—	—	I become violently angry.
—	—	—	—	I daydream of doing violent things, of injuring people.
—	—	—	—	I am upset by so much drugs around me.
—	—	—	—	I feel that I need drugs of some kind.
—	—	—	—	I drink too much alcohol.
—	—	—	—	I feel that I could not fit into American society back home at the present time.
—	—	—	—	I am having difficulty getting along with my wife.
—	—	—	—	I am having difficulty getting along with my children.
—	—	—	—	I am having difficulty getting along with my girlfriend.
—	—	—	—	I have difficulty forming any deep, personal relationship.
—	—	—	—	I have difficulty with superior officers.
—	—	—	—	I have difficulty with other soldiers.
—	—	—	—	Other: _____
—	—	—	—	Other: _____

Your Personality

Please use the scale below to give a description of yourself. Do not spend too much time on any one item. Put an "X" in the column that gives the best description of you.

Not at all	Slightly	Moderately	Very	
_____	_____	_____	_____	Active
_____	_____	_____	_____	Complaining
_____	_____	_____	_____	Dependable
_____	_____	_____	_____	Domineering, bossy
_____	_____	_____	_____	Easy-going
_____	_____	_____	_____	Frightening
_____	_____	_____	_____	Generous

Not at all	Slightly	Moderately	Very	
————	————	————	————	Good-looking
————	————	————	————	Healthy (good physical health)
————	————	————	————	Humorous
————	————	————	————	Independent
————	————	————	————	Industrious, hard-working
————	————	————	————	Intelligent
————	————	————	————	Interested in others
————	————	————	————	Irritable, gets angry easily
————	————	————	————	Masculine
————	————	————	————	Moody
————	————	————	————	Nervous
————	————	————	————	Practical
————	————	————	————	Punishing
————	————	————	————	Rational, unemotional
————	————	————	————	Religious
————	————	————	————	Responsible
————	————	————	————	Self-confident
————	————	————	————	Shy
————	————	————	————	Strict
————	————	————	————	Stubborn
————	————	————	————	Submissive
————	————	————	————	Warm
————	————	————	————	Worthy of respect

Your Ideal Personality

Use the scale below to give a description of the personality that you would like to have if you could change yourself any way you want. Put an "X" in the column that gives the best description of the personality you would like to have.

Not at all	Slightly	Moderately	Very	
————	————	————	————	Active
————	————	————	————	Complaining
————	————	————	————	Dependable
————	————	————	————	Domineering, bossy
————	————	————	————	Easy-going
————	————	————	————	Frightening

Not at all	Slightly	Moderately	Very	
———	———	———	———	Generous
———	———	———	———	Good-looking
———	———	———	———	Healthy (good physical health)
———	———	———	———	Humorous
———	———	———	———	Independent
———	———	———	———	Industrious, hard-working
———	———	———	———	Intelligent
———	———	———	———	Interested in others
———	———	———	———	Irritable, gets angry easily
———	———	———	———	Masculine
———	———	———	———	Moody
———	———	———	———	Nervous
———	———	———	———	Practical
———	———	———	———	Punishing
———	———	———	———	Rational, unemotional
———	———	———	———	Religious
———	———	———	———	Responsible
———	———	———	———	Self-confident
———	———	———	———	Shy
———	———	———	———	Strict
———	———	———	———	Stubborn
———	———	———	———	Submissive
———	———	———	———	Warm
———	———	———	———	Worthy of respect

*Family Experiences During Childhood
and Adolescence*

How many brothers and sisters do you have? _____

How many are older than you? _____

Did your parents live together all the time while you were growing up?

Check one: ___ Yes ___ No

If no, how old were you when the separation began? _____

How long did the separation last? _____

In general, how would you describe the relationship between your parents when you were living with them? Check one:

___ Very good

___ Somewhat good

___ Indifferent

___ Somewhat bad

___ Very bad

In general, how would you describe your own relationship with your father?

BEFORE YOU WERE 12 YEARS OLD   AFTER YOU WERE 12 YEARS OLD

___ Very good   ___ Very good

___ Somewhat good   ___ Somewhat good

___ Indifferent   ___ Indifferent

___ Somewhat bad   ___ Somewhat bad

___ Very bad   ___ Very bad

In general, how would you describe your own relationship with your mother?

BEFORE YOU WERE 12 YEARS OLD   AFTER YOU WERE 12 YEARS OLD

___ Very good   ___ Very good

___ Somewhat good   ___ Somewhat good

___ Indifferent   ___ Indifferent

___ Somewhat bad   ___ Somewhat bad

___ Very bad   ___ Very bad

In general, how did you get along with your brothers and/or sisters?

BEFORE YOU WERE 12 YEARS OLD   AFTER YOU WERE 12 YEARS OLD

___ Very good   ___ Very good

___ Somewhat good   ___ Somewhat good

___ Indifferent   ___ Indifferent

___ Somewhat bad   ___ Somewhat bad

___ Very bad   ___ Very bad

8

DEMOGRAPHIC AND PRE-SERVICE VARIABLES AS PREDICTORS OF POST-MILITARY SERVICE ADJUSTMENT

E. ROBERT WORTHINGTON, Ph.D.

INTRODUCTION

In 1972 the United States terminated active participation in the Vietnam conflict, the longest war in our history. This complex struggle in Southeast Asia had been fraught with economic, cultural, political, educational, and social problems unprecedented in our history. The consequences of this controversial war are still being argued by social and behavioral scientists and the plight of the Vietnam era veteran is still receiving considerable attention. Until recently very little scientific investigation had been conducted regarding the readjustment process of veterans. Prior to 1973 the information that had been published was primarily descriptive and anecdotal. The popular media had depicted the Vietnam veteran as suffering from a variety of reentry adjustment problems ranging from mild to serious. Since this time the veteran has been scrutinized by the scientific community inquiring into his post-service adjustment. The prevailing perspective is that stress disorders among Vietnam veterans are primarily a direct function of combat service in particular and military service in general. We take ex-

The opinions and assertions contained herein are the private views of the author and are not to be construed as official or as reflecting the views of the Department of the Army of the Department of Defense.

This selection is an extension of a paper presented at the 84th Annual American Psychological Convention, Washington, D.C., September 1976.

The author wishes to acknowledge the assistance and contributions rendered by A. E. Worthington and Dr. A. Schopper in the preparation of this manuscript.

173

ception to this view and argue that pre-service factors account for more of the variance in post-service psychosocial adjustment than various military service experiences, including combat.

MILITARY EXPERIENCE AND ADJUSTMENT

Behavioral scientists who assert the existence of widespread post-service maladaptive behaviors on the part of Vietnam era veterans feel these behaviors are related to military training and experiences. Shatan (1971) explained that "good Americans" were turned into "mass executioners" as a result of modern combat training. The outcome, Shatan (1972) believes, is an unconsummated grief of soldiers which deprives them of any meaning in their current existence. He labels this "post-Vietnam-syndrome." These symptoms do not occur immediately; nine to 30 months elapse before the veterans begin to exhibit such changes as apathy, cynicism, alienation, depression, mistrust, insomnia, restlessness, and impatience (Shatan, 1973). Although Shatan admits that he has no scientific studies to support his belief, he maintains that ". . . impressive evidence suggests that thousands of combat veterans experience severe psychic suffering and tens of thousands may be experiencing milder suffering that is never recognized" (1973, p. 645).

Horowitz and Solomon (Chapter 13) report that the delayed stress response often begins after termination of the real environmental stresses and after a latency period has passed. This unresolved stress leads to violent impulses and feelings of shame and guilt. In concurrence with Shatan, a theory of pathology is assumed in the absence of scientific inquiry. These assertions, Horowitz and Solomon agree, must be regarded as preliminary and speculative.

Egendorf (1975) and Lifton (1975) report the success of therapeutic rap sessions with veterans who talked about feelings of guilt, pain, and torment. Lifton (see Chapter 10) believes that these feelings are a reflection of the veteran survivors reacting to the inhumane actions of the Vietnam War. He also warned, however (Lifton, 1973), that his samples were not representative since the combat veterans he interviewed also shared his anti-war sentiments.

Some studies support the thesis that the veteran's perception of the extent and intensity of his combat involvement is related to his overall adjustment to civilian life. For instance, a study conducted in New England (O'Neill & Fontaine, 1973) revealed that 70 percent of a random sample of veterans in various colleges reported experiencing difficulty adjusting to civilian life. The Veterans Administration has conducted extensive research regarding the Vietnam era veteran and readjustment. Charles Stenger (1974), a senior VA psychologist, stated that there was reason to believe that the readjustment process was more difficult for Vietnam era veterans than for their predecessors. He felt that special readjustment problems faced by the returning Vietnam veterans were added to the adjustment problems they already shared with non-Vietnam veteran peers. Stenger feels that while it is theoretically possible that some veterans may exhibit all of the post-Vietnam syndrome, the VA mental health professionals have not found this to be the case. He feels there is more evidence of character and behavior disorders which reflect a cultural tolerance of acting-out behaviors.

In contrast, however, there is an equally large group of studies which conclude that current adjustment problems among Vietnam veterans are related to factors other than just combat. Although acknowledging that combat can be highly stressful, they believe that no evidence exists which concludes that combat stress is the primary cause of long-term psychosocial problems.

Further, a comparative study of veterans and nonveterans in a western university (Hassener & McCary, 1974) revealed that veteran students viewed their military tours as favorable and helpful toward success in college. The veteran students reported satisfying relationships with fellow students and being well accepted on campus. The investigators also found that the veteran students experienced difficult times regarding social adjustments because they were older and had encountered more unique life experiences. Another study in the midwest (Enzie, Sawyer, & Montgomery, 1973) examined the manifest anxiety level of recently returned Vietnam combat veterans in comparison to a random sample of male undergraduate students. The study revealed that the veteran sample did not have higher levels of anxiety than did the undergraduate sample.

Borus (1974), a Harvard psychiatrist, felt that reports of post-service civilian maladjustment were not the results of scientifically controlled studies. His own investigations suggested that only a small minority of veterans had some record of maladjustment. His contention was that some of the later readjustment problems might be more related to ongoing problems than to military service. In a military study, Borus (1975) reported findings of a sizeable number of Vietnam veterans who had difficulty readjusting to the stateside military. He emphatically pointed out that a generalization of this to all Vietnam veterans was false.

Starr (1973), an investigative reporter for Ralph Nader's Center for Study of Responsive Law, reached the following conclusions regarding the "post-Vietnam-syndrome": There is no significant evidence indicating widespread violence among veterans and there is no significant evidence that violence among veterans is more frequent than violence among young working-class males. While agreeing that some veterans do encounter disorientation, anger, resentment, rage, and bewilderment, he states that there are no studies to indicate how widespread these behaviors might be.

Salt Lake County Study of Vietnam Veterans

In order to contrast these two competing perspectives, we will first present the results of an earlier investigation conducted in 1972-73 to examine feelings reported by Army veterans who had returned to civilian life (Worthington, 1973, 1976c).

The sample consisted of 147 male Army veterans living in Salt Lake County, Utah, who had been released from active duty within twelve months of the study (April 1972-March 1973). The sample represented 75 percent of the total population of Army veterans available in the county for the study. These 147 veterans represented 90.7 percent of the veterans contacted. The list of veterans was compiled with the assistance of a U.S. Army Reserve Headquarters. The original list contained a total population of 227 veterans. Of these 227 veterans, 33 could not be located or contacted, 32 had left the county or never returned upon completion of their Army tour, 9 refused to participate, and 6 could not or would not complete the study.

The investigation was based on the theory of anomie since certain factors seen as relevant variables in the concept of anomie (i.e., confusion, anxiety, frustration, helplessness, and social isolation) were also noted in the adjustment process of recently returned veterans. An attempt was made to demonstrate a relationship between anomic feelings reported by these veterans and specified antecedent conditions or events (i.e., military service).

Two independent variables were selected: whether or not the veteran liked his service tour and whether or not the veteran served in Vietnam. These factors were manipulated statistically utilizing a multiple analysis of variance program (MANOVA) to examine their relationship to the veteran's responses to several classes of dependent measures (scores on self-report evaluations of adjustment which were seen as factors of anomie). Four of these measures were taken from the Elmore Scale of

Anomie (Elmore, 1965). The fifth measure was the total Positive Score of the Tennessee Self Concept Scale (Fitts, 1964) and the sixth measure was the Socialization Scale of the California Psychological Inventory (Gough, 1956). These adjustment scales were incorporated into a self-report questionnaire (see Appendix 8-A). Included as a part of this questionnaire was a 26-item, 131-response biographic/demographic questionnaire.

The findings of this study found no support for the thesis that the veteran's post-service adjustment was related to having served in Vietnam. Differences did exist on measures of adjustment between veteran groups on their like or dislike evaluation of their service tours, regardless of where they served (Worthington, 1976).

A second phase to the above study was conducted in 1973-74 (Worthington, 1977). This portion of the investigation examined the information obtained in the 26-item biographic/demographic questionnaire. The responses were evaluated to determine if any possible biographic or demographic relationships to post-service adjustment existed.

A one-way analysis of variance (ANOVA) was performed on each one of the three adjustment scales (i.e., the Elmore Scale of Anomie, the Tennessee Self Concept Scale, and the Socialization Scale of the California Psychological Inventory) utilizing the categories (i.e., different responses) inherent in each of the biographic/demographic questions as the independent variable. An analysis of the data was used to determine if any response to an item in the biographic/demographic questionnaire was significantly different from the other responses. In this study 11 of the 26 items were identified as being related to adjustment differences, based on an .05 (or higher) alpha level for all three adjustment scales. These 11 items related to post-service adjustment (on all three scales) were: (1) post-service marital status (i.e., single, married, divorced, or widowed); (2) post-service religious affiliation (i.e., none, Latter-Day Saint, Protestant, Catholic, other); (3) post-service educational level (i.e., non-high school graduate, high school graduate, some college or trade school, college graduate, graduate work); (4) post-service occupation (i.e., laborer, blue collar, tradesman, white collar, professional, unemployed); (5) type of service (i.e., drafted, enlisted Regular Army, enlisted through a reserve program, reserve officer, Regular Army officer); (6) rank upon discharge (i.e., E-1 to E-3, E-4 to E-5, E-6 to E-9, Warrant Officer, Commissioned Officer); (7) disciplinary action during service (i.e., none, Article 15, Summary Court Martial, General Court Martial); (8) educational or vocational status prior to service (i.e., in high school, in college or trade school, unemployed, working, waiting for draft); (9) age upon entering the service (i.e., 17 or younger, 18, 19, 20, 21 or older); (10) legal or school authority problems prior to entering the Army (i.e., no trouble, trouble with school authorities, trouble with legal authorities—juvenile, misdemeanor, felony); (11) time spent away from home prior to service (i.e., Church mission, school, employment, travel, prior military service, none).

The results suggest that high adjustment scores (reflecting "good" adjustment) were positively related to post-service marriage and professional occupational status while the reverse was also found; low adjustment scores (reflecting "poor" adjustment) were related to marital problems. In addition, poor adjustment was also associated with the following post-service and service factors: (1) no religious affiliation; (2) being high school dropout; (3) being unemployed; (4) having served as an enlisted man; (5) not being promoted or being demoted during service tour; and (6) having received some type of disciplinary action while in the Army. The results showed, however, statistically significant correlations between post-service adjustment scores and several pre-service factors. These factors include: age, higher educational level, lack of problems with the law or school authorities, and having spent time away from home prior to Army service.

Thus, post-service adjustment problems could be attributed to social, educational, or vocational problems not connected with military service as well as to problems which might be related to military experiences. The findings also suggest that those veterans who might be experiencing post-service adjustment problems could be the same soldiers who also had adjustment problems during and before their military service. The study lends support to the theory that problems in the veteran's current lives might be more related to maladaptive behavior patterns than to military service, especially service in Vietnam.

PRE-SERVICE EXPERIENCE AND ADJUSTMENT WITHIN THE MILITARY

These findings are not inconsistent with other research being conducted with active duty servicemen or Vietnam era veterans and factors related to adjustment. Goodwin, Davis, and Robins (1975) studied drinking patterns and problems of 451 Army enlisted men after their return from Vietnam. Four pre-service predictors of alcohol abuse were noted: early age of drinking, school troubles, low educational level, and a father with a history of alcohol abuse. A study of narcotic use and addiction was conducted with 898 Vietnam veterans (Helzer, Robins, & Davis, 1975/76). The authors feel their study confirms the importance of a history of deviant behavior in predicting a willingness to try narcotics and a propensity to increase the involvement. Robins (1974), in an examination of veterans' drug use three years after Vietnam, stated that the strongest predictor of post-Vietnam arrests, depression, unemployment, and divorce was a history of drug usage both during and before Vietnam. Nace, O'Brien, Mintz, Ream and Meyers (Chapter 5), in a study of alcohol and drug abuse in the Vietnam veteran, found that post-discharge criminality, alcohol and drug abuse, and depression are accounted for by pre-service experiences as well as addiction status while in Vietnam.

The U.S. Navy has conducted several studies examining relationships between future performance and biographic/demographic data. Gunderson and Arthur (1966), for example, reported that relationships were found between incidence of mental illness of male Naval enlisted personnel and demographic factors such as age, length of service, rank and occupational specialty. Plag and Goffman (1966) found that three variables—age, level of schooling, and general intelligence—were significantly related to military effectiveness in the Navy. Similarly, Arthur (1971) found that pre-service variables of age, educational level, intelligence, school and civil disciplinary record, and home stability were highly predictive of success within the Navy while standard psychiatric selection interviews had only minimal predictive validity.

A study conducted in an Army Airborne Division attempted to create a behavioral profile for predicting "problem" soldiers (Timmerman, 1974). Variables of personality, background, and intelligence were collected and analyzed on both a "problem soldier" and "non-problem soldier" sample. The conclusions were that 12 variables of adjustment, background, and intelligence had a relatively high degree of predictive ability. These variables were able to identify the soldier who had disciplinary problems after entering an Army troop unit.

An Air Force investigation led to the development of a Symptom Checklist (Short & Stankus, 1974), a 50-item paper-and-pencil questionnaire. This checklist sampled a wide variety of symptoms including sleep problems, interpersonal difficulties, and phobias. It was found to be an effective tool for evaluating the emotional stability of basic trainees being considered for sensitive future assignments.

STUDY OF ADJUSTMENT TO ARMY BASIC TRAINING

The following study (Worthington, 1976b) addresses various biographic variables found in successful and unsuccessful samples on an Army training post conducting both basic combat training (eight weeks) and advanced individual training (eight weeks). This research was based on the concept that civilians with a high potential for not being able to adjust in their initial phases of military training may be identified early by examining their pre-service backgrounds for evidence of maladaptive behavior patterns. Biographic/demographic data were gathered on 75 trainee soldiers who were referred to the post Mental Hygiene Consultation Service (MCHS) for evaluation during the summer of 1975. These men were considered unsuitable for retention and recommended for administrative discharge from the Army based on their inability to adapt to the military training or environment. This group was seen as the unsuccessful soldiers. The successful group was comprised of soldiers who were in the last days of basic or advanced training. Biographic/demographic information was assembled from a self-report questionnaire which was part of another study conducted at the same time (Worthington, 1976a). The data on the successful soldiers were collected from a sample of 1,489 soldiers questioned in the next to last week of their training. A comparison of the biographic/demographic data from the two groups showed that many, if not most, of the trainees reporting difficulty adjusting to military training also reported family problems, trouble in school, poor interpersonal relations, and spotty work records.

The results of this study support earlier findings and suggest that a relationship existed between adjustment during initial stages of Army training and pre-service adjustment behavior patterns. The Army trainee who was unable to complete Basic or Advanced Training because of an inability to adjust reported a pre-service background of disruptive personal and family existence. The mean educational level of the unsuccessful soldier was lower (10.8 years) than that of the successful soldier (11.7 years), yet when his schooling terminated his average age was a year older than would be expected. Less than half (49 percent) of the unsuccessful group graduated from high school compared to 83 percent of the successful group. The marital patterns revealed more married, divorced, and remarried men in the unsuccessful soldier group (29 percent versus 17 percent). More of the unsuccessful group entered the Army from the labor market (80 percent were working and 20 percent were in school) while 40 percent of the successful group entered straight from school and 60 percent were working. Familial information from the unsuccessful group revealed more traumatic upbringing. Almost two-thirds of this group (61 percent) had been without one or two parents. Most of the missing parents (42 percent) were the consequences of divorce or separation which occurred when the mean age of the trainee was eight. A high incidence of family psychiatric problems (43 percent) was also reported by the unsuccessful group.

Of the total soldiers recommended for discharge by MHCS personnel, 53 percent were based on personality evaluations of immaturity, maladjustment, anxiety, and stress. An examination of their pre-service history does not make it difficult to understand why. The background of both the unsuccessful soldier and his family was highly indicative of very poor adjusting or coping resources; families failed, marriages broke down, schooling was seen as nonproductive and terminated early. The soldier's life after entering active duty was not better; failure occurred again.

Conclusions

The major thesis of this paper is that pre-service conditions account for much of the variance in veteran's adjustment. The Salt Lake County study presented data which indicated that soldiers who experienced difficulty in readjusting after their military tour also showed evidence of difficulty during and prior to their Army service. Those veterans who reported experiencing no difficulty readjusting to civilian life were the same veterans who reported success in their Army career and who also denied any conflicts or problems in coping with life prior to entering the Army. On the other hand, those veterans who reported experiencing more difficulty in readjusting to civilian life also reported a lack of success during their military service and a history of pre-service adjustment problems.

A review of the published research suggests that pre-service adapting behaviors may be the best predictors of service success. The findings of the research project conducted by the author at a large Army training post indicated that a relationship did exist between adjustment behaviors during the initial phases of Army training and pre-service adjustment behaviors. Those soldiers who were unable to successfully finish basic training because of an inability to adjust also reported a pre-service history of unsuccessful personal and family coping mechanisms. The recruit who failed in basic training had also failed in civilian life before entering the Army.

It is not difficult to conclude that the results of research available today present substantial evidence that veteran adjustment complications are related to a lifelong pattern of coping. Perhaps, though, this is a simplistic way to avoid the real issue; the problem may be that many young people were inducted into a situation (the military and, for some, combat) that was beyond their capability to endure without resulting problems. Maybe they were barely able to continue, holding on as long as there was support from friends also facing the same difficulties. Possibly, upon release, the multitude of supportive resources were no longer present and, once again, these young men were left to cope as best they could. This time, however, they were thrust, ill-prepared prior to military service, into a world they found even more hostile and foreboding. Could this not exacerbate their already deficit coping skills and make life even more difficult to endure?

The problem is not only why some veterans find it difficult to readjust to the mainstream of life but, more important, what can be done now? It will be years before social scientists can examine the Vietnam era veteran from an uncontaminated vantage point. Until then we will have to proceed in light of the data and evidence currently available. It is the contention of this researcher that there is insufficient evidence to support the concept of a massive "delayed stress syndrome." The data available to date seem to support the theory that adjustment problems are more related to previous maladaptive behaviors than to military experiences.

APPENDIX 8-A

BIOGRAPHIC DEMOGRAPHIC QUESTIONNAIRE

1. Vietnam service: Yes ___ No ___

2. Age _____

3. My present employment status is:

   1. unemployed
   2. work part-time
   3. work full-time
   4. in on-the-job training program
   5. unable to work due to disability

4. My present student status is:

   1. not a student
   2. part-time student
   3. full-time student
   4. correspondent course student
   5. accepted into a school program but have not begun yet

5. My annual income is:

   1. $3,000 or less ($250 or less per month)
   2. $3,001 - $5,000 (more than $250 but less than $418 per month)
   3. $5,0001 - $10,000 (more than $417 but less than $835 per month)
   4. $10,000 - $15,000 (more than $834 but less than $1,250 per month)
   5. over $15,000 (over $1,250 per month)

6. My marital status is:

   1. single
   2. married
   3. divorced or separated
   4. widowed

7. My religious affiliation is:

   1. none
   2. LDS
   3. Protestant
   4. Catholic
   5. other

8. Looking back at your service tour, how would you describe your feelings:

   1. I hated the Army *ALL* of the time.
   2. I hated the Army *MOST* of the time.

3. My tour was bad.
4. My tour was not too bad.
5. No feelings one way or another.
6. My tour was okay.
7. My tour was good.
8. I really enjoyed the Army *MOST* of the time.
9. I really enjoyed the Army *ALL* of the time.

9. My educational level is:

1. did not graduate from high school
2. graduated from high school
3. some college/university/trade school
4. graduated from four-year college/university
5. graduate work at college/university

10. My occupation is:

1. laborer
2. blue collar worker
3. tradesman
4. white collar worker
5. professional
6. unemployed

11. Since your release from the Army have you ever been in trouble with legal authorities for:

1. no trouble with legal authorities
2. moving traffic violations (more than one)
3. narcotic usage
4. alcohol usage
5. misdemeanor
6. felony

12. My type of service was:

1. drafted—US
2. enlisted—RA
3. served through a reserve program
4. officer—RA
5. officer—USAR

13. When I got out of the Army my rank was:

1. E-1 to E-3
2. E-4 to E-5
3. E-6 to E-9
4. Warrant Officer W1 to W4
5. O1 or higher

14. My main job in the Army concerned:

    1. troops
    2. staff (intelligence, operations, etc.)
    3. administration (personnel, clerks, etc.)
    4. logistics (supply, food, POL, etc.)
    5. technical (signal, medical, aviation, etc.)

15. I received the following disciplinary action while in the Army:

    1. None
    2. Article 15
    3. Summary Court Martial
    4. Special Court Martial
    5. General Court Martial

16. My discharge (type of release from active duty) was:

    1. honorable
    2. general
    3. undesirable
    4. bad conduct
    5. dishonorable

17. I served in:

    1. only the United States
    2. Vietnam
    3. Korea or South East Asia other than Vietnam
    4. Europe
    5. other

18. My type of service was:

    1. combat (served in a line unit in combat)
    2. combat support (served in a unit directly supporting a combat unit in combat)
    3. service support (served in non-combat duty but in a combat zone, i.e., Vietnam or Korea)
    4. did not serve in a combat zone

19. I received the following combat decoration (s):

    1. Medal of Honor or Distinguished Service Cross
    2. Silver Star, Distinguished Flying Cross, or Bronze Star with "V"
    3. Air Medal with "V" or Army Commendation Medal with "V"
    4. Foreign decoration for valor
    5. Purple Heart
    6. none

20. I received the following decoration (s) for meritorious service:

    1. Distinguished Service Medal or Legion of Merit
    2. Bronze Star

    3. Joint Service Commendation Medal or Army Commendation Medal
    4. Foreign decoration for meritorious service
    5. none

21. I served in Vietnam:

    1. never served
    2. less than 6 months
    3. 6 - 12 months
    4. 13 - 18 months
    5. over 18 months

22. I served in the Army:

    1. less than 6 months
    2. 6 - 12 months
    3. 13 - 24 months
    4. 25 - 36 months
    5. over 36 months

23. Before I went into the Army I was:

    1. in high school
    2. in college/trade school
    3. unemployed
    4. working
    5. waiting for the draft

24. When I joined the Army my age was:

    1. 17 or younger
    2. 18
    3. 19
    4. 20
    5. 21 or older

25. Before joining the Army I:

    1. was never in any trouble with any authorities
    2. was in trouble with school authorities
    3. was in trouble with juvenile authorities
    4. was in trouble with the law for minor problems (misdemeanor)
    5. was in trouble with the law for major problems (felony)

26. Before joining the Army did you ever spend any length of time (six months or more) away from your family and home such as:

    1. LDS Church mission
    2. school (not in home town)
    3. employment (not in home town)
    4. extended travel
    5. prior military service

6. other
7. before joining the Army I had never been away from my home for any length of time.

27. Before joining the Army I was:

    1. single
    2. married
    3. divorced or separated
    4. widowed

28. My sex is:

    1. male
    2. female

Note: Items 8 and 17 were included only to establish the independent variables. They were not used as part of the 26-item survey.

9

THE VIETNAM POW VETERAN: IMMEDIATE AND LONG-TERM EFFECTS OF CAPTIVITY

EDNA J. HUNTER, Ph.D.

INTRODUCTION

The former prisoner of war who escaped or was released by his captors is also a Vietnam veteran—with war experiences very different from the typical veteran from Southeast Asia. The prisoner of war's battle was not only a fight for daily survival, but also a fight against psychological coercion, physical torture, boredom, humiliation, feelings of helplessness, and oftentimes extreme mental depression. Different also was his hero reception by the American public upon return and the care and attention he received in the years following return. It would not be unexpected that the process of reintegration back into family, job, and society would also vary from that which the ordinary Vietnam veteran experienced.

In past years, particularly since the end of World War II, organized attempts have been made by researchers to document the immediate and long-term effects of the prisoner of war (POW) experience. Each captivity experience, we must remember, is clearly unique in terms of the nature of the captive, captor culture, length and conditions of internment, attitudes toward the war, and many other factors. Nonetheless, the environment of POW captivity typically combines a potent blend of physical hardship and privation, as well as enormous psychological stress and trauma, and there appears to be a consistency with which captivity effects appear across time and across widely divergent settings and populations of POWs.

Moreover, the physical and emotional trauma of captivity are likely to leave a residue of psychic scar tissue that never altogether heals (Segal, Hunter & Segal, 1976). It would not be unexpected that the

188

physical stresses of the South Vietnam POW experience and the over-whelming psychological stresses of the North Vietnam experience would be reflected in differential residual symptomatology manifested by the men both at the time of release and over time. Moreover, the latency and degree of incarceration effects could be expected to be tempered by the time of capture and the duration of captivity.

Two years prior to the POWs' release, Arthur (1971) pointed out that follow-up studies of concentration camp victims and American prisoners of war of the Japanese, North Koreans and North Vietnamese indicate that permanent psychic and psychophysiological damage can occur to adult human beings if they are subjected to prolonged malignant and cataclysmic stress. Segal has also emphasized that the cumulative weight of findings from existing follow-up studies leads to the conclusion that the extraordinary stresses of incarceration are related to a heightened vulnerability to physical and psychological health problems over the long term (Segal, 1974).

Such heightened vulnerability can perhaps explain the delay, sometimes as long as five to ten years, in appearance of symptoms in POW populations that seemed remarkably free of pathology immediately upon release from captivity. Thus, we must concur with Nefzger's (1970) position that long-term studies of prisoners of war are justified, if for no other reason than to answer administrative questions that can be answered only by observation.

It was recognized by the Department of Defense that the return of the American POWs from Southeast Asia in 1973 presented a unique opportunity for a long-range investigation of POWs and their families. Among other things, a comprehensive study would provide an understanding of the full impact of the POW experience, not only upon the man's physical, psychological, and social adjustment following return, but also upon his family members, during and after separation. Finally, it was recognized that such a study would show how men and families cope with stress and crises, and determine characteristics of those individuals and families who seem to be able to successfully cope during and after incarceration, regardless of degree of stress or adversity.

Prior to the return of the POWs from Southeast Asia, the Army, Navy, and Marine Corps cooperated to set up such a research effort. Thus, in April 1972, the Center for Prisoner of War Studies was established in San Diego, California. Its multidisciplinary professional staff is now in the fourth year of a comprehensive longitudinal study of the residuals of captivity and family separation for the 241 Army, Navy, and Marine Corps prisoners returned in 1973. In addition, comparison subjects were carefully matched with the 138 Navy returned POWs and their families. Both groups will be followed year by year in order to determine, among other things, precisely what psychosocial variables appear to be linked to captivity-related stress. Efforts are currently underway to select comparison groups for the Army and Marine POWs. This chapter describes specifically the experience of the American POWs held for varying periods of time in Southeast Asia from 1964 through early 1973. It also examines how both they and their families coped with captivity and separation and their initial adjustment to reunion.

The number of POWs returned from the war in Southeast Asia (766) was very small indeed when compared with the numbers held captive in Korea (7,140) or during World War II (130,201). The men returned from Southeast Asia (as of 31 December, 1976) were a highly select group compared with the POWs of earlier conflicts. The majority were officers, and as a group they were older and more highly educated.

Of those men captured in the North, all but one were air crew members. Five hundred ninety-one Americans, including 25 civilians, were repatriated in early Spring, 1973. An additional 84 men, held prisoner anywhere from 36 hours to five and one-half years, escaped or were released prior to 1973. The military group who returned in 1973 included 325 Air Force, 77 Army, 26 Marine Corps, and 138 Navy POWs.

The first American shot down over North Vietnam in August of 1964 was Lt. Everett Alvarez, USN, and he was the *sole* captive of the North Vietnamese for almost six months. Then, from February 1965 until November 1968, the prisoner of war population grew steadily, and with the increasing number of men taken, captor treatment worsened. Because of the bombing halt in 1968, no Americans were captured in North Vietnam from that time until the resumption of bombing in December 1971. *Those men captured prior to the bombing halt spent more time in captivity than any other Americans in history;* they spent three years longer than any of the more recent shootdowns of 1971, 1972, and 1973 (Rowland, 1975a, b).

THE CAPTIVE EXPERIENCE: TIME AND LOCATION

Throughout the Vietnam conflict, the prisoner of war situation was typically conceptualized as a unidimensional experience. With the return of the men in 1973, however, it became readily apparent that this was not true. Two important factors must be considered both in describing the captivity experience and in attempting to understand the physical and psychosocial residuals of the Vietnam POW experience: location of capture and time of capture. Men captured and detained in North Vietnam underwent an experience which was quite different from the experience of those captured in the South. A number of men were captured in the South but were later sent to the North.

Moreover, men captured prior to 1969 had a much more stressful experience than those who became POWs subsequent to October 1969 —a point in time when the treatment of the prisoners took a definite turn for the better. The definitive explanation for this change is unknown, but it can probably be attributed to some combination of three factors: (a) the death of Ho Chi Minh in September 1969; (b) statements made about harsh prisoner treatment by two POWs released in August of 1969; and (c) the efforts on the part of the POW/MIA families to bring world attention to the plight of the men. Perhaps the Vietnamese had also come to realize that the POWs were important politically for post-war bargaining leverage.

Whatever the reasons, torture dropped off considerably, camp routine changed, and the POWs began receiving three meals a day—at least in camps in the North. It was not until 1970, however, that the North Vietnamese released a list of Americans detained by them. Only then did some of the families know for the first time that their husbands, sons, or fathers were actually alive. Thus, the families, like the men, experienced very different separation experiences, depending upon whether or not their men had been captured prior or subsequent to late 1969.

The POW experience in South Vietnam, as mentioned earlier, differed considerably from that in the North, and differed even for those men in the South from one area to another. Confinement facilities in the South, for example, normally consisted of bamboo cages elevated on stilts, in which the men were confined most of the time. This was in contrast to the more permanent prison structures in the North. In the South the POWs were sometimes chained to their cages or to trees, except when on work details, cleaning their cages, or washing clothes. Some men were kept in caves or bunkers. Conditions were primitive. Most of the camps were near the end of the supply lines. Thus, food and medical supplies were often short or nonexistent. The POWs in the South generally suffered less torture and brutality and fewer interrogations and indoctrinations than those captured in the North. However, the men in the South were faced literally with trying to *survive* from day to day. Thus, while those held in the South suffered an experience marked by severe physical deprivation and concern for basic personal survival, those in the North reported an experience characterized by borderline food and living conditions and by physical torture, as well as psychological mistreatment for interrogation and propaganda purposes (Berg, 1974).

Coercion in Captivity

The odds for survival were much higher for men captured in the North. There, however, virtually all American POWs spent their first days of captivity in solitary confinement, and many spent much longer periods alone. Forty percent spent over six months in solitary; 20 percent from one to two years; 10 percent over two years; and *four POWs spent over four years in solitary confinement.*

In 1966, with the increased tempo of the war, the prisoner population increased dramatically, and treatment worsened. During these early years the Vietnamese appeared determined to exploit the American POWs for propaganda purposes. Demands were placed upon them for propaganda tapes, press interviews, and letters to their fellow pilots and congressmen denouncing America's participation in the war, actions which were contrary to the Military Code of Conduct.

In July of 1966, the prisoners were threatened with war crimes trials. Unable to obtain information through normal interrogation, the Vietnamese began a program which included the use of ropes, leg and wrist irons, and other methods of severe torture. The severely injured were denied medical treatment, and some men even had previous injuries aggravated in order to force submission. No prisoner of war withstood "the ropes" without complying in some fashion with the desires of the captor. For many of the POWs, the fact that they could be forced to cooperate with their captors against their will was quite unexpected and was a powerful source of intense and long-lasting feelings of depression and guilt. The POWs held in the North were not allowed to work as those in the South had to do in order to survive. Any outside exercise was rare, although men usually instituted their own program of physical exercise within their cells.

Systems of Resistance

The POW's existence was a lonely, monotonous and incredibly boring one, against which they fought with two powerful, covert weapons: a

POW military organization based upon seniority or rank, and a communication code to pass messages between walls.

While solitary confinement was the most psychologically devastating treatment, perhaps the most continuously morale boosting and most important aspect of captivity for survival was communication. Most returnees cite this ability to communicate, even when in solitary confinement, as the one thing that kept them going throughout their captivity (Deaton, Berg, Richlin & Litrownik, in press). They were not only able to communicate from room to room, but also from building to building, compound to compound, and from one end of the camp to the other. They passed current events brought in by new arrivals, policies of the senior officer, data on who was in camp, as well as movie plots, foreign language lessons, poems, prayers and biblical scriptures. Intrapersonal communication was another important factor. Some men reported that captivity gave them the opportunity to sort out and reorder their values and come to know themselves better.

Hence, despite the severe deprivation and stress of foreign incarceration, some benefits did accrue to some of the POWs (Rowland, 1975a, b).

THE CAPTIVE EXPERIENCE: PSYCHOSOCIAL CONSEQUENCES

Individual Coping Patterns

What factors determine who dies and who survives captivity? Certainly, climate, living conditions, work load, medical care, and captor treatment are some of the factors. Kushner (1974), a prisoner himself in South Vietnam, reduced the remaining variables in survival to the individual mental states of the prisoners, their individual reactions to stress, and the individual training and constitutions.

According to Kushner, the survivors tended to be those who kept active, kept clean, maintained a sense of humor, worked hard, and in general coped with their environment. Those who did not survive, on the other hand, refused or resisted the captive environment. These men drowned themselves in self-pity, refused to contribute to camp life, usually were depressed, withdrawn, helpless, and had to be forced to work and bathe. Thus, the POWs who survived long-term captivity could be classed as a highly "select" group. They would be expected to possess stronger basic personalities with fewer post-return adjustment problems, all other factors being equal, than war veterans in general.

The Effects of Solitary Confinement

As noted earlier, extended periods of solitary confinement were a unique aspect of the Vietnam POW experience. Social isolation has been rated by the POWs themselves (Vohden, 1974) as one of the three most important sources of stress in captivity. The stress engendered by solitary confinement was exceeded only by the amount of stress produced by the event of capture itself and the stress which resulted from physical torture during captivity. Various studies have found that solitary confinement was associated with significantly more abnormal psychiatric ratings for presence of feelings of guilt and ambivalence (Hunter, 1976b). At the time of their release from captivity, those men who had been subjected to prolonged periods of solitary confinement were more likely to show lower suggestibility, higher superego development, and higher need for achievement. Physiologically, the men who had spent extensive time in solitary also tended to appear older than their chronological ages according to reports made by the examining physicians.

Personal Values and Captivity

Do basic values shift during captivity? One study of POWs' values found that the majority of the POWs "perceived" that their value system had changed significantly as a result of the captivity experience (Rutledge, Hunter, & Dahl, in press). Actual data from that study, however, indicated that perhaps rather than an overall shift in one direction or another, there may have been substantial reordering of the importance of certain values. The POWs differed significantly from their matched controls on only the one value, power, with the POWs scoring lower. Also, for those men who had experienced prolonged solitary confinement, scores on the value of wealth were significantly lower.

Many of the wives of the POWs reported to researchers from the Center for POW Studies that their greatest surprise at homecoming was how little their husband's basic personalities had actually changed during the long, stressful years of captivity.*

When the men returned, the wives expected much change and found little. The husbands, on the other hand, expected little change in their

---

* As noted elsewhere in this volume, however, value shifts may not appear—like stress symptoms—until years later.

wives and families, and found much. It is little wonder that a substantial part of the post-repatriation reintegration adjustment was staged within the family arena.

Resistance Posture and the POW

Considerable attention has been focused on the relationship between the POW's resistance posture in captivity and the POW's ability to survive incarceration (Hunter, Plag, Phelan, & Mowery, 1976; Hunter & Phelan, in press; Naughton, 1975; Segal, 1957). Relating resistance posture to the time spent in captivity, age, and amount of solitary confinement, Hunter and colleagues found that men held captive longest were more likely to avoid actions which might be used by the captor for propaganda purposes and were less inclined to bargain with the captor; older men tended to report firmer resistance postures; men with longer periods of solitary confinement were more reluctant to bargain with the captor; and harsh captor treatment was significantly related to the firmer resistance posture (Hunter *et al.*, 1976). Thus, it is apparent that the manner in which the POW relates to the captor is associated with the treatment received, and, consequently, to his odds for survival and post-release adjustment.

SEPARATION EFFECTS ON THE FAMILY

It would be surprising indeed if the years the POW spent in solitude and privation did not reverberate in the world to which he returns. Since the manner in which families coped with the major part of the separation period appears to be related to their adjustment to reunion, let us begin our discussion of family adjustment with the crisis of casualty.

Patterns of Reaction to Notice of Capture

One of the fascinating early observations of the Center's staff was the recognition of the similarity between the captured husband and his waiting wife in terms of their experiences and feelings in adjusting to their dissimilar situations following casualty (Berg, 1974). Typically, the POW described the process of adjustment to capture as a cycle which began with psychological shock and numbing, followed by a period of several days or weeks of hyper-alertness and intense interest in even the most trivial details of the prison environment and his captors. Then ensued a period of weeks, months, or even years of mental depression, which finally culminated in a conscious decision to survive, to make the best of things, to become active again—a process which parallels the normal process of grieving (Kubler-Ross, 1969), which it indeed was. The man grieved over the loss of his freedom; the wife grieved over the loss of her husband.

Analogous to the man's process of adjusting to his capture, initially the wife too was psychologically numbed by the news of her husband's casualty. As the shock wore away, she put forth an intense effort to learn everything possible about the circumstances of his capture, whether he had been injured, or if he were still alive. When all sources of information were exhausted, the wife also entered a depressed phase, just as the POW had done. However, the wife did not lose her freedom as her husband had; in contrast, she suddenly found herself with both freedom and new responsibilities she had never before known. Moreover, over time, she learned to cope admirably with that newfound independence, and as the months and years passed, she became more and more reluctant to relinquish it (McCubbin, Hunter, & Dahl, 1975). Personal indepth interviews by the Center's staff in 1972, prior to the men's release, indicated this depressed stage for the wife usually ended sometime between the second or third year following casualty. At that point in time, she typically made a conscious decision that, in order to cope with the marital limbo she was in, she had to quit "marking" time in place and get on with living." She then perhaps became very active in POW/MIA organizations, returned to school, or went to work. She sometimes moved off the military post where she had waited during the initial months or years and purchased a home in the civilian community and perhaps began dating.

Coping with the captivity of her husband, to some extent, meant closing out his role within the family system. She might adopt other coping styles, however. Just as Deaton and colleagues (Deaton, Berg, Richlin & Litrownik, in press) studied the various mechanisms the men used in coping with captivity, McCubbin and associates found a variety of coping patterns—some functional and others dysfunctional—which wives utilized in dealing with family separation. These patterns appeared to be related to the wife's background, perceived quality of marriage, husband's background, his motive for going to Southeast Asia, the stresses experienced by the wife during separation, and the family's preparation for separation (McCubbin, Dahl, Lester, Benson & Robertson, 1976).

The marital relationship of the repatriated captive is clearly vulnerable to the stresses of separation. McCubbin, Hunter and Dahl (1975) have highlighted adjustment problems which were found among families of Vietnam POWs. After prolonged absences, many of the wives experienced extreme ambivalence and guilt immediately prior to their husbands' return. Family reunions were indeed stressful.

Recent studies by the Center for POW studies, like Hill's (1949) classic WWII study, have shown that maintenance of the father's role in the family unit during separation was an important factor in the reintegration process (McCubbin, Dahl, Lester, & Ross, 1975). Three other variables which McCubbin and associates found uniquely related to family reintegration were (a) the wife's assessment of the marriage before casualty, (b) the degree of wife's emotional dysfunction during separation, and (c) the length of the marriage at the time of the POW's casualty. In other words, the better the wife's satisfaction with the marriage and the longer the marriage at the time of casualty, and the fewer emotional problems the wife experienced during the separation period, the more likely the family would remain intact after the POW's return.

Children, too, had to cope with the captivity of their fathers, and their success in doing so reflected, to a large degree, their mother's ability to cope successfully with this stressful family crisis. Two or three years following father's release, however, the Center's studies suggest that father-absence continued to have a profound and generally negative effect upon these children when compared to general population norms—effects apparently not offset by father's return (Dahl, McCubbin, Lester, & Hynds, 1976). Until these POW/MIA children are contrasted with a matched group, however, we do not know if they really differ from any other comparable group of military children.

POST-CAPTIVITY ADJUSTMENT

An Overview

Following an unpopular war, the POW released from Southeast Asia returned to country, family, and career. While still in captivity, the POW, his mind sometimes clouded by captor recriminations and maltreatment, frequently weighed the possibility that he would return to the United States in total disgrace. What were some of his other thoughts and feelings? His family would be waiting, of course, but there would be no future career in the military, no more flying the

TABLE 1

Common Diagnoses Established at Operation Homecoming
for Army, Navy and Marine Corps POWs*

Diagnosis	PERCENT Army (N = 77)	Navy (N = 138)	Marine Corps (N = 26)
Helminthiasis	77	88	96
Refractive Errors	29	52	58
Hearing Impairment	40	48	46
Peripheral Nerve Injury	39	46	31
Malaria	34	< 5	12
Dermatophytosis	39	25	19
Nutritional Deficiencies	55	11	15
Amoebiasis	22	38	27
Spondylitis Osteroarthritica	9	28	23
Trauma to Skeletal System:			
Fractured Vertebrae	18	26	15
Deranged Knee	< 5	16	< 5
Deranged Shoulder	< 5	9	12
Fractured Radius & Ulna	< 5	7	< 5

* Data from Spaulding, R. C. "Diagnostic trends in Navy RPWs: Homecoming diagnoses compared with summary data from the first and second year follow-up examinaitons." Paper presented at the 3rd Annual Joint Meeting Concerning POW/MIA Matters, San Diego, Ca., Nov. 1975. In Spaulding, R. C. (Ed.), 1976, p. 13.

planes he loved to fly. Unexpectedly, the POW came back to a well-planned homecoming with all the hoopla of a hero's welcome; he was perhaps the *only* hero of the Vietnam conflict. He not only had a career, but he was also given every advantage to pursue it—a choice of assignments, a return to school for a higher degree, back into a cockpit for the majority who were qualified, and, for some of the POWs, another promotion and perhaps a coveted command.

Filling the role of hero was not without an added portion of guilt and doubt. The POW, his self-esteem bruised by captivity, suffered from depression-produced feelings as he often ruminated about the past and all the other men who did not return. Perhaps those making the decisions in Washington were not fully aware of his behavior while in captivity. Could he really handle a command after being in a time capsule for so many years as the world sped on without him? Perhaps he should continue his education rather than taking a command. In spite of personal and family commitments he felt obligated to tell about his experience to anyone who might request a personal appearance— Boy Scouts, church, civic groups, etc.—even if it meant further separations from his family. He slipped quickly from sensory deprivation to sensory overload.

There is no doubt that captor treatment received as a POW had at times made him feel something less than human, with a concomitant lowering of self-esteem. However, his comments upon return indicated that he believed he had learned what is important in life, citing, for example, family, friends, education, and learning to play a musical instrument. One tends to denigrate such things as power and wealth when they are beyond one's reach. And then the POW returned; he could now achieve all those prisoner-of-war dreams; he again had the power to make decisions and to control his own life. But can he? He has already achieved the one goal in life he has had for many years— freedom. Unless he finds another worthwhile goal quickly, life may become meaningless, especially if freedom is not quite as sweet as he had so long fantasized it would be. Undoubtedly, the physical and psychological residuals the POW brings back with him, coupled with the psychosocial events he meets upon his return, combine, at least in part, to determine the course of his future adjustment. It should be noted that for almost a third of the married returnees there were, in fact, no families waiting when they arrived home.

The Homecoming

Physical problems. First let us examine the physical illnesses and injuries diagnosed in the group of 241 Army, Navy, and Marine Corps returned POWs at the time of Homecoming (see Table 1, Spaulding, 1976). It should be noted that the 138 Navy POWs and 10 of the Marine Corps officer-aviators spent their entire captivity in North Vietnam. All 77 Army men and the remaining 16 Marine Corps POWs were captured in South Vietnam. Eventually the majority of this second group were moved into the Northern camps, but 20 percent spent their entire captivity in the South. The differential diagnoses made at homecoming for the three services reflect differences in location of capture, age, and education. The most common diagnosis at the time of homecoming for POWs held either in the North or the South was helminthiasis (worms). Prisoners held in the South had both more diagnoses, and different types of diagnoses: e.g., malnutrition, malaria, transient situational reactions, and skin diseases (Berg & Richlin, in press).

The group held in the North was noteworthy for the types of injuries received. Many suffered injuries when their planes were shot down, and these injuries were usually orthopedic in nature. In contrast, injuries for the group held in the South were acquired either in fire fights or in the crash of a helicopter. In a captivity situation, even a minor injury can be life threatening because of the danger of infection. Injuries sustained at capture had their greatest influence during the first several weeks after capture. As time passed, however, the role of capture injuries in the POW's survival lessened. Peripheral nerve injury was also greater in the North due to the use of the "ropes" for coercion. When one considers the intense physical and psychological pressures applied, it is perhaps surprising the POWs held in the North did not show a higher degree of psychopathology. Berg and Richlin (in press) cite several factors which may have ameliorated the deleterious effects of maltreatment of those held by North Vietnam (e.g., well-organized leadership and communication, group support for those "broken" by the captor, and greater maturity).

Psychiatric problems. With regard to psychiatric evaluations at the time of homecoming, diagnoses of *neurosis* were given to five percent of the returning Army and Navy POWs and to 15 percent of the Marine Corps men. The more severe diagnosis of transient situational disturbance was received by five percent of the Navy POWs, 15 percent of the Marines, and 25 percent of the Army group. Whether the greater psychiatric symptomatology for the Army and Marine populations is a service-related difference or a location-of-captivity difference is still unclear. It should perhaps also be noted that two men committed suicide in the months shortly after return (one Marine and one Air Force POW). Subsequently, a Navy man was killed in a single-car automobile accident. Aircraft accidents have also claimed the lives of two more POWs—one Air Force and one Navy POW.

Evaluations Two-Years Post-Captivity

Physical problems. Navy and Marine Corps POWs return annually to the Naval Aerospace Medical Institute and Laboratory at Pensacola, Florida, for medical follow-up examination; Army returnees go to Brooke Army Medical Center, San Antonio, Texas. Examinations include a searching interim history, a thorough physical examination, a complete battery of blood studies including serologies for malaria and other Southeast Asia parasites, special x-rays, stress studies for heart disease, studies of lung functions, and studies of the organs of balance. The psychiatric portion of the study, in addition to the usual psychiatric interviews, includes extensive psychological testing. Special consultations include dental, ear, nose and throat, eye, hearing, and other specialties as indicated, e.g., orthopedic, surgery, dermatology, and urology, etc. For the second-year follow-up the Halstead-Reitan test for organic brain damage was added to the protocol, and certain blood chemistry, vestibular, and visual studies were deleted. Matched comparisons undergo the same examination and tests that the POWs receive (Spaulding, 1976).

Because analyses of the second-year Army medical follow-up data were incomplete at the time of this writing, we can only examine how Navy and Marine Corps POWs were faring two years subsequent to release. Generally, according to the examining physicians, the men were doing well physically, with most abnormalities occurring in the same areas as previously, except for parasites where the number of diagnoses had decreased considerably. Perhaps the major problems were the orthopedic problems: dislocations, fractures and injuries of the extremities, and injuries of the spine. However, at the two-year point in time, only one man had been retired because of the severity of his injuries. Past investigations of the prisoner of war experience have suggested there is a delayed onset of symptomatology for the survivor of captivity. Thus, we ask: Are the number of medical problems decreasing or increasing for these men over time? Based upon medical data available for 81 returned POWs for the first three examination periods (homecoming, 1974, and 1975), there had been a total of 241 diagnoses for the Navy and Marine POWs on whom data were available—an average of 2.78 diagnoses per man. Of these, 73 diagnoses were consistent for the first- and second-year follow-up examinations, but were *not* present at homecoming. A total of 128 diagnoses were established for the first time at the second-year follow-up; that is, they were *not* present at the two prior examination periods. Thus, in this group of Navy and Marine POWs, although many diagnoses present at homecoming were successfully treated, during the first two years subsequent to release from captivity, it would appear that *there has been a trend of increasing number of new physical symptoms* not evidenced immediately following return (Spaulding, 1976).

Psychiatric evaluations. Psychiatric diagnoses received two years subsequent to release, based upon 102 Navy and Marine Corps POWs are

TABLE 2

Psychiatric Diagnoses for Navy and Marine Corps
POWs Two Years Post-Return*
(N = 102)

Diagnosis	Percent
Marital Maladjustment	19
Obsessive-compulsive personality	17
Hysterical personality	10
Depressive Neurosis	10
Anxiety Neurosis	8
Alcoholism	8
Adjustment Reaction	8
Schizoid Personality	6
Schizophrenia	2

* Data from O'Connell, P. F. "Trends in psychological adjustment: Observations made during successive psychiatric follow-up interviews of returned Navy-Marine Corps POWs." Paper presented at the 3rd Annual Joint Meeting Concerning POW/MIA Matters, San Diego, Ca., Nov. 1975. In Spaulding, R. C. (Ed.), 1976, p. 16.

shown in Table 2 (O'Connell, 1976). Navy psychiatrists found that length of captivity was indeed a factor in whether or not the POW received a psychiatric diagnosis. The longer the captivity duration, the more likely the POW would receive a psychiatric diagnosis two years post-release. However, it was also apparent that those men who had predisposing factors in their past histories were four times more likely to receive a psychiatric diagnosis than those who did not (O'Connell, 1976). Most of the Navy returned POWs appeared to be doing quite well psychiatrically two years subsequent to return. Based upon psychiatric examinations, for those who were having problems most of the symptoms appeared related to the marital relationship. Pathology related etiologically to the marital relationships had increased from 28 to 38 percent from the previous year (1974). Next in importance to marriage were etiological events related to childhood and the captivity experience.

Diagnoses etiologically related to captivity factors, unlike those related to marriage, decreased during the previous year from 24 percent to 10 percent. It is noteworthy that there were significantly more psychiatric diagnoses two years post-return for those Navy POWs who had never married than for those who were either married or had married and later divorced. Also of interest was the finding that those men who elected to return to school following repatriation were more likely to receive psychiatric diagnoses than those who went immediately to a full-time active duty assignment. In some instances, returning to school may have been a means of avoiding problems associated with or apprehensions about the ability to handle a duty assignment satisfactorily. Of those Navy POWs who showed definite psychiatric deterioration during the period from the first-year follow-up to the second-year follow-up examination, depression was the most common diagnostic picture, with a suggestion that an obsessive-compulsive personality pattern was a predisposing factor (O'Connell, 1976). Interestingly, those men who showed no change between the first- and second-year follow-up examinations received fewer psychiatric diagnoses than either the group that changed for the better or those men who changed for the worse.

THE POW FAMILY

Divorce. Almost 30 percent of the Army, Navy, and Marine Corps POWs who had been married prior to captivity were faced with marital dissolution within the first year after return. Many of these were marriages of short duration or problem marriages prior to casualty. Actually, the rate is not too different from divorce rates in general within the United States today. Typically, however, divorce rates within the military are lower than those for the general population; when compared with the divorce statistic for the matched comparison group, the POW rate was two to three times higher. At the point in time three years post-release, we looked to see how many in each group had experienced at least one marital dissolution since date of casualty. We found that 32.3 percent of the Army, 25.0 percent of the Marines, and 27.9 percent of the Navy POWs had experienced marital dissolution compared with only 11.1 percent of the comparison group for the Navy sample* for the same time period (Hunter, 1976a).

Family integration. As mentioned previously, maintenance of a husband/father role within the family was found to be an important factor for successful family reintegration following return (McCubbin *et al.,* 1975). We have also noted that, ironically, successful coping for the wife during the separation period required at least a partial "closing out" of the father's role through reassignment of his tasks to other fam-

---

* Matched comparison for the Marine Corps and Army POWs had not yet been selected at the time the analyses were made.

ily members. It was, then, predictable that major adjustments in family roles would have to occur in the initial weeks and months after repatriation in order for successful reintegration to take place.

Preliminary comparisons between the family role structure of Navy POW families and matched control families showed some interesting differences. Three years subsequent to return, the POW families, as a group, were significantly more "female-centered" or matriarchal than the more "traditional" control families. In other words, even though the POW father had returned to the family many months before, not all his previous roles had been reassumed by him. The wife of the POW was still performing some of the roles or family tasks that were more likely, in the group of comparison families, to be performed by the husband (Hunter, 1976a). Other between-group differences were apparent from these comparative studies. For example, the family of the POW was less independent and less cohesive, according to reports of the wife of the POW, when compared with the comparison families. The wives of the returned POWs also perceived their husbands' career adjustment as lower than did the wives of the matched controls in judging their husbands' job performance.

One final noteworthy finding should perhaps be mentioned here. It was found that the amount of solitary confinement the POW experienced during captivity was highly related to his perception of how well he was doing in his career three years subsequent to return. The longer the period of solitary, the lower the POW's perceived career adjustment (Hunter, 1976c). Before we put too much credence in this relationship, however, we must look further for objective measures of how well he is performing his job. Because these returned POWs, as a group, appeared to be trying to "make up for lost time" during the years immediately following release from captivity and because they tended to set extremely high expectations for themselves, they may have been performing more than adequately even though they perceived they should be doing better. Again, it would appear there may be more problems in the post-return period for either the POW who over-achieves or the one who becomes depressed and gives up than for the middle-of-the-roader who sets more realistic goals for himself.

Resistance posture in captivity and later adjustment. Differences between the POW and his wife regarding the performance of and agreement on family roles and tasks have been used in the Center's studies as measures of family reintegration (Hunter, 1976c); e.g., the greater the discrepancies between spouses as to who performed which roles, the poorer the reintegration. Findings from these studies also indicated that the extremely firm resisters during captivity did not appear to be reintegrating within the family as quickly as those who had assumed more moderate resistance postures. However, there was no relationship found between either resistance posture or harsh captor treatment and the POWs' subsequent personal, marital, or career adjustment. The effects of those two captivity variables (resistance posture and harsh captor treatment) were reflected only in the area of father-child adjustment, where they were associated with higher disagreement between the parents regarding child discipline (Hunter, 1976c).

The POWs' children. Although the absence of the father in a military role poses difficult problems for any child, when the father is a POW in a long and unpopular war, there are additional burdens imposed by the situation. Mothers must cope not only with their own problems and feelings but also with those of their children. A recent study by Dahl and McCubbin (1976) of the personal and social adjustment of the children of returned prisoners from Vietnam revealed that the children were significantly below the norms on overall adjustment. However, we must caution that until these preliminary findings are compared with the data for the comparison group children, we will not know if the POW's children are really any different from any other group of military children. Preliminary between-group comparisons would indicate they may not be.

Father-child relations within the POW family have been shown to be highly related to the father's perceived abuse in captivity (McCubbin, 1976). In other words, the more stressful the captivity experience was viewed by the POW, the more difficult it appeared to be for him to reestablish close and satisfying father-child relationships after return. It was expected that POW father absence would show differential effects on children as a function of age and sex of a child. However, the Center's studies to date have been unable to establish any significant relationships between sex of child and age of child at the time of the father's casualty and satisfactory father-child relationships in the postreturn period, although such relationships may yet become apparent in later phases of these longitudinal studies.

CONCLUSIONS

This chapter has presented a few of the preliminary findings of the longitudinal studies of the 241 Army, Navy, and Marine Corps prisoner of war veterans released from Southeast Asia in 1973. These studies are being carried out at the Center for Prisoner of War Studies in San Diego, California, and have as their primary goal the achievement of a better understanding of the multidimensional impact of captivity upon the men and their families. Preliminary findings indicate that incarceration by a foreign power has both immediate and long-term effects which may become manifest only after a latency period of several months or years. Both the events of casualty and reunion have been shown to be stressful family crises. To quote one physician who has followed the POWs closely during the three years subsequent to their release from captivity: "It is now apparent that the process of recovery from the stress of shootdown, capture, captivity, and repatriation appears to *require,* among other things, recovery of self-esteem through reintegration with the group: the POW group, the military, the family, and society. . . . To the degree that there is failure, there will be . . . psychopathology. We are by nature 'beingwith' creatures" (O'Connell, 1976, pp. 21-22). Perhaps this statement explains the extremely deleterious effects of prolonged solitary confinement on the POW—effects which after three years echo throughout his relationships with himself, his family, and his fellow-workers. Although the Center's studies may at times appear to focus heavily on psychopathology, they can also afford new insights both into the manner whereby POWs are able to survive their ordeal and into the ways in which the ordeal of captivity served to strengthen them and build new resources—both for the men and their families.

Section III

TREATMENT IMPLICATIONS

The final section is, perhaps, the most important part of the volume in its attempt to provide useful information on treating stress disorders. Collectively the five papers attempt to explicate the salient features and strategies for treating veterans with combat-related stress disorders.

The first chapter, by Robert Lifton, serves as an appropriate introduction to the section and the chapters to follow. In a straightforward manner Lifton provides important insights into the psychology of helping and healing by first describing his approach to the treatment of Vietnam veterans: confrontation, reordering, and renewal. He views the veteran as a survivor of war and describes a method of treating the veteran within the context of self-help rap-groups composed of other veterans.

Chapter 11 presents Egendorf's clinical work with veterans and extensive discussions with colleagues over the last eight years. The first section deals with common conceptual fallacies that can hamper therapists' work with veterans. The second part discusses numerous issues and conflicts associated with treating veterans and offers concrete suggestions for therapists to deal with these issues and conflicts. Egendorf concludes by raising the question of how psychotherapy can provide a healing antidote to the experience of war, and presents an experiential perspective illustrated with cases of clients he has worked with.

The first part of Sarah Haley's chapter reports on a study assessing the incidence of Post-Combat Stress Response Syndromes discussed by Horowitz and Solomon in this section. The results of the study suggest that the occurrence of combat-related stress disorders is much more pervasive among Vietnam veterans than expected. The latter portion of the paper provides some specific treatment strategies for mental health practitioners working with clients diagnosed with stress disorders.

The chapter by Mardi Horowitz and George Solomon is an abridged version of their paper, "A Prediction of Delayed Stress Response Syndromes in Vietnam Veterans," which appeared in a special issue, *Soldiers in and After Vietnam*, in the *Journal of Social Issues* (1975, *31* (4), 67-80). Based on the authors' experiences in working with Vietnam veterans in a clinical setting and on the theoretical writings of the first author *(Stress Response Syndromes*, New York: Aronson, 1976), the paper provides important insights on combat-related stress reactions. The authors believe that substantial numbers of Vietnam veterans in the coming years will experience mild to severe stress reactions which can be traced to combat stress.

Chapter 14 by Duncan Stanton and Charles Figley focuses on the veteran's interpersonal relationships. After a brief discussion of theoretical orientations to the treatment of Vietnam veterans with combat-related stress disorders, they focus on the family system. Among other things, they suggest that the disorder is often enmeshed within a variety of interpersonal problems, and that the family system has the potential for both maintaining and eliminating the disorder. Specific family treatment issues are discussed and a number of treatment modalities are suggested.

10

ADVOCACY AND CORRUPTION IN THE HEALING PROFESSION

ROBERT JAY LIFTON, M.D.

In looking at the professions, one does well, I think, to hold to the old religious distinction between the ministerial and the prophetic. One should not assume, as many do, a simple polarity in which the sciences are inherently radical or revolutionary and the healing professions intrinsically conservative. The professions must minister to people, take care of them, and that is a relatively conservative process. But there are prophets who emerge from the healing ministrations of the professions—Freud is a notable example—with radical critiques and revolutionary messages. Moreover, even "pure scientists" (in biology or physics, for example) spend most of their time ministering to the existing paradigm and strongly resist the breakthrough that is inevitably charted by the prophets among them. There are ministerial and prophetic elements in both the healing professions and the sciences.

But one must also distinguish between the professions, which have profound value in their capacity for continuity and renewal, and professionalism, the ideology of professional omniscience, which in our era inevitably leads to technicism and the model of the machine. The necessity for such a distinction becomes painfully clear if one looks at the situation that prevailed for psychiatrists in Vietnam. I want to take that situation as a starting point for a broader discussion of these dilemmas and their moral and conceptual ramifications. For the fact is that, in such extreme situations, the professional may be no better able than his soldier-patient to sort out the nuances of care and professional commitment on the one hand, and moral (or immoral) action on the other.

Reprinted with permission from *The Social Psychology of Military Service*, N. L. Goldman and D. R. Segal (Eds.). Beverly Hills: Sage Publications, 1976, pp. 45-64.

Central to my view of the present predicament of the professions is the psychology and the spirit of the survivor. The concept of the survivor derives in my work from the study I did in Hiroshima (Lifton, 1968) a little more than ten years ago, and has been fundamental to my subsequent thought. I define a survivor as one who has touched, witnessed, encountered or been immersed in death in a literal or symbolic way and has himself remained alive. Let us assume that we as professionals share the national "death immersion" of not only Vietnam but the related Watergate-impeachment process and that our ways of surviving them can have significance for us in our work. We may then discover that we are not entirely removed from the constellation of psychological patterns that I found Hiroshima survivors to share to a rather striking degree with survivors of Nazi death camps, the plagues of the Middle Ages, natural disasters, and what Kurt Vonnegut calls "plain old death."

THE CONCEPT OF THE SURVIVOR

The concept of the survivor includes five patterns. The first is the survivor's indelible death image and death anxiety. This "death imprint" often has to do with a loss of a sense of invulnerability. The second pattern, that of death guilt, is revealed in the survivor's classic question, "Why did I stay alive when he or she or they died?" The question itself has to do with a sense of organic social balance: "If I had died, he or she would have lived." That image of exchange of one life for another is perhaps the survivor's greatest psychological burden. A third pattern is that of desensitization, or what I call psychic numbing, the breakdown of symbolic connectedness with one's environment. Numbing is a necessary protective mechanism in holocaust, but can become self-perpetuating and express itself in sustained depression, despair, and apathy or withdrawal. A fourth survivor pattern has to do with the "death-taint," as experienced by others toward survivors and by survivors themselves, resulting in discrimination against them and mutual suspicion and distrust. Central to this pattern is the survivor's "suspicion of counterfeit nurturance," his combination of feeling in need of help and resenting help offered as a reminder of weakness. (This kind of suspicion occurs not only in holocaust but in any situation in which "help" is offered by the privileged to the downtrodden or oppressed, as in white-black relations; one can readily find models for this pained interaction in parent-child relationships.)

The fifth pattern is fundamental to all survivor psychology and encompasses the other four. It is the struggle to be able to find form and significance in one's remaining life experience (see Langer, 1942, 1953, 1962; Cassirer, 1944, 1946). This formulative struggle is equally visible in more symbolic experiences of holocaust, those of surviving ways of life one perceives to be "dying." In that sense rapid social change makes survivors of us all.

In examining our healing professions in relationship to these survivals, especially that of the psychiatric death encounter in Vietnam, we should keep in mind two general survivor alternatives. One can retreat from the issues raised by the death immersion and thereby remain bound to it in a condition of stasis (or numbing). Or one can confront the death immersion and derive insight, illumination, and change from the overall survivor experience (Lifton, 1973a). The latter response to some kind of experience of survival has probably been the source of most great religious and political movements, and of many breakthroughs in professional life as well.

A related issue is that of advocacy, which in our profession applies both to investigation and therapy, and is crucial to issues of professional renewal. I came to my work with Vietnam veterans from two directions, from prior antiwar advocacy and from professional concern with holocaust deriving from my research in Hiroshima. In the work with veterans I sought to combine detachment sufficient to enable me to make psychological evaluations (which I had to do at every step) with involvement that expressed my own commitments and moral passions. I believe that we always function within this dialectic between ethical involvement and intellectual rigor, and that bringing our advocacy "out front," and articulating it makes us more, rather than less, scientific. Indeed, our scientific accuracy is likely to suffer when we hide our ethical beliefs behind the claim of neutrality and see ourselves as nothing but "neutral screens." The Vietnam War constitutes an extreme situation, in which the need for an ethical response is very clear. But we have a tradition of great importance in depth psychology, much evident in Freud, of studying extremes in order to illuminate the (more obscure) ordinary.

VETERANS' RAP GROUPS

I want to focus now on my experience over the last three years with "rap groups" of antiwar veterans and then to generalize from that experience about professional issues around advocacy and corruption.

The veterans' rap groups came into being because the veterans sensed that they had more psychological work to do in connection with the war (Lifton, 1973a). It is important to emphasize that the veterans themselves initiated the groups. The men knew that they were "hurting," but did not want to seek help from the Veterans Administration, which they associated with the military, the target of much of their rage. And though they knew they were in psychological pain, they did not consider themselves patients. They wanted to understand what they had been through, begin to heal themselves, and at the same time make known to the American public the human costs of the war. These two aspects of the veterans' aspirations in forming the groups—healing themselves while finding a mode of political expression—paralleled the professional dialectic of rigor and advocacy mentioned earlier. Without using those words, the veterans had that combination very much in mind when they asked me to work with them.

I called in other professionals (Chaim Shatan did much of the organizing) in the New York-New Haven area to assist us in the rap groups. I also participated with the veterans in the Winter Soldier Investigation of 1971, the first large-scale public hearing at which American G.I.'s described their own involvement in war crimes. From the beginning the therapeutic and political aspects of our work developed simultaneously. It seemed natural for us to initiate the rap groups on the veterans' own turf, so to speak, in the office of the Vietnam Veterans Against the War—and to move to the "neutral ground" of a theological seminary when problems of space and political in-fighting developed at the VVAW office. The men wanted to meet where they were comfortable and where they could set the tone. With many stops and starts and much fluidity in general, a sizable number of these rap groups have formed, in New York City and throughout the country (Lifton, 1973a). The one that I have been part of has been meeting continuously since early in 1971.

We made plans for weekly two-hour meetings, but the sessions were so intense, with such active involvement on the part of everybody, that they would generally run for three or four hours. I also interviewed many of the men individually in connection with the research I initiated then and subsequently published. From the beginning we avoided a medical model: We called ourselves "professionals" rather than "therapists" (the veterans often referred to us simply as "shrinks"), and we spoke of rap groups rather than group therapy. We were all on a first-name basis, and there was a fluidity in the boundaries between professionals and veterans. But the boundaries remained important nonetheless; distinctions remained important to both groups; and in the end the healing role of professionals was enhanced by the extent to which veterans could become healers to one another and, in some degree, to professionals also. Equally important, there was an assumption, at first unspoken and later articulated, that everybody's life was at issue; professionals had no special podium from which to avoid self-examination. We too could be challenged, questioned about anything—all of which seemed natural enough to the veterans but was a bit more problematic for the professionals. As people used to interpreting others' motivations, it was at first a bit jarring to be confronted with hard questions about our own and with challenges about the way we lived. Not only was our willingness to share this kind of involvement crucial to the progress of the group, but in the end many of us among the professionals came to value and enjoy this kind of dialogue.

As in certain parallel experiments taking place, not only in psychological work but throughout American culture, we had a clearer idea of what we opposed (hierarchical distancing, medical mystification, psychological reductionism that undermines political and ethical ideas) than of what we favored as specific guidelines. But before long I came to recognize three principles that seemed important. The first was that of *affinity*, the coming together of people who share a particular (in this case overwhelming) historical or personal experience, along with a basic perspective on that experience, in order to make some sense of it (the professionals entered into this "affinity," at least to a certain extent, by dint of their political-ethical sympathies and inclination to act and experiment on behalf of them). The second principle was that of *presence*, a kind of being-there, or full engagement and openness to mutual impact—no one ever being simply a therapist against whom things are rebounding. The third was that of *self-generation*, the need on the part of those seeking help, change, or insight of any kind to initiate their own process and conduct it largely on their own terms so that, even when calling in others with expert knowledge, they retain major responsibility for the shape and direction of the enterprise. Affinity, presence, and self-generation seem to be necessary ingredients for making a transition between old and new images and values, particularly when these relate to ultimate concerns, to shifting modes of historical continuity or what I have elsewhere called symbolic immortality (1973b).

I do not want to give the impression that everything went smoothly. There were a number of tensions in the group, one of them having to do with its degree of openness and fluidity. Openness was an organizing principle: In the fashion of "street-corner psychiatry," any Vietnam veteran was welcomed to join a group at any time. Fluidity was dictated by the life-styles of many of the veterans, who traveled extensively around the country and did not hold regular jobs. Professionals too were unable to attend every session. We established a policy of assigning three professionals to a group, with arrangements that at least one come to each meeting—but professionals became so involved in the process that there were usually two or all three present at a given group meeting.

When a veteran would appear at the group for the first time, obviously ill at ease, he would be welcomed by the others with a phrase, "You're our brother." Still, everyone came to recognize that such a policy could interfere with the probing of deep personal difficulties. A similar issue developed around the question of how accessible we would be to the media. Veterans wanted to make known the human costs of the war as part of their antiwar commitment, but after permitting a sympathetic journalist to sit in on a few of the sessions they came to recognize that group process could be interfered with by the presence of even a sensitive outsider. We eventually arrived at the policy that only veterans and professionals could be present during group sessions, but that the group could on occasion meet with interested media people after a session was over. That solution served to protect the integrity of the group while conveying to those journalists a rather vivid sense of both the impact of the war and the nature of the rap group experience.

There was also a tension among the professionals between two views of what we were doing. In the beginning a majority of the professionals felt that the essential model for our group sessions was group therapy. These professionals argued that the men were "hurting" and needed help and that if we as therapists offered anything less than group therapy we were cheating the men of what they most needed. I held to a second model which was at first a minority view. This position, while acknowledging the important therapeutic element of what we were doing, emphasized the experimental nature of our work in creating a new institution—a sustained dialogue between professionals and veterans based on a common stance of opposition to the war in which both drew upon their special knowledge, experience and needs. This model did not abolish role definition—veterans were essentially there to be helped and professionals to help—but it placed more stress on mutuality and shared commitment.

We never totally resolved the tension between these two models in the sense of all of us coming to share a single position. The veterans tended to favor the second model but did not want to be short-changed in terms of help they wanted and needed. There was a continuing dialectic between these two ways of seeing what we were doing. But those who held to the second model—which related to other experiments taking place in American society with which the veterans identified—tended to stay longer with the project. Those professionals who conceived the effort in a more narrowly defined therapeutic way, and who I suspect were less politically and ethically committed to an antiwar position, tended to leave.

Of course there were differences in professional style even within these two models. Some professionals were particularly skilled at uncovering the childhood origins of conflicts. I was seen as an authority on issues of death-and-life-continuity and on social-historical dimensions around death and survival. As a personal style, my impulse was to be something of a mediator and the group soon came to see me in that way. The group recognized and accepted differing personal styles and it was interesting to us as professionals to observe reflections of ourselves in the responses to us not only of veterans but of other professionals sharing the experience of a particular group. The veterans began with almost no knowledge of group process but they learned quickly. The focus of the group was from the beginning on the overwhelming experience of the war and on residual guilt and rage. In the process of examining these issues the men looked increasingly at their ongoing life struggles, especially their relationships with women, feelings about masculinity, and conflicts around work. There was a back-and-forth rhythm in the group between immediate life situations and war-related issues, with these gradually blending in deepening self-examination that was generally associated in turn with social and political forces in the society.

For all of us in the group there was a sense that the combination of ultimate questions (around death and survival) and experimental arrangements required that we call upon new aspects of ourselves and become something more than we had been before. Central to this process was the changing relationship between veterans and professionals. At moments the veterans could become critical of the way professionals were functioning. There was one bitter expression of resentment by a veteran who felt that the interpretations made by a professional were too conventional and tended to ignore or undercut issues very important to him. The group discussed the matter at great length. I agreed in part with the veteran, but also tried to point out that the interpretation was made in good faith. At another point one of the veterans spoke very angrily to me because I was occupied with my note-taking. I was trying to record the words of the veterans precisely because, as we had discussed earlier, I was in the group not only as a healer but also as an investigator who would write about the experience. When we discussed the matter it became clear that the veterans had no difficulty accepting that dual role. What they objected to was my not being fully "present" with them as I focused on taking notes. I thought about that and decided they were right. I ceased my note-taking and from that point on made notes only at the end of each session, a well-established pattern in the practice of psychotherapy that I had to relearn. There were, of course, many other conflicts as well, but there was also an essential feeling of moving toward authentic insight. By taking seriously such issues, as they were raised, we maintained a double level of individual-psychological interpretation and shared actuality. Taking that actuality seriously contributed to the sense of everyone's "presence."

One additional experience, not frequently encountered in healing endeavors, is worth mentioning. About six months after we initiated the groups a non-white veteran—we were not certain whether he was American Indian or Puerto Rican—came to a session and spoke rather movingly about his struggles to sustain himself and a baby left with him by a girlfriend who deserted him. He came to a second meeting but fled after just five minutes. We wondered at his behavior, and some weeks later discovered an explanation for it. Though he did not again appear in the group, he came to the VVAW office and confessed to another veteran that he had been an FBI informer. He stayed only long enough to say that he was sorry for what he had done and felt especially badly because he had liked the rap group very much. When we discussed all this in the group, reactions varied from wondering what arcane matters the FBI might have imagined we were discussing (though we concluded that he had probably been simply sent to the VVAW office and had somehow wandered into our session), to the rekindling of bitter resentment at official America, to an uneasy sense that betrayal from within —by veterans themselves (and by inference, by oneself)—was all too evident a possibility.

A COMMON SURVIVAL

The rap groups represented a struggle on the part of both veterans and psychological professionals to give form to what was in many ways a common survival, a survival for the veterans of a terrible death immersion and for the professionals of their own dislocations in relationship to the war and the society. During our most honest moments, we professionals have admitted that the experience has been as important for our souls as for theirs, for the rap groups have been one small expression (throughout the country they and related programs have probably involved, at most, a few thousand people) of a much larger cultural struggle toward creating what I have termed animating institutions (Lifton, 1973a, 1973c). Whether these emerge from existing institutions significantly modified or as "alternative institutions," they can serve the important function of providing new ways of being a professional as well as relating to professionals. While such institutions clearly have "radical" possibilities, they can also serve a genuinely conservative function in enabling those involved to find a means of continuing to relate, however critically, to the existing society and its other institutions, as opposed to retreating in embittered alienation, destructiveness, or self-destructiveness. In this and other ways the rap group experience seemed to me a mirror of psychohistorical struggles of considerable importance throughout the society.

A compelling example was the rap group's continuous preoccupation with struggles around maleness. I described these struggles in a chapter of my book entitled, somewhat whimsically but not without seriousness, "From John Wayne to Country Joe and the Fish." The men were very intent upon examining what they came to call "the John Wayne thing" in themselves—a process actively encouraged if not required by girlfriends and wives often active in the women's movement. The essence of the issue for the veterans was their deepening realization that various expressions of super-maleness encouraged in American culture were inseparable from their own relationship to war-making. They probed unsparingly the sources and fears beneath their male bravado in enthusiastically (in many cases) "joining up" and even seeking out the war. The insight that gradually imposed itself on them was that only by extricating themselves from elements of "the John Wayne thing"— notably its easy violence on behalf of unquestioned group loyalty, and male mystique of unlimited physical prowess always available for demonstration—could they, in a genuine psychological sense, extricate themselves from the war. Two significant psychological alternatives were available to them from the youth culture of the 1960s: the image of a male being no less genuinely so for manifesting tenderness, softness, aesthetic sensitivity, and awareness of feelings; and the overall social critique of war, warmaking, and the warrior ethos. It was particularly the latter that Country Joe MacDonald and his rock group (Country Joe and the Fish) gave ecstatic expression to in their celebrated song, "I Feel Like I'm Fixin' to Die Rag." A frenzied and bitter evocation of the absurdity of dying in Vietnam, the song propels one to the far reaches of the grotesque: "And it's 1, 2, 3, 4, what are we fighting for?/ Don't ask me I don't give a damn. . . . Well there ain't no time to wonder why/ Whoopee we're all gonna die." And a little later in the song: "Well come on mothers throughout the land/Pack your boys off to Vietnam/Be the first one on your block/ To have your boy come home in a box." Ironically and significantly, the "Fixin' to Die Rag" was probably the most frequently played song by men serving in Vietnam, and it is very likely that this expression of the utter absurdity and grotesqueness of dying in Vietnam will become *the* song of the Vietnam War.

The personal transformation the veterans experience (barely suggested here) can thus be seen to have had both introspective and extrospective elements. The men constantly look inward, but they also look outward at their society both in relationship to having been drawn into the war and to what they perceived as a dubious welcome upon their return. This extrospective aspect of personal change is always important—not only in experimental institutions like the rap groups but in ordinary psychotherapy and ordinary living—but is often denied or ignored because of the implicit assumption that psychological experience, being internal, is totally self-contained. It was precisely this dual vision that enabled many veterans to develop what I came to see as an animating relationship to their sense of guilt (Lifton, 1973a). In contrast to static (neurotic) forms of guilt and immobilizing self-condemnation, animating guilt can provide energy toward change via the capacity to examine the roots of that guilt in both social and individual terms. I believe that these distinctions around guilt, when pursued further, have significance both for depth-psychological theory and for the ethical questions at issue in this discussion (Lifton, 1972).

CHAPLAINS AND SHRINKS

Guilt and rage were fundamental emotions that we explored constantly in the groups. But the men had a special kind of anger best described as ironic rage toward two types of professionals with whom they came into contact in Vietnam, chaplains and "shrinks." They talked about chaplains with great anger and resentment as having blessed the troops, their mission, their guns and their killing: "Whatever we were doing—murder, atrocities—God was always on our side." Catholic veterans spoke of having confessed to meaningless transgressions ("Sure, I'm smoking dope again. I guess I blew my state of grace again") while never being held accountable for the ultimate one ("But I didn't say anything about killing"). It was as if the chaplains were saying to them, "Stay within our moral clichés as a way of draining off excess guilt, and then feel free to plunge into the business at hand."

The men also pointed to the chaplain's even more direct role of promoting false witness. One man spoke especially bitterly of "chaplains' bullshit." He illustrated what he meant by recalling the death of a close buddy—probably the most overwhelming experience one can have in combat—followed by a combined funeral ceremony-pep talk at which the chaplain urged the men to "kill more of them." Another who had carried the corpse of his closest buddy on his back after his company had been annihilated described a similar ceremony at which the chaplain spoke of "the noble sacrifice for the sake of their country" made by the dead. It is not generally recognized that the My Lai massacre occurred immediately after the grotesque death from an exploding "booby trap" of a fatherly, much-revered noncommissioned officer, which had been witnessed by many of the men. That ceremony was conducted jointly by a chaplain and the commanding officer, the former blending spiritual legitimacy to the latter's mixture of eulogy and exhortation to "kill everything in the village." A eulogy in any funeral service asks those in attendance to carry forward the work of the dead person. In war, that "work" characteristically consists of getting back at the enemy, thereby providing men with a means of resolving survivor guilt, and a "survivor mission" involving a sense not only of revenge but of carrying forth the task the fallen comrade could not see to completion. In Vietnam, the combination of a hostile environment and the absence of an identifiable "enemy" led to the frequent manipulation of grief to generate a form of false witness, a survivor mission of atrocity (Lifton, 1973a).

The men spoke with the same bitterness about "shrinks" they had encountered in Vietnam. They described situations in which they or others experienced an overwhelming combination of psychological conflict and moral revulsion, difficult to distinguish in Vietnam. Whether one then got to see a chaplain, psychiatrist, or an enlisted-man-assistant of either, had to do with where they were at the time, who was available, and the attitudes of the soldier and the authorities in his unit toward religion and psychiatry. But should he succeed in seeing a psychiatrist he was likely to be "helped" to remain at duty and (in many cases) to carry on with the daily commission of war crimes, which was what the ordinary G.I. was too often doing in Vietnam. Psychiatry for these men served to erode whatever capacity they retained for moral revulsion and animating guilt. They talked in the rap groups about ways in which psychiatry became inseparable from military authority.

But in their resentment of chaplains and psychiatrists the men were saying something more. It was one thing to be ordered by command into a situation they came to perceive as both absurd and evil, but it was quite another to have that process rationalized and justified by ultimate authorities of the spirit and mind—that is by chaplains and psychiatrists. One could even say that spiritual and psychological authority was employed to seal off in the men some inner alternative to the irreconcilable evil they were asked to embrace. In that sense the chaplains and psychiatrists formed an unholy alliance not only with the military command but also with the more corruptible elements in the soldier's psyche, corruptible elements available to all of us, whether soldier or chaplain or psychiatrist.

This "double agent" problem arises even in wars that are more psychologically defensible (such as World War II), where the alliance between spiritual-psychological authority (chaplains and shrinks), on the one hand, and the soldier's inner acceptance of killing, on the other, is buttressed by at least a degree of belief in the authenticity (or necessity) of the overall enterprise. Even then, ethical-psychological conflict occurs in everyone concerned—there is the "Catch 22" described by Heller, according to which one's very sanity in seeking escape from the environment via a psychiatric judgment of craziness renders one eligible for the continuing madness of killing and dying. But in Vietnam, that alliance took on a grotesquery extraordinary even for war, as priest and healer, in the name of their spiritual-psychological function, undermined the last vestiges of humanity in those to whom they ministered.

We can then speak of the existence of a "counterfeit universe" in which pervasive, spiritually reinforced inner corruption becomes the price of survival. In this sense the chaplains and psychiatrists were just as entrapped as the G.I.'s. For we may assume that most of them were reasonably conscientious and decent professionals—much like the writer and reader of this chapter—caught up in an institutional commitment in this particular war.

When the men spoke harshly, in our group, of military psychiatrists, we professionals of course asked ourselves whether they were talking about us. In some degree they undoubtedly were. They were raising the question whether *any* encounter with a psychiatrist, even in a context which they themselves created, and into which we were called, could be any more authentic than the counterfeit moral universe psychiatrists had lent themselves to in Vietnam.

THE ISSUES OF PROFESSIONAL INTEGRITY

I want to move now to some reflections about psychiatry in more ordinary situations. The rap group experience raised questions about the extent to which everyday work in our profession, and the professions in general, tends to wash away rather than pursue fundamental struggles around integrity—the extent to which the special armor of professionals blocks free exchange between them and the people they intend to serve.

In the rap group experience I found the issue of investigative advocacy more pressing and powerful than in other research I have done.＊ This was partly because veterans and professionals alike were more or less in the middle of the problem—the war continued and we all had painful emotions about what it was doing, and what we were doing or not doing to combat it.

But I also came to realize that, apart from the war, the work had important bearing upon a sense of long-standing crisis affecting members of all the professions—a crisis the war in Vietnam both accentuated and illuminated but by no means created. We professionals, in other words, came to the rap groups with our own need for a transformation in many ways parallel to, if more muted than, what we sought to enhance in veterans. We, too, sometimes with less awareness than they, were in the midst of struggles around living and working that had to do with intactness and wholeness, with what we have been calling integrity.

One source of perspective on that struggle, I found, was a return to

---

＊ In contrast, my Hiroshima work, in which I also experienced strong ethical involvement, was retrospective and in a sense prospective (there were immediate nuclear problems, of course, but we were not in the midst of nuclear holocaust); my study of Chinese thought reform dealt with matters of immediate importance but going on (in a cultural sense) far away; and my work with Japanese youth had much less to do with overwhelming threat and ethical crisis (Cf. Lifton, 1961, 1970a, 1970b).

the root ideas of profession, the idea of what it means to profess. Indeed, an examination of the evolution of these two words could provide something close to a cultural history of the West. The Latin prefix *pro* means forward, toward the front, forth, out, or into a public position. *Fess* derives from the Latin *fateri* or *fass,* meaning to confess, own, acknowledge. To profess (or be professed), then, originally meant a personal form of out-front public acknowledgment. And that which was acknowledged or "confessed" (until the sixteenth century) had to do with religion: with taking the vows of a religious order or declaring one's religious faith. But as society became secularized, the word came to mean "to make claim to have knowledge of an art or science" or "to declare oneself expert or proficient in" an enterprise of any kind. The noun form *profession* came to suggest not only the act of professing, but also the ordering, collectivization, and transmission of the whole process. The sequence was from *profession* or religious conviction (from the twelfth century) to a particular order of *professed persons,* such as monks and nuns (fourteenth century) to "the occupation which one possesses to be skilled in and follow," especially "the three learned professions of divinity, law, and medicine" along with the "military profession." So quickly did the connotations of specialization and application take hold that as early as 1605 Francis Bacon could complain: "Amongst so many great foundations of colleges in Europe, I find strange that they are all dedicated to professions, and none left free to Art and Sciences at large" (Lifton, 1973a).

Thus the poles of meaning around the image of profession shifted from the proclamation of personal dedication to transcendent principles to membership in and mastery of a specialized form of socially applicable knowledge and skill. In either case the profession is immortalizing—the one through the religious mode, the other through works and social-intellectual tradition. And the principles of public proclamation and personal discipline carry over from the one meaning to the other—the former taking the shape of examination and licensing, the latter of study, training, and dedication. Overall, the change was from advocacy based on faith to technique devoid of advocacy.*

---

* One can observe this process in the modern separation of "profession" from "vocation." Vocation also has a religious origin in the sense of being "called by God" to a "particular function or station." The secular equivalent became the idea of a personal "calling" in the sense of overwhelming inclination, commitment, and even destiny. But the Latin root of vocation, *vocare,* to call, includes among its meanings and derivatives: vocable, vocation, vouch; advocate, advocation, convoke, evoke, in-

To be sure, contemporary professions do contain general forms of advocacy: in law, of a body of supra-personal rules applicable to everyone; in medicine, of healing; and in psychiatry, of human principles of psychological well-being and growth. But immediate issues of value-centered advocacy and choice (involving groups and causes served and consequences thereof) are mostly ignored. In breaking out of the premodern trap of immortalization by personal surrender to faith, the "professional" has fallen into the modern trap of pseudo-neutrality and covert immortalization of technique. As a result, our professions are all too ready to offer their techniques to anyone or anything. I am not advocating a return to pure faith as a replacement for the contemporary idea of what profession means. But I am suggesting that the notion of profession needs to include these issues of advocacy and ethical commitment. The psychiatrist in Vietnam, for example, whatever his intentions, found himself in collusion with the military in conveying to individual G.I.'s an overall organizational message: "Do your indiscriminate killing with confidence that you will receive expert medical-psychological help if needed." Keeping in mind Camus' warning that men should become neither victims nor executioners, this can be called—at least in Vietnam—the psychiatry of the executioner (Camus, 1946). I do not exempt myself from this critique, as I served as a military psychiatrist in the Korean War under conditions that had at least some parallels to those we are discussing.

Three well-known principles of military psychiatry developed during recent wars are *immediacy* (a soldier is treated as soon as possible), *proximity* (close to the combat area), and *expectancy* (everyone under treatment is from the beginning made to expect that he will return to duty with his unit). There is a certain logic to these principles. Their use very often does eliminate or minimize the secondary gains from illness and the chronic symptomatology that would otherwise ensue when men are sent to the rear to undergo prolonged psychiatric hospitalization, as well as feelings of failure and unmanliness that become associated with eventual medical discharge from the military. One psy-

---

voke, provoke, and revoke. Advocacy is thus built into the original root and continuing feel of the word vocation; and vocation in turn is increasingly less employed in connection with the work a man or woman does. If we do not say profession, we say "occupation," which implies seizing, holding, or simply filling in space in an area or in time; or else "job," a word of unclear origin that implies a task, activity, or assignment that is, by implication, self-limited or possibly part of a larger structure including many related jobs, but not, in essence, related to an immortalizing tradition or principle.

chiatric report from Vietnam describes the use of these principles and the assumption that those requiring treatment "had run into some difficulty in interpersonal relations in their units that caused them to be extruded from these groups," so that "The therapeutic endeavor . . . was to facilitate the men's integration into their own groups (units) through integration into the group of ward patients" (Bloch, 1969).

The approach seems convincing, until one evaluates some of the conditions under which atrocities occurred or were avoided. I spent ten hours interviewing a man who had been at My Lai and had not fired nor even pretended he was firing. (Among the handful who did not fire most held their guns in position as if firing in order to avoid the resentment of the majority actively participating in the atrocity.) Part of what sustained this man and gave him strength to risk ostracism was his very distance from the group. Always a "loner," he had as a child been raised near the ocean and engaged mainly in such solitary activities as boating and fishing. Hence, though an excellent soldier, he was less susceptible than others to group influence, and in fact remained sufficiently apart from other men in his company to be considered "maladapted" to that immediate group situation (Lifton, 1973a). One must distinguish between group integration and personal integrity—the latter including moral and psychological elements that connect one to social and historical context beyond the immediate. Group integration can readily undermine integrity—in Vietnam for both the soldier and the psychiatrist who must grapple with his own struggles to adapt to a military institution with its goals of maximum combat strength, and to a combat situation of absurdity and evil. No wonder that, in Vietnam, he found little ethical space in which to move. The clear implication here is that the psychiatrist, no less than the combat soldier, is confronted with the important question of the group he is to serve and, above all, the nature and consequences of its immediate and long-range mission. To do that he must overcome the technicist assumption we fall into all too easily, namely: "Because I am a healer, anything I do, anywhere, is good." It may not be.

THE PROFESSIONAL ROLE

I wonder how many colleagues shared my sense of chilling illumination in picking up the October, 1971 issue of *The American Journal of Psychiatry* and finding in it two articles by psychiatrists about Vietnam: one entitled "Organizational Consultation in a Combat Unit"

(Bey and Smith, 1971), and the other "Some Remarks on Slaughter" (Gault, 1971). The first lives up to its title in providing a military-managerial view of the psychiatrist's task. The authors invoke a scholarly and "responsible" tone as they describe the three principles of combat psychiatry and trace their historical development. They then elaborate their own "workable method of organizational consultation developed and employed in a combat division in Vietnam." The method combines these principles of military psychiatry with "an organizational case study method" recently elaborated for industry at the Menninger Foundation, which, according to the authors, has bearing on possible developments in community psychiatry. Their professional voice sounds tempered, practical, and modest as they tell of their team approach (with trained corpsmen), of interviews with commanding officers, chaplains, and influential noncoms, and acknowledge that commanders "were far better prepared to work out solutions to their problems than me, since their area of expertise was in administration and fighting whereas ours was in the area of helping them to see where their feelings might be interfering with their use of these skills."

It was enough for psychiatric consultants to serve as an "observing ego" to the particular military unit. To back up that position they quote, appropriately enough, from an article by General W. C. Westmoreland recommending that the psychiatrist assume "a personnel management consultation type role." The title of that article by General Westmoreland—"Mental Health—An Aspect of Command"—makes quite clear just whom psychiatry in the military is expected to serve.

The authors' combination of easy optimism and concern for everyone's feelings and for the group as a whole makes one almost forget the kinds of activities the members of that group were engaged in. Reading that lead article in the official journal of the national organization of American psychiatrists gave me a disturbing sense of how far this kind of managerial technicism could take a profession, and its reasonably decent individual practitioners, into ethical corruption. What is most significant about the article is that the authors never make mention of the slightest conflict—in themselves and their psychiatric team any more than in the officers and men the team deals with—between group integration and personal integrity. Either they were too numbed to be aware of such conflict, or (more likely) they did not consider it worthy of mention in a scientific paper.

Gault's article was a particularly welcome antidote, even if a bit more hidden in the inside pages. As his title makes clear, Gault's tone is informed by an appropriate sense of outrage. Significantly, his vantage point was not Vietnam but Fort Knox, Kentucky, where he examined large numbers of men returning from combat. He was thus free of the requirement of integration with a combat unit, and we sense immediately a critical detachment from the atrocity-producing situation.

Gault (1971) introduces the idea of "the psychology of slaughter," combining the dictionary definition of that word ("the extensive, violent, bloody or wanton destruction of life; carnage") with a psychological emphasis upon the victim's defenselessness ("whether . . . a disarmed prisoner or an unarmed civilian"). He can "thus . . . distinguish slaughter from the mutual homicide of the actual combatants in military battle." He sets himself the interpretive task of explaining, how "relatively normal men overcame and eventually neutralized their natural repugnance toward slaughter." He is rigorously professional as he ticks off six psychological themes or principles contributing to slaughter, and yet his ethical outrage is present in every word. His themes are: "The enemy is everywhere . . . (or) the universalization of the enemy"; "the enemy is not human . . . (or) the 'cartoonization' of the victim"; the "dilution" or "vertical dilution" of responsibility; "the pressure to act"; "the natural dominance of the psychopath"; and "sheer firepower . . . (so that) terrified and furious teenagers by the tens of thousands have only to twitch their index finger, and what was a quiet village is suddenly a slaughterhouse."

Gault sensitively documents each of these themes in ways very consistent with experiences conveyed to me during rap groups and individual interviews. He ends his article with illustrative stories: of prisoners refusing to give information being thrown out of helicopters as examples to others; of a new combat commander who refused to shoot a 12-year-old "dink" accidentally encountered by the company while setting up an ambush, and thereby deeply jeopardized himself with his own men, who in turn saw the whole company jeopardized by the survival of someone who might, even as a prisoner, convey information about the ambush. Gault admits he does not know "why similar experiences provoke so much more guilt in one man than in another," and, still professionally cautious (perhaps overly so), remains "unwilling to attempt to draw any large lessons from my observations." At the end he insists only that "in Vietnam a number of fairly ordinary young men have been psychologically ready to engage in slaughter and that moreover this readiness is by no means incomprehensible."

One senses that these stories made a profound impact upon him, that he became a survivor of Vietnam by proxy and that the article was his way of giving form to that survival as well as resolving his own integration-integrity conflict as a morally sensitive psychiatrist in the military at the time of the Vietnam War.* He was able to call forth his revulsion toward the slaughter (and, by implication, his advocacy of life-enhancing alternatives) as a stimulus to understanding and to bring to bear on the Vietnam War a valuable combination of professional insight and ethical awareness.

We do not have follow-up studies on psychiatrists and their spiritual-psychological state after service in Vietnam. I have talked to a number of them, and my impression is that they find it no easier to come to terms with their immersion in the counterfeit universe than does the average G.I. They too feel themselves deeply compromised. They seem to require a year or more before they can begin to confront the inner contradictions they experienced. They too are survivors of Vietnam, and of a very special kind. I know of one or two who have embarked upon valuable survivor missions, parallel to and partly in affiliation with that of VVAW as an organization. But what is yet to emerge, though I hope it will before too long, is a detailed personal account by a psychiatrist of his struggles with group integration and individual integrity, and with the vast ramifications of the counterfeit that this paper only begins to suggest.

Put simply, American culture has so technicized the idea of psychiatric illness and cure that the psychiatrist or psychoanalyst is thrust into a stance of scientifically based spiritual omniscience—a stance he is likely to find much too seductive to refuse entirely. Anointed with both omniscience and objectivity, and working within a market economy, his allegedly neutral talents become available to the highest bidder. In a militarized society they are equally available to the war-makers.

The Technicist Model

The technical model in psychiatry works something like this: A machine, the mind-body function of the patient, has broken down; another machine, more scientifically sophisticated—the psychiatrist—is called upon to "treat" the first machine; and the treatment process itself,

---

* This assumption that the article was an expression of Gault's own survivor formulation, which I made originally only on the basis of reading it (and, of course, on my experience, personal and professional, with the psychology of the survivor), was strongly confirmed by a brief talk he and I had when we met as members of a panel on Vietnam veterans at a psychoanalytic conference.

being technical, has nothing to do with place, time, or individual idiosyncrasy. It is merely a matter of being a technical-medical antagonist of a "syndrome" or "disease." Nor is this medical-technical model limited to physicians—nonmedical psychoanalysts and psychotherapists can be significantly affected by it. And the problem is not so much the medical model as such as it is the technicism operating within that model.* The technicism in turn feeds (and is fed by) a denial of acting within and upon history.

To be sure no psychiatrist sees himself as functioning within this admittedly overdrawn model. But its lingering technicism is very much with us and can have the catastrophic results we have observed. Even psychological groups bent on breaking out of this technicism, such as some within the humanistic psychology movement (or "third force"), can be rendered dependent upon it by their very opposition, to the point of being unable to evolve an adequate body of theory and practice of their own.

An alternative perspective, in my judgment, must be not only psychohistorical, but also psychoformative. By the latter I mean a stress upon the process of inwardly re-creating all that is perceived or encountered (1973b). As in the work of Langer (1942, 1953, 1962) and Cassirer (1944, 1946) and others (Collingwood, 1956; Whitehead, 1948, 1958) my stress is upon what can be called a formative-symbolic process, upon symbolization rather than any particular symbol (in the sense of one thing standing for another). The approach connects with much in twentieth-century thought, and seeks to overcome the nineteenth-century emphasis upon mechanism, with its stress upon breakdown of elements into component parts—an emphasis inherited, at least in large part, by psychoanalysis, as the word itself suggests (Vankelovich & Barrett, 1970; Kuhn, 1962; Whyte, 1944). Twentieth-century technicism could be described as an aberrant (and in a sense nostalgic) re-creation of nineteenth-century mechanism. In contrast, a focus upon images and forms (the latter more structured and more enduring than the former) and upon their continuous development and re-creation gives the psychiatrist a

---

* In this sense I am in sympathy with Szasz (1961) and Laing (1960, 1961) in their stress on the repressive uses of the medical model, but also with Humphrey Osmond's defense of the enduring, human core of the medical model, which has "stood the test of millennia" (Osmond, 1970) and contains still untapped resources for us. I believe that the medical model of disease and healing is still needed by psychiatrists, at least in some of our work and thought, but that it must itself be liberated from its technicist fetters.

way of addressing historical forces without neglecting intrapsychic concerns.

The antiwar passions of a particular Vietnam veteran, for instance, had to be understood as a combined expression of many different psychic images and forms: the Vietnam environment and the forces shaping it; past individual history; the post-Vietnam American experience, including VVAW and the rap groups and the historical forces shaping these; and the various emanations of guilt, rage, and altered self-process that could and did take shape. Moreover, professionals, like myself, who entered into the lives of these veterans—with our own personal and professional histories, personal struggles involving the war, and much else—became a part of the overall image-form constellation.

Psychiatrists have a great temptation to swim with an American tide that grants them considerable professional status but resists, at times quite fiercely, serious attempts to alter existing social and institutional arrangements. As depth psychologists and psychoanalysts we make a kind of devil's bargain that we can plunge as deeply as we like into intrapsychic conflicts while not touching too critically upon historical dimensions that question those institutional arrangements. We often accept this dichotomy quite readily with the rationale that, after all, we are not historians or sociologists. But the veterans' experience shows that one needs extrospection as well as introspection to deal with psychological conflicts, particularly at a time of rapid social change. And I believe that a general psychological paradigm of "death and the continuity of life" (Lifton, 1973b) helps us to achieve this dual perspective, and to recognize the interplay of psychological and moral elements in relationship to ultimate commitments and our involvement in that interplay.

All this points toward the need for a transformation of the healing professions themselves. In my work with veterans I restated a model of change I had elaborated in earlier work, based on a sequence of confrontation, reordering, and renewal (Lifton, 1961, 1973a). The idea is worth stating at least as a model—not with any expectation of instant transformation, but with the recognition that, here and there, people are already pursuing it, and will undoubtedly continue to do so in forms we have not yet imagined. Confrontation for the veterans meant confronting the idea of dying in Vietnam, often through the death of a buddy. For psychiatrists it would mean confrontation of our own concerns about death, mortality and immortality, and our professional struggles with them. Reordering meant the working through of difficult emotions around guilt and rage; for psychiatry this would mean seeking animating relationships to the same emotions in ourselves and recognizing and making use of our experience of despair (Farber, 1966). Renewal for veterans meant a new sense of self and world, including an enhanced playfulness. The professional parallels are there, and much can be said for the evolution of more playful modes of investigation and therapy.

I want to conclude with two quotations. The first is from Stanley Milgram, who performed controversial experiments on the willingness of people to cause pain and even endanger the lives of others, when authoritatively requested to do so. Whatever one's view of the scientific and moral aspects of these "Eichmann experiments," one of Milgram's own conclusions is worth thinking about: "Men are doomed if they act only within the alternatives handed down to them" (1963, p. 377).

And finally, Joseph Campbell, perhaps American's most distinguished student of mythology, said: "A god outgrown becomes immediately a life-destroying demon. The form has to be broken and the energies released" (1956, p. 43).

11

PSYCHOTHERAPY WITH VIETNAM VETERANS: OBSERVATIONS AND SUGGESTIONS

The military years, and particularly the time spent at war, are likely to constitute an important phase of any veteran's life. This chapter is intended to aid psychotherapists in becoming more sensitive to the implications of military experiences for later life and in dealing with them when treating Vietnam veterans.

In writing this chapter, I will be drawing on what I know from having served with the Army for a year in Vietnam and from having reflected on that experience repeatedly as a client in therapy, as a therapist with other veterans, and as a member of an interdisciplinary research team on a study entitled "Veterans and Controls: Impact of the Vietnam War.*

Authors always worry about being misunderstood. In my case, the fear is that the emphasis here on veteran status and military experiences will be taken as either an argument or an excuse for an exaggerated focus on this part of people's lives. Therapists concerned about preserving a balance in the attention given to various developmental periods and areas of functioning can be reassured. My aim is not to

I am grateful for the helpful comments on earlier drafts of this chapter made by a number of colleagues: Florence Pincus, Chaim Shatan, John Talbott, Jerome Fine; Julie Spain and Susan See.

* This study began in September 1974 and received funding from the Russell Sage Foundation, the Hazen Foundation, the Boehm Foundation and the National Council of Churches. Major grants were later provided by the National Institute of Mental Health and the Veterans Administration. The author is one of five co-principal investigators for this work, which is being conducted at the Center for Policy Research, 475 Riverside Drive, New York, N.Y. 10027. Data to be collected consist of four-hour interviews with 1200 males, ages 22-35, with samples in four locations nationally and with stratifications for race, education, military service and age.

upset that balance, but rather to add to it an understanding of how the military past may still be functioning now. Therapists who, on the other hand, are excited by a presentation that invokes the intricate relation between politics and history on the one side and psychology on the other should proceed with caution.

It would be a mistake to conclude from the following that any Vietnam veterans who seek psychotherapy ultimately do so because of their war experiences. Nor should a therapist take the emphasis here to mean that psychotherapy with Vietnam veterans *must* deal explicitly with their war experiences before termination. Responding therapeutically to the veteran's reluctance to discuss troubling experiences is one matter. It is an entirely different matter for a therapist, armed with a fixed notion of what makes people tick, to dictate an agenda. Except under unusual circumstances, the latter practice is simply bad therapy.

OBSTACLES FOR THERAPISTS

Therapeutic progress with veterans depends, in part, on the therapist's refusing to accept uncritically certain common biases and misconceptions about Vietnam. These potential obstacles are distinct from the highly personal attitudes and prejudices usually included under the rubric of countertransference. It may be useful to discuss a number of them before making positive suggestions.

Seeing Veterans as Villains or Victims

Vietnam veterans generally have strong feelings and maintain entrenched attitudes about the war and their role in it. A therapist, too, is likely to have been affected by the polarized attitudes spread throughout the country during the war. These include the insistence that "no normal person could have been involved in atrocities," or the equally questionable but contrary belief that "people in the military were no more than pawns." Either of these views may be expressed in very subtle forms. After speaking with a veteran, a therapist might feel, for example, "If it had been me, *I* wouldn't have gone," or "If I had gone, *I* wouldn't have done what *he* did," or "If I had done something like that, *I* wouldn't have tied myself in such neurotic knots about it." In contrast, yet still inauthentically, a therapist might "set up" a veteran as victim or idol, in that the veteran "has suffered so much" or "has borne so much so nobly" or "has, at least, seen and lived some real adventures."

While the war was going on, people generally related to its protagonists and antagonists either by passing judgment or romanticizing them. These tendencies, though now muted, are still with us. This means that therapists need to be careful to avoid being taken over by such attitudes, which distort and simplify the complexity of human experience.

Equating War Neuroses with Compensation Neuroses

Some (Dancey, 1960; Kalinowski, 1950) purport that post-war psychological distress among veterans is wholly conditioned by the disbursement of disability pensions. This reduction of veteran problems to an artifact of public policy is tantamount to focusing on only one of the aspects of a veteran's situation and ignoring the rest.

Present policies regarding veterans unquestionably have a distorting effect that can be understood in psychological as well as in sociological, political and economic terms. The individual therapist must, of course, be mindful of these distortions. But the argument that "war neurosis" is *nothing but* "compensation neurosis" has been more than adequately answered by follow-up studies that document "traumatic neuroses" appearing years and decades after World War II among veterans for whom compensation was not an issue (Futterman & Pumpian-Mindlin, 1951; Archibald & Tuddenham, 1965).

Misinterpreting Research

Some therapists are frank enough to say outright, "Don't bother with the war. If it wasn't that, it would've been something else. The predisposing factors are what's important." Those who adopt this predisposition and thesis (cf. Chapter 8) cite various research findings of significant correlations between pre- and post-war indices of functioning. When the correlations are high, or when they account for more variance than measures associated with military service do, the tempting conclusion is that "the war does not matter."

With respect to the variables measured, such a conclusion may or may not be correct. But whatever the variables are, this attitude is altogether inappropriate for clinical work, for two reasons: First, in psychotherapy, what matters to the individual veteran is of primary importance. What he cares about and how he sees his experiences are the most crucial data for the therapist. It may be interesting to compare an individual veteran's perspective with what other veterans feel or with the picture that researchers develop of veterans in general. But second-hand or aggregate accounts can never do justice to the richness of one person's experience. For this reason, conclusions drawn from quantitative research are, at best, of secondary importance in clinical work.

A second factor places further limits on the direct applicability of quantitative research findings as guidelines for psychotherapy. In life and in therapy, in contrast to what is usually assumed in research, the present can never be fully explained as a product of the past. Each moment of living brings its own possibilities for creative uniqueness. This must be true if change and growth through therapy are to be feasible in the first place. Furthermore, the unique potential of any present moment includes the possibility of looking freshly at the past. This opportunity, when taken, is what allows a patient to accord to a past moment that was glossed over in the living of it some of the uniqueness that now seems appropriate in retrospect. This means that, in a very real way, the present can also determine the past, and further fresh looks to come in the future can determine it too.

Research based on the assumption that the present is a product of the past cannot, therefore, say reliably whether or how much the war matters—for an individual veteran or for veterans as a group. The truth is that we have yet to receive the final word on this matter. And our present estimates will only improve if we remain open to continual revisions.

Assuming That "the War" Is Only an Abstraction

Clinicians are generally well prepared to respond to patients' difficulties arising from such experiences as personal insults, rejection, the loss of a friend through death, and family conflict. Confronted by the trauma of war itself, however, many therapists erroneously believe that what is "really" going on is something else "more concrete."

Part of the misunderstanding stems from identifying the "real" problems of life with those that most people bring to treatment. Psychotherapy usually focuses on everyday concerns, like growing up, getting along with people and growing old. Anything removed from these topics may be misconstrued as secondary, elaborated or abstracted.

People who live through catastrophic events, like sensitive people who are "touched" by suffering even at a distance, may be genuinely troubled by questions that seem extraneous to what is "real" for most others. This is understandable if one sees that catastrophic upheaval disturbs the very foundations of life in the world, which are taken for granted in everyday life. The veteran who perseverates about clashing armies, blooded nations, conspiracy in high places, the fate of humanity itself—as well as the one who falls deathly silent on such matters—may very well be trying to address his pain to those realms where meaning was once secure for him, but is no longer.

Failing to Comprehend the Intrinsic Conflict of War

Therapists might be more responsive to veteran trauma if they could appreciate that war, in itself, may be problematic quite concretely for the person swept up in it. Like any other conflict that arises in living, the conflict of war does not necessarily cease with the event that evoked it.

War is only possible in a particular frame of mind—one that "absolutizes" experience. A soldier fights "to the end." He must either cooperate by risking his life or risk punishment by death. The struggle against the enemy is for the highest stakes. Ultimate sacrifice hangs in the balance. Human relationships take on extreme intensity during war, but so does everything else—including the extremes of indifference and hedonism of soldierly pastimes.

This "absolutizing" becomes a problem for soldiers or veterans who reflect enough to have it turn back on itself. In this turn the soldier sees that the ultimate cooperation is not only with his compatriots. The collusion is with the enemy as well or the battle cannot go on. Men go to war, in part, to prove their worth, only to be shown by it, if they open their eyes, the utter insignificance and expendability of any human life. A soldier stakes everything to end the fight by fighting. But then, why fight at all? All reason slips away and one is left having risked everything for nothing. It is this dawning sense of "everything for nothing" that makes soldiers at war so desperate for "support back home," and that has left many veterans of Vietnam so bitter that they did not get it.

Ultimately, then, treatment of Vietnam veterans raises the question of how psychotherapy can provide a healing antidote to the individual's experience of war and its aftermath. This question provides the backdrop for the positive suggestions that follow in the next section of this chapter. It will be raised explicitly again in the third part and in the conclusion.

RESPONDING TO THE ISSUES

This part of the chapter discusses a few issues that are likely to arise in psychotherapy with Vietnam veterans. All of the following must be qualified, however, by noting that little justice can be done in such a short space to the huge variation in subjective experience from veteran to veteran.

The suggestions to therapists presented here are all instances of two principal therapeutic objectives: listening to and exploring military experiences. First, *listening:* It is easy to say "Listen!" but hard to do it. With some men, it might mean being there with them attentively as they go over painful details session after session until the pain eases and some firmer grasp on the experience develops for them. Others might need, in addition to being heard, the gentle reassuranace that they do not have to try to "get it all out" at once, that at difficult moments in therapy the option is always open to take a break and come back to the hard part after a rest.

Second, *exploring:* By this I mean asking questions like, "What was that like for you?" In some cases the responses may lead to a very definite event, trauma or association that seems to account for much of the psychological pressure of the war experiences. It may be a buddy's death, a sin of commission or omission, a lie incorporated by a veteran into his "war stories" that he cannot bear to give up, etc. But one must be careful not to fall into the form of mechanistic thinking that expects a cure to be achieved once and for all when this seeming "core" is brought to light and "abreacted."

Work with many veterans will not lead to such a "core," unless, of course, the therapist's view of what the core "really is" is imposed and "bought" by the veteran. Furthermore, even for those with whom a more extensive exploration does lead to some very major psychological factor "behind" the war's importance, one must not be seduced into thinking that the exploration is over for all time.

Although exploring in this way has no absolute endpoint, it does have a goal—the exploration itself. Crucial is the slow but sure learning that, contrary to one's worst fears, painful memories can be brought to light, cherished but brittle perspectives on life and the world can be allowed to bend and give, and a haunting past can, to some extent, be communicated, shared and allowed to open further onto a more liveable present.

Reluctance to Communicate

Many veterans believe they cannot communicate what it was really like serving in the military—especially in Vietnam—to anyone who was not there. What lies "behind" this belief varies greatly. Some will appear resentful and bitter, for example, that "nobody knows or want to know"; some will express their despair over the impossibility of sharing the burden of the experience; others will pride themselves on having known and seen what most people cannot fathom; still others will say that the whole thing is "no big deal."

Diagnosticians may be quick to note that veterans who hold such attitudes may be avoiding the very form of relating that will make things easier for them. This diagnostic truism may not, however, constitute a therapeutic response. A therapist who emphasizes how the veteran is making his own problems may very well be experienced as yet another of society's representatives who deny the reality of the war and the very real consequences it has in people's lives.

To avoid this bind, therapists can attempt to initiate a dialogue beyond subtle accusations and self-accusations by saying something like: "I don't know whether you are interested in talking about your experiences in the military, or whether you consider them relevant to what you want to get out of your coming here. I feel, though, that it would help me understand you better if I hear from you about *that* part of your life."

A therapist who puts it this way can easily take "no" for an answer, while still having registered clearly an unpressured invitation. If the veteran's response *is* "no," one could then say, "Fine, we certainly don't have to get into that. And you may *never* want to. I just would like you to know that if you *ever* feel that it's something you want to explore, I'm willing to get into it with you."

Of course, many veterans will not say "no," will not need to be asked about it so gingerly; they will jump right in. The next question for the therapist, then, is how to prepare for what he or she is likely to hear.

Preparing to Listen

Some therapists like to prepare themselves for working with people whose experiences are unfamiliar by reading the professional literature (see also Egendorf, 1977; Lifton, 1973a; Mantell & Pilisuk, 1975; VA, 1972; Chapter 4 for a review of the research). For those who prefer writings by people who were in Vietnam, there are fiction and autobiographies by Caputo (1977), Hugett (1973), Kovic (1976) and Stone (1973), as well as poem and story collections written, edited and published by Vietnam veterans of the First Casualty Press—*Free Fire Zone* (1975); *Winning Hearts and Minds* (1972). Regardless of the amount and type of reading or what you know already about veterans, the best preparation is first to dwell for a time on whatever you *do* know. Then ask what, in your *own* experience, might need to be taken into account before you can respond as fully as you might like as a veteran's therapist.

The answer(s) to that question will be highly personalized, but probably categorizable under two general headings. The first has to do with what veterans are like. Some have killed, raped, burned people's homes, or witnessed these and other gruesome events. One whole set of potential therapist reactions that can hamper the capacity to listen includes sentiments like horror, pain, hurt, pity, guilt, fear, etc. Therapists differ according to which aspects of their clients' experiences are disturbing and what form the disturbance takes. Those who resisted or otherwise avoided the draft may feel some mixture of guilt, disdain, and defensiveness on hearing a veteran complain that antiwar protesters dragged out the war and almost got him killed. Female therapists may be sensitive to the very common accounts veterans give of prostitution and sexual abuse of women by G.I.'s.

A second source of difficulty for therapists may be their own image of themselves as members of a helping profession. Although therapists are usually well trained to recognize when feelings such as lust, jealousy and anger arise in them, they are generally less skillful at discerning and acknowledging sentiments such as hate, disgust, repugnance, condescension, and contempt. Work with veterans may very well call up such feelings, and therapists need to be prepared to see these "negative" reactions in themselves, the better to "deal with" them in such a way that therapeutic work can proceed. This "dealing with" has to take into account the therapist's need to feel reasonably comfortable in order to be effective. But one must also keep in mind that many veterans' worst fear is that they will never be able to open up to anyone who was not in the war without the other person being shocked or disgusted.

Excessive Feeding Off War Experiences

In contrast to the apparent reluctance described above, some veterans may seem wrapped up with their war experiences to the exclusion of anything else. They may talk a great deal about their military past and volunteer a flood of information. What they say might be a perseverative rehashing of events that represent serious traumata to them. Or their talk may seem like highly systematized, defensive maneuverings, paranoid style. A strong temptation for therapists working with such people is to search for ways to make them stop this excessive fixing on one part of their past.

My own experience has been that therapy is much more effective when the negatives—for example, what to *stop* doing—are translated by the therapist into some positive direction. This might amount to no more than formulating a question that opens the possibility of some realm beyond present limitations, as in the following approach: Veterans who talk about the war in a perseverative or paranoid way can be seen as similar, in one important respect, to those who tell their war stories impersonally, as if they were not even touched by what happened. With all of these veterans, one may infer that they lack skill and understanding as to how to deal with their experiences beyond familiar, well-entrenched boundaries. A therapist may avoid provoking more "resistance" by addressing this deficiency directly rather than interpreting it. For example, one might say, "From the way you emphasize and keep talking about it, I know there's something very important to you in all that." And then, "Of course, being in Vietnam probably made some kind of impact on everybody who was there. But what is the special meaning it has for you?" One could also say, "You've already told me a lot. Maybe it would help to limit additional details for now and try to understand the importance all that has for you." Attempts to push people beyond boundaries they have established for themselves are usually less effective than invitations to peek over the other side.

Vividness: Signs of Vitality

Therapists who work with veterans may note that war memories, years later, can be surprisingly vivid and even fresher than the events that happened the day before or the previous week. For some veterans this contrast between sharp memories of military years and vaguer recollections of the time since then underscores the anti-climactic quality of their post-war lives. They may come to therapy hoping, in part, to find release from the feeling of being overly domesticated, or hemmed in, not unlike the way so many originally went off to Vietnam, as happens in all wars, to flee the ennui of civilian life.

Through therapy, some of these men will find a new quest for themselves in psychological inquiry. For them, self-scrutiny, or "the journey inward," may provide a more civil adventure, with its own risks and rewards, triumphs, and defeats. In such cases it will be fairly easy for the therapist to initiate a line of questioning like: "What is it like for you when this feeling comes on of having to bug out (or blow up or run away or do whatever the problematic response is)?" Other queries can follow like, "What brings this on?" "What's happening with you that this suddenly feels as if it's the only way to handle things?" With men who learn quickly to ask these kinds of questions of themselves, ennui may soon give way to curiosity. The hemmed-in feeling may then diminish as new psychological "territory" opens for them and realizations develop of actual options available to them.

Others, however, will not be so ready to convert to the practices of psychological self-exploration. With them it is particularly important that the therapist be sensitive to the vividness of old memories as a sign that in addition to whatever flatness, enervation or closed-off feeling may mark this person's present existence, some spark of life is still accessible. This is a clue to therapists to hear and acknowledge not only whatever horror may be evident in what a veteran recalls, but also whatever might be exciting, enlivening and thrilling about these memories.

Listening for this vital or "positive" aspect can open up important therapeutic possibilities even when the vivid memories carry such deadening or "negative" feelings as disappointment, hurt, disaffection, or self-castigation. In such cases, it is useful first to acknowledge these negative feelings, by saying, for example, "I can tell that's really upsetting for you," or "That certainly sounds like it was a big blow." A next step might be to point to the positive aspects that "go with" the negative reaction to the situation, as in "You must have wanted such-and-such pretty badly," or "You obviously cared a lot about that," or "It sounds like that was quite important to you." By acknowledging the hurt, pain, or other "negative" feeling first, the therapist avoids the possibility that the next comment, which points to the "positive" aspect, will be experienced as "jumping ahead" or as "missing the point."

Once it is established that the veteran *did* care very much about something "back then," or that he really *did* "get into things" at one time, one can ask what it is that keeps him from bringing the same care or energy to life now. And as this inquiry proceeds, it would probably be helpful to bring back the vivid memories from time to time as long as these remain a principal mode of access to vital feelings.

Intimacy and Authority

Like others, veterans can be troubled by difficulties with relationships, particularly with those they are close with or responsible to. It is even likely that as the war recedes in memory, the strains felt in connection with people at home and at work will become, if they have not already, the most common immediate complaints that veterans bring to treatment (see Chapter 14).

As with most other areas of therapeutic work with veterans, the focus on present relationships may or may not include explicit reference to military experiences. In any event, it will be useful for the therapist to be aware of how military experiences may be part of what colors and influences present difficulties in living. By way of illustration, following are three themes that commonly crop up when veterans explore their difficulties in the relating with others.

1. *Sex in the Military.* The military world denigrates women and treats sex as a commodity even more blatantly than the civilian world does. Men were "socialized" into the Vietnam era military through a training ritual which included castigation for not being "man" enough by being called "pussies" and "cunts" (see Chapter 4 and Eisenhart, 1975). Prostitution was not only accepted but openly encouraged. Generally, sex was viewed as a bodily indulgence to be paid for or "ripped off," to "have a good time," or to "get your rocks off," rather than as an expression of a loving relationship based on openness and trust.

2. *Authority in the Military.* Military orders are given for reasons, but rarely, and to a much lesser degree than obtains in civilian life, do these reasons include the welfare, respect, feelings, and good will of the people who are subject to the orders. Soldiers soon become accustomed to being disregarded and learn to expect that those "over" them do not have their interests at heart. Predictably, resentments run high. The military way of dealing with them is to provide rationalizations (frustration is considered a good tool for whipping men into shape) and "releases" (drunkenness and brawls are sanctioned in their appropriate place and time; drugs were never openly sanctioned, but they were widely available and sought for sedative effect all the same). In all of this, little or no attention is given to developing ways in which superiors and subordinates can communicate, cooperate, and engage in give and take.

Revulsion with this pattern may, to a limited extent, lead a man to search out a civilian career outside of highly regimented and bureaucratized institutions. But the effect of military experience is often to leave men with the routine expectation, at some level, that any hierarchical structure is exactly like the military. Resignation to this expectation may be "adaptive" for veterans who find work in police and fire departments, the civil service and large corporations. But if the resignation is not complete, or if it becomes necessary for a veteran to try to live beyond regimentation, that routinized expectation and whatever is associated with it may make his life quite painful and difficult.

3. *Legitimated Murder.* The issue of greatest importance here has literally to do with life and death. A civil existence becomes possible among people when they share at least a minimal respect for life. The military way is to call this into question. During the Vietnam era, we were ordered to shriek "Kill! Kill!" as we ran headlong and thrust bayonets into rubber, human surrogates. We were taught to sing, "I want to go to Vee-yet Nah-am and kill the Vee-yet Cah-ong" as we marched. Some hundreds of thousands of us (nobody knows precisely how many) had to take this further when actually thrown into the slaughter.

In working with veterans, therapists may be called on to help men free themselves from these psychic legacies. Some may view what is needed as an analysis of veterans' transference to the military. Others may call for an extinction of maladaptive behaviors. I prefer to approach the matter experientially, since this allows for easier communication with someone going through the process. From this perspective, the freeing comes with greater sensitivity, as in learning to distinguish subtle variations in what formerly appeared monolithic. Equations like "women =bitches to fuck" or "people over you=ass holes" or "once a killer, always a killer" fade. These are supplanted by finer gradations in both thought and feeling as one comes to sense more acutely the evolving complexity of one's life.

Attachments to Military Ways

Years later, veterans may be living in subtle ways as if they were still in the military. Attachments to these ways generally fall into one of two basic categories: (1) ideological attachments and (2) distortions in the feeling mode or capacity to feel.

1. *Ideological Attachments.* Men have lived and even thrived in military institutions for millenia. Many today still do. Some argue that it is a "good deal"—high pay, abundant benefits, a chance to see the world. Others find that military life provides self-respect, a sense of accomplishment and the satisfaction of living beyond the humdrum life of folks at home.

Many Vietnam veterans cling to the positive aspects of military life nostalgically and pride themselves on living according to the lessons the military taught them. Problems may arise for them, however, when they fail to differentiate clearly the aspects that are inappropriate for civilian living. Wives and children may not respond well when told "Learn respect!" with the tone a sergeant uses with a private. A therapist need not deprecate military discipline, or any other positively valued aspect of military life. What matters is the need to bring a veteran's attention to the ways in which certain military approaches to situations fit poorly in civilian life. A therapist might say to a veteran: "It's good that you still appreciate how well you worked out ways to manage your life there in the military. But now we're seeing together that those ways are not always well suited to deal with what is going on in your life at present. It looks like you'll have to be creative and come up with a few new ways of dealing with things now."

2. *Distortions in the Feeling Mode.* Men who disavow any ideological attachment to the military may still be bound up with it at a "deeper" level. As with ideological attachment, the difficulty here may also be described as veterans living *as if* they were still in the military. Another similarity is that the difficulty diminishes as the capacity develops to distinguish what may have been appropriate during the military years and the different kinds of responses appropriate for current living. But the important distinction between ideological and feeling mode attachment is that the former involves desires that are readily accessible to awareness. The latter may not be experienced as involving any desire and may not even be subject to conscious recognition as a problem.

In the literature difficulties in the feeling mode are often referred to as "blocked" or "numbed" feelings. Too frequently, however, the description of the problems involved is limited to invoking mechanistic metaphors which do little to clarify how a therapist should respond. The standard accounts leave too much room for the mistaken belief that some mechanism or "thing" is doing the blocking or numbing, and that the therapist has to "remove the block" or "numbing agent" to effect a cure. I prefer to formulate what is problematic in "distortions of feeling" as in the following section.

Experiential Formulation

The feeling mode refers to the capacity to "get a feel for" or "have a sense of" something—for example, an event, person, or situation. This must be clearly distinguished from the specific sentiments we call "feelings," such as anger, love, frustration. These sentiments arise through the capacity to feel, but the sentiments themselves do not constitute that capacity.

It is also important to recognize the feeling mode as the source of the basic data of *any* experience. One *knows* what someone's face looks like, not because one has available a well worked out description of it, but because one has a feel or sense of it. There may be a clear visual memory, too. But when this memory is "lost," it is a felt sense that must be called upon to let one know whether attempts to recall it have come up with the right one. Similarly, one does not need a proof that no two situations are exactly alike. One *knows* this directly, by an "inner" observation of the data that one can sense or feel directly.

From an experiential view, the difficulty veterans have with the capacity to feel may be understood as arising in one of two ways (or both). Some veterans may have developed a *trained incapacity to feel* by virtue of military indoctrination. The value placed on toughness can easily encourage the practice of not attending to the subtle feel of whatever is associated with pain and discomfort, on the one hand, or with tenderness and softness on the other. Veterans who seem "masochistic" in courting danger, seeking fights, taking risks, and so on, may be doing so, in part, as a result of not being able to sense what is hurtful to them. Similarly, complex situations such as intimate relationships, for which standardized rules of behavior cannot be worked out beforehand, may be particularly difficult and frustrating for these men. Knowing what is happening in such situations depends on access to the subtle cues that are only communicated at the feeling level.

Others may have arrived at a similar predicament after having been "freaked" by the feeling evoked in them in some particular situation. In order to avoid being "freaked" again, they may have cultivated the capacity to *in*attend to what is felt directly. One can hear veterans say, for example, "The first time I saw a guy killed, I couldn't believe it. After that, it didn't bother me anymore. I didn't feel anything really."

Responding to Distortions in the Feeling Mode

When informed of the patient's military history, therapists can tailor their approach to current problems with that background in mind. To the extent that the emphasis on toughness has been influential, a therapist can respond to a veteran's complaints, whatever they are, by saying something like, "It may be that more is happening here than is readily obvious. This might not be easy at first, but see if anything you can feel inside can give us a clue to something going on that we haven't identified yet." In effect, the therapist repeatedly directs the veteran's attention to immediate sense data as a way of helping him acquire or relearn the capacity to feel.

To the extent that a fear of some particular sentiment or another seems important, whether the fear is accessible to awareness or not, the therapist can ask if the veteran has a sense that some particular kind of situation is hard for him to handle. If so, the inquiry can proceed by exploring this difficulty, as in asking what makes it so difficult, or what would make it easier.

Often the fear is of a sentiment like getting too attached or getting too angry. These may be associated with military experiences, such as, "I learned back in Nam that you don't get too close to people because you don't know who's going to be next to get killed," or "I saw for myself that you get in big trouble if you get too pissed off—you could go beserk and kill somebody." Often, however, the link with earlier experiences may not already be established. Developing such a link, whether with military or other experiences, and then distinguishing between the situation that gave rise to the fear and the present, may be helpful. But this is not essential—therapy can proceed simply by discussing the fear itself, by asking, "What makes that feeling so bad?" or "What makes you feel you can't handle that?" and then, "What might you do to make that more manageable for yourself?" This approach works directly by helping veterans to "feel their way" with sentiments they formerly related to as "too much" for them to handle.

It *is essential* to see that dealing with the fear alone is unlikely to be sufficient. If the problem has really become a "trained incapacity to feel"—however it began, the relearning will be necessary before "numbed" veterans can feel their way on their own.

Dealing with Trauma

Some veterans will come to psychotherapy complaining that their lives have never been the same since military experience. A portion of these men will talk about themselves in ways that resemble some or all of the descriptive elements of the diagnosis "post-traumatic stress disorder," as proposed for the revised Third Edition of the American Psychiatric Association's Diagnostic and Statistical Manual (DSM III): "reexperiencing of the traumatic event, decreased involvement with the external world ('psychic numbing'), hyperalertness, insomnia, guilt feelings, impaired memory and concentration, avoidance of situations resembling the traumatic event" (with the possibility of other manifestations such as "nightmares," "flashbacks," and "angry outbursts" (Shatan et al., 1977).

Some of the veterans who seem this way will generally be willing to explore with a therapist the experiences they believe to be linked with their difficulties. Though achieving a resolution through therapy may be quite difficult with them, beginning the therapeutic process will be fairly straightforward.

Others, particularly those who are notably "detached," will be much more difficult to engage at all. Though obviously troubled, "detached" veterans may insist that they do not have problems or, if they *do* admit to feeling some discomfort, may be at a complete loss to explain or do anything about it.

Men I have worked with who are detached in this way often become more engaged in therapy when I "opened up" about myself in a measured way. In effect, I attempt to "model" how to reflect on one's experience: "I know I end up feeling cut off from things when something has turned me off, or when it feels like more than I can handle. Does anything like that ever happen for you?" At times the response that comes back may sound "intellectualized" or "abstracted," as when veterans register some political or philosophical complaint about "the way this society is" or "the problem that people have." Rather than dismiss such complaints, I try to listen first and ask questions later. If these "abstractions" are repeated over and over, however, and the veteran shows signs of not being able to take them further on his own, the therapist can help by saying sensitively: "I hear what you say, but I don't get what that *feels* like to you. Why don't you stop for a moment, get a feel for what you're talking about for yourself, and then say what the crux of it is for you."

A word of caution is in order with respect to two therapeutic strategies that have been often celebrated in connection with work with veterans and other victims of trauma: (1) assisting men to recover "lost" memories and (2) encouraging men to "abreact" or "cathart" or "ventilate" strong emotion. As traumatized people heal, it is very often the case that they will experience something that they will then describe in common-sense language as memories "coming back." Also, these instances of "recall" are likely to be associated with strong emotion that the person will feel moved to express. But therapists can easily confuse things, cart before the horse style, when they "go after" memories or strong affects, as if these concomitants of the healing process are the curative agents themselves.

Summary of Therapeutic Responses

Veterans, like other survivors of other catastrophic events (see Krystal, 1968; Lifton, 1967, Chapter 10), may remain desperately in need of re-creating some sense of communal relatedness for many years afterwards, even for the rest of their lives. Therapists can help with this most effectively by listening and by providing the support and encouragement for veterans to explore realms of their experience that they cannot yet fathom on their own.

Survivor experiences also throw into question "internal" bonds, the ways people have of making sense out of their lives. War does not "fit" into standard life categories, particularly when it is a controversial, "lost" war, which cannot easily be filed away as a "necessary evil."

People who survive a war may make known in some way this difficulty of making sense of what they have lived through. The commonly heard phrase "Nobody who wasn't there can really understand" may be giving voice to the speaker's *own* difficulty in understanding. Therapists can help men come to grips with what baffles them, in part, by supporting their spontaneous attempts to *express* what the experience has been about for them—through writing, painting, photography, talk, or whatever mode is preferred.

It is worth noting again the emphasis given in this chapter to many veterans' need to regain the capacity to feel. The approach suggested is, in effect, a way of responding *both* to difficulties in understanding or grasping the meaning of one's experience and to problems with distortions in feeling. One can see this connection by noticing that meaning and feeling are both rooted in sense—*making* sense, in the first instance, and *responding* to what is sensed in the second. Though conceptually intricate, the relations among sense, feeling, and meaning can be established quite straightforwardly in practice. All one need do is help a veteran "get in touch" with himself with questions like, "How is that for *you?* What's the feel of it?" There, in his own concretely felt sense of things, he can discover the relation directly.

Some therapists who have worked with Vietnam veterans have, as a deliberate therapeutic strategy, involved themselves more actively in a veteran's life than they usually would with other clients. It is a good rule for therapists to be mindful of what they are doing, and on what basis, whenever they set aside their accustomed ways of working with people. It is just as good a rule that therapists be alert to situations that require innovative responses (Lifton, 1973a, and in Chapter 10).

PSYCHOTHERAPY: AN ANTIDOTE TO THE
INDIVIDUAL EXPERIENCE OF WAR

Now I will turn to general issues and, in particular, to the question raised earlier: How can psychotherapy provide a healing antidote to the individual's experience of war? As an introduction to this final part, I will first make some remarks about therapy itself.

The Ethical Thrust of Psychotherapy

Therapists make a unique contribution to interactions with patients and clients by assuming a particular posture toward experience and by helping the people they work with to learn how to take this pose themselves. One aspect of the therapeutic attitude consists of openness, empathy, and nonjudgmental receptivity. Another aspect involves the continually renewed willingness to entertain whatever arises in the interaction as a subject of reflection. Not everything needs to be reflected upon, but everything potentially *may* be, including the other person's comments and behaviors, the exchanges between both people, as well as the therapist's own comments, behaviors and feelings.

This openness to reflection is what I mean by the ethical thrust of psychotherapy. It is a thrust in that it provides an active direction for the interaction. It is ethical, rather than merely technical, in that it derives from the age-old moral vision that values self-scrutiny as a way of addressing the limitations humans impose on themselves.

The reflective attitude works therapeutically, first, because it takes anything that can present itself to awareness as a potential starting point for exploration or open inquiry. Conflicts, pitched battles, even the most dire pains, cease being mere objective oppressions when transformed, through reflection, into subjects of interest as well. In this light nothing is rigid, fixed, or immutable for all time, even suffering.

Secondly, with patience, reflection yields discovery. Crystalized attitudes, beliefs, habits, and embodied rigidities may offer a kind of comfort and security. But they obscure the infinitely rich realm of experience which consists of all that can be sensed directly when awareness is unbiased by the various forms that prejudgment can take. It is through contact with this wider realm that broadened perspectives on self and world can evolve. And this evolution proceeds when we suspend adherence to old crystalizations of experience and allow ourselves, through reflection, to see things freshly.

Open Reflection and the "Polarizing" of War

With this formulation as background, it may be possible to offer a perspective on what, in my experience, is the special relation between therapy and war. Soldiers who begin a reply to their commanders, "Well, I thought that . . ." are often interrupted and told, "Stop. That's wrong from the start. You're not paid to think. Just do what you're told!" Here one sees an essential part of military training, for war requires a certain absence of thought. As described above, war involves a drawing of absolute boundaries and a sacrificing of human life for a point of view that sees all good on this side and all evil on that.

Such boundaries do not withstand reflection. Knowledge of that fact must be available in at least a minimal way to a commander who gives the order not to think. A similar knowledge, embraced explicitly, is part of what informs the extraordinary thirst for learning and self-scrutiny that some veterans develop who have seen firsthand the ultimate consequence of unreflective action and are revolted by it. These are the men who become prized students, model therapy candidates, and the authors of works of art that transform the horror of ultimate destruction into creative inspiration.

In the light of reflection, the slogans and battle cries of war become questionable impositions that arbitrarily divide the human race and split people's minds. Veterans who comprise, in effect, a *second* group, may resist probing or questioning their experience for this very reason. Having seen life sacrificed and having risked their own for a doctrine, a principle or an idea, many men are understandably frightened of how all that might appear if brought into fresh light. Therapists who work with such men will need to exercise particular patience and gentleness so that change can come slowly and without posing too great a threat.

A *third* group of veterans may come to therapy after having begun to reflect on their war experiences and encountering a conflict they cannot resolve. I will describe below an instance of a man with such a conflict and sketch briefly how a group I was in responded to him.

In the final sections below I will compare the example of the veteran I know with a case excerpted from the literature dating from World War II. This comparison is intended to clarify further what I mean by open reflection. It is also designed to illustrate how the process of reflection can be truncated by a therapist—in this instance, through adherence to an institutional agenda, rather than a therapeutic one, and through a narrow application of dynamic theory.

A Vietnam Veteran Who "Froze"

One man who came to the veterans' rap group I was in for a number of years talked one night about feeling haunted by an act of cowardice. He and his unit had been pinned down in a fire fight toward the end of his year in Vietnam. One of the men in his unit was wounded and lying on the ground not too far from where he was taking cover. When he saw the man get shot, his first impulse was to go out under fire to bring him back. But then, quite suddenly, he froze and could not move for what he felt to be a very long time.

This incident had happened five years previously. It was still quite vivid and bothered this man enough for him to have disturbing nightmares about it. Essentially, he could not forgive himself.

We asked him about that time in his life, and he spoke easily in response. Early in his tour in Vietnam he had been quite enthusiastic about the war. But that feeling diminished sharply and steadily during the months he spent there. Seeing people die was part of the change. Also, he became confused by the conflict between the warmth he felt for the Vietnamese guide he worked closely with and the sense that had been instilled in him, and continually reinforced by racist slurs all around him, that *any* Vietnamese was the enemy. Another crucial ingredient was his loss of trust in his commanders for their repeatedly shoddy and reckless handling of his unit. In fact, the incident that troubled him came about after his commander had allowed the men to smoke marijuana while on patrol and then wander, randomly, over an open field. This made them easy prey for the ambush that eventually occurred.

When we played his story back to him, he saw before long what had been immediately apparent to some of us. He had kept the way he was viewing his "freezing" isolated from the way his perspectives on the larger situation had been developing at the time of the incident. Once he saw this, he felt relieved and many other things became clearer to him.

Without being fully aware of what was happening with him in Vietnam, this man had become progressively more disenchanted with the pre-packaged view of the war that had formed the basis of his enthusiasm. Then, suddenly, at a moment of crisis, when his life was at stake and he expected himself to act without question, as he had been trained, this growing sense of profound disillusionment took over. In the military's terms, and in terms of his earlier enthusiasm, this *was* an act of cowardice. But in the terms that he was evolving, which he had not acknowledged directly before that night in our group, this non-act represented the first sign of rebellion, a refusal to risk his life anymore. With the beginnings of reflection, the rationales for mindless obedience lost their hold on him. Only when he was able to reflect further on what had happened did he see the event as his frustrated attempt to come into his own.

A World War II G.I. With "The Jitters"

Grinker and Spiegel (1945), in their classic account of war neuroses and treatment during World War II, describe many cases of similar "freezing." In one of them, a B-27 door gunner had become extremely anxious after a raid over Poland and could barely bring himself to join his crewmates for later missions. He did not know what was bothering him, so he was submitted to treatment with pentobarbital, which helped him recall the raid as a low-flying strafing mission. He was able to remember seeing an old man on the ground. This had suddenly reminded him of his grandfather. It was then that he froze and couldn't shoot, after which he developed a severe case of "the jitters."

The attending psychiatrists drew evidence from this man's history for concluding that the problem consisted of the projection of the ambivalence he had always felt toward authority figures onto the enemy civilian. They reported that following the patient's achieved insight and abreaction, he was able to return to duty.

The Two Cases Contrasted

Despite the many differences in historic settings, immediate situation and therapist objectives, these two cases bear an important similarity. Both reactions came with an incipient sense of horror, transgression, or absurd twist in the previously accepted order of things. The difference in how these veterans were treated can be attributed to many factors. For present purposes, it is enough to see that Grinker and Spiegel, deliberately or unknowingly, turned their backs on the underlying intelligence and perceptiveness inferable from the gunner's response. They emphasized instead its "irrationality." Serving as secular catalysts for the man's moral catharsis, they helped him shore up the fabric of an otherwise tenuous world-view that made murder legitimate. In effect, Grinker and Spiegel encouraged the gunner to discount the image that came to mind that equated his victim with his own blood relation, thereby dismissing his own intimations that universal human relatedness cannot be refuted by a declaration of war. They may have been performing their job effectively, but that kind of work does not qualify as open reflection.

In the case of the Vietnam veteran, it is clear that open reflection is not predisposed to responding exclusively to psychopathology. Therapists may be called on to help men see the ways in which an experience that came as an emotional breakdown in one context may have been the first breakthrough of a wider, and ultimately more livable perspective on life.

It is also evident in the Vietnam veteran's case that open reflection may serve to loosen further a man's hold on the official interpretation of events. This is another restatement of the peculiar suitability of the psychotherapeutic process as an antidote to war. But this is not because therapy is an organizing arm for antiwar partisans. Organizing, in that sense, proceeds on a much more narrow agenda than the ethical thrust of therapy. Rather, the healing power of therapy in the wake of war is that ultimately it teaches men how to pass beyond the mere translation of one set of battle lines into another set, so that the struggles of life may be redefined into new and less destructive terms.

CONCLUSION

The goal of this chapter has been to communicate to psychotherapists some of what I have learned to date in working with Vietnam veterans. As this is work in progress, the formulations recorded here are tentative. The title is meant quite literally: these are suggestions, nothing more.

In several respects this has departed from a standard clinical discussion. First, I have interspersed theoretical digressions among the technical suggestions. This is not due, however, to a simple fascination with concepts. Throughout the chapter I have cautioned, in effect, that complacent psychologizing will lead one to miss the import of the veteran experience. How clinicians view that experience fundamentally influences how they respond to it. Taking up *theory*, the Greek word for *viewing* or *looking at*, offers the possibility of bringing fresh illumination to clinical practice, much the way therapy seeks through reflection to illuminate living.

The need for this theoretical reorientation is rooted in history, which brings me to the second major departure here. Repeatedly, I have referred to matters that would ordinarily be classed beyond psychology as history, sociology, or philosophy. I have done so on the conviction that psychology, narrowly circumscribed, is incapable of apprehending fully the question of a healing antidote to war. In fact, all of the modern disciplines have established themselves by splitting off as separate forms of inquiry into human experience. This insistence on separateness constitutes the fragmented view that humanity holds of itself, a factionalism embedded in the presuppositions of separate disciplines.

The crucial point here is that this fragmented view "educates" in such a way as to provide fertile grounds for the polarizing frame of mind of war. Only by leaving behind the piecemeal explanations of experience, and by taking up the search for a unified understanding, can formal inquiry identify what lies beyond the polarizing mentality that promotes war.

A third departure is the emphasis on the ethical thrust of psychotherapy. I have underscored this point in the last part because the historical challenges in the wake of Vietnam—the moral dilemmas the war poses for an American conscience—can be very much alive in psychotherapeutic work with veterans. When they are, both therapist and patient need the confidence that the process they are engaged in is adequate to the task. In discussing how therapy, as open reflection, undercuts the divisiveness or vestigial warring and polarizing within minds and human relationships, I have tried to suggest a basis for just such confidence.

Although history is a collective process, no person or group can free another from historical burdens. It is up to an entire generation to determine how the legacy of Vietnam is to be passed on. But if that legacy is to be transformed from a curse and a nightmare, individuals, singly and together, will have to do the hard work of reflecting on what that experience has been.

12

TREATMENT IMPLICATIONS OF POST-COMBAT STRESS RESPONSE SYNDROMES FOR MENTAL HEALTH PROFESSIONALS

SARAH A. HALEY, M.S.W.

INTRODUCTION

During the past seven years I have evaluated, treated or supervised the treatment of more than 500 Vietnam combat veterans at the Boston VA Outpatient Clinic. A majority exhibited varying degrees of the delayed stress response syndrome delineated in Section I above. These veterans represent a range of pre- and post-service levels of adjustment, but each in his own style has had to cope with the impact of combat on his life. Although the Vietnam veterans seen in the Boston Veterans Administration Outpatient Clinic are certainly a small percentage of the total who served in Vietnam, my clinical and teaching experience with these men has given me an insight into why we do not know more about these veterans.

If, as Aeschylus stated, "In war, truth is the first casualty," then most certainly information about the civilian readjustment process of three million Vietnam veterans has been a first order casualty of the post-Vietnam war era. Such needed information would attempt to integrate preservice adjustment, degree of combat involvement, and civilian readjustment, predicting the percentage of combatants with delayed or chronic stress syndromes. This would aid mental health professionals in planning effective treatment. The seminal works of Bourne (1970a, 1970b) and the present volume are important first steps.

This paper is dedicated to the memory of Dr. Elvin Semrad. He taught us by example and by inspiration to seek the source of our patients' pain and to be with them as they mourn their losses.

The situation, however, is not unique to veterans of the Vietnam war. In a 20-year follow-up of World War II veterans, Archibald and Tuddenham (1965) noted that:

> The impact of the great war has not been fully revealed two decades after its termination. The combat fatigue syndrome which was expected to vanish with the passage of time has proved to be chronic, if not irreversible in certain of its victims. Nor can the persistent disorder be dispelled as compensation neurosis, since many have never received compensation and are only now appearing for treatment as aging exacerbates their stymptoms. The syndrome is apparently found in different parts of the world and among victims of different kinds of stress, although it may be called by different names. . . . There is reason to believe that the symptoms following from sufficiently severe traumatic stress may persist over very long intervals if indeed they ever disappear (p. 475).

Further, Hocking (1970), in a review of the stress literature, concluded that although individuals varied in their ability to adjust to differing degrees of stress, subjection to prolonged, extreme stress results in the development of neurotic symptoms in virtually every person exposed to it.

Horowitz, in his book *Stress Response Syndromes* (1976), drawing on clinical, field and experimental studies, concludes that major stress events tend to be followed by involuntary repetition in thought, emotion and behavior. These responses tend to occur in phases of denial/numbing and intrusive repetition of some aspect of the event. These phases may alternate with periods of successful warding off or resolution of many of the conflictual aspects of the event.

The controversy over stress response syndromes, however, has been reflected in the psychiatric nomenclature. Shatan, Haley and Smith (1977) discuss the American Psychiatric Association's Diagnostic and Statistical Manual (DSM), noting that presently there is no official diagnostic category for stress disorders of some duration. Horowitz (1976) has suggested that perhaps, as the long-term syndrome is traced, ". . . it seems to lose its connection with an immediate stress event and gain connections to conflicts and character traits present before the event" (p. 27). Another possible reason may be the countertransference difficulties of clinicians when confronted with the patient's and, by extension, one's own vulnerability to catastrophic stress. I will develop this point in the discussion of the treatment issues with combat veterans.

A category of "post-traumatic disorder" will be reinstated in the upcoming DSM III. This disorder will include both man-made and natural catastrophes. Mental health professionals involved with combatants have worked with the DSM III Task Force to delineate post-combat stress response syndromes. They believe that, regardless of premorbid personality, the ego may suffer an overwhelming catastrophic stress. This stress, characteristically, has an intrusive and enduring impact, discrete symptom syndrome, clinical course and treatment outcome which can be distinguished from other clinical entities (e.g., Reaction Depression). Without a diagnostic classification of Stress Response Syndromes, the onus of psychic responsibility lies on the survivor; thus, the reasoning tends to be "if only he/she were made of sterner stuff, he/she would have made a better adjustment."

Here I will report a survey initiated to investigate the extent to which delayed and/or chronic stress response syndromes were diagnosed among our veteran population. The latter part of the chapter will address the treatment implications and the potential countertransference difficulties for the therapist.

DESCRIPTION OF THE STUDY

The Mental Health and Behavioral Sciences Service of the Boston Veterans Administration Outpatient Clinic is the primary source for outpatient psychiatric care for veterans in the metropolitan Boston area. The Outpatient Clinic includes a Drug Dependency Treatment Center and a Center for Problem Drinking to which most veterans are referred directly. Consequently, the majority of veterans making direct application for treatment to the Mental Hygiene Unit do not have a presenting difficulty of substance abuse. The service has a psychoanalytic orientation and offers individual, group, marital, and family therapy, as well as psychotropic drugs when indicated.

A survey of the intake records of the Mental Hygiene Unit from November 1974 to November 1975 was conducted for the purpose of gaining clinical data on the incidence of Vietnam veterans diagnosed with post-combat stress reactions.* The clinic has five intake teams who evaluate veterans on a walk-in and extended evaluation basis. At the conclusion of the evaluation, an APA DSM II diagnosis is entered in the intake log and in the veteran's medical treatment folder and a treat-

---

* These data have been presented to the DSM-III task force directly and in the symposium "Traumatic War Neurosis and DSM-III" American Orthopsychiatric Association annual meeting, Atlanta, Georgia, March 10, 1976 (Shatan, et al., this volume).

ment plan delineated. In reviewing the intake log, it was noted that often an "informal" or "soft" diagnosis of "traumatic war neurosis" or "post-Vietnam syndrome" was also entered. In the absence of a stress disorder diagnostic category, another APA diagnosis was assigned, but the treatment plan devolved from the informal, working diagnosis.

Method

The intake log indicates diagnosis, disposition, period and type of military service.* The Vietnam era refers to any military service between 1964 and 1974 and not specifically to Vietnam duty. In total, 676 Vietnam era veterans were seen in intake evaluation for either brief service or application for treatment between November 1974 and November 1975. A review of the records indicated that 130 had seen Vietnam duty and, of those, 90 had been involved in combat.

The development of post-combat stress response syndromes in Vietnam veterans has been described by Neff (1975b) as a syndrome consisting of (1) a depression, (2) explosive aggressive reactions, (3) sleep disturbances accompanied by traumatic nightmares, (4) startle responses to stimuli associated with previous life threatening experiences, (5) constriction of ego interests and adaptive functions, and (6) disassociative reactions (i.e., "flashbacks"). Neff's typology was used in the present study along with the DSM II classification.

Results

Upon examination of the records of the 90 combat veterans and/or interviews with the intake team or therapist, 67 veterans had a majority of the six symptoms of this syndrome. Only 30 of these veterans were service-connected for a nervous condition. The remaining 37 were eligible, on an adjunctive basis or under PL 93-82, for outpatient care to obviate hospitalization.

The 67 Vietnam combat veterans who demonstrated varying degrees of post-combat stress response syndrome were assigned approximate APA DSM II diagnoses as indicated in Table 1. A diagnosis of Anxiety Reaction, Depressive Reaction, Mixed Anxiety/Depressive Reaction and/or Adult Situational Reaction accounted for 58 of the 67 veterans, and it was in these cases that most often an informal diagnosis of traumatic war

---

* Hospitals' data on military service experiences are not collected—for example, the number of veterans who were in combat or other stress producing situations.

TABLE 1

Diagnoses of Vietnam Combat Veterans Presenting Varying
Degrees of Post-Combat Stress Response Syndrome

N = 67

APA DSM II Diagnosis	Number
Depressive Reaction	27
Anxiety Reaction	22
Mixed Anxiety/Depressive Reaction	6
Adult Situational Reaction	3
Schizophrenic Reaction	3
Psychoneurosis	2
Psychophysiological Skin Reaction	2
Manic/Depressive Psychosis	1
Passive/Aggressive Personality Disorder	1
Schizoid Personality	1

neurosis or post-Vietnam syndrome was indicated as the stressor. Of these 67 veterans, only four carried psychotic diagnoses and, with this group, stress reactions to the Vietnam experience were interlaced in schizophrenic and manic/depressive symptomatology. Of the remaining 63 veterans, all of whom have varying degrees of post-combat stress reaction and of whom 58 carry a reactive diagnosis, the following range of ego assessments was represented: passive/dependent or passive/aggressive personality disorder, 21; borderline personality, 14; characterological disorders—other, 7; and psychoneurosis, 21 (depressive—11, obsessive/compulsive—7, anxiety—2, hysterical—1).

SIGNIFICANCE OF THE FINDINGS

The significance of these findings dramatizes Neff's (1975b) observation that Vietnam veterans are "invisible patients with an invisible (nonexistent) illness." The veteran, often skeptical of the "system," may find that when he does present himself for psychiatric help, his symptoms do not "add up" to an officially recognized diagnostic entity. The negative ramifications for veterans have been far-reaching. As Shatan (Chapter 3; 1974) and others have noted, veterans have often been denied treatment and service-connected psychiatric disabilities by the Veterans Administration because technically they had no illness. On the other hand, the VA treats the veteran (e.g., with a diagnosis of depressive reaction), but the diagnosis would be linked to the veteran's preexisting psychic vulnerability rather than to the impact of combat as a catastrophic stress. Thus, veterans most damaged in the Catch-22 of this paper debate have been those who have been denied treatment/disability because their combat-related stress disorders were adjudged to be conditions that existed prior to their military experience!

Enlightened practitioners, however, seem to provide needed services in spite of outdated procedures. The inclusion and availability of a category of post-traumatic disorder in the upcoming DSM III will enable clinicians to assign a more accurate diagnosis which in turn should lead to more effective treatment planning.

Beyond nomenclature shortcomings, however, is an even more insidious factor in the failure to recognize, diagnose and treat post-combat stress response syndromes. Quite frequently, therapists and treatment facilities avoid the questions which would render the trauma available for therapeutic intervention because of negative countertransference difficulties and a lack of appreciation that stress syndromes may be chronic or have a delayed onset (Haley, 1974). In the next section, I will discuss my observations of this unfortunate situation.

TREATMENT IMPLICATIONS

Overview

Breuer and Freud (1895) noted that there was frequently a latent period between the occurrence of a stressful event and the onset of symptoms. Similarly, Horowitz and Solomon (Chapter 13) have predicted that civilian mental health professionals will begin to see stress response syndromes in Vietnam veterans over the next years. If they overlook the etiological importance of their military history, they will encounter difficulties in establishing treatment for these men.

It is uncertain whether this is due to a lack of knowledge about long-term stress disorder or simply avoidance. Van Putten and Emory (1973) of the Brentwood VA noted that there was "almost a collusion between veteran and therapist not to talk about Vietnam" (p. 698). In presenting our data to more than 30 community and university psychiatric staff conferences and in consultation within the Veterans Administration, I have been impressed by the incidence of a negative countertransference set toward Vietnam veterans. This set is manifested by attitude (e.g., "veterans are junkies"; "these are character disorders") and by avoidance behaviors.

The denial and avoidance which have been described as characteristic of Vietnam veterans are only matched in my experience by the denial and avoidance of mental health workers. One cannot know that one is treating a Vietnam combat veteran, let alone assess the meaning and impact on him of that experience, unless one has taken a history. Examples of these avoidance behaviors generally fall into two categories: (1) detailed psychosocial histories and elaborate dynamic formulations with a total absence of a military history; or (2) a military history either volunteered or elicited but not integrated into a dynamic formulation which most typically relies solely upon a genetic reconstruction.

The treatment program I am suggesting for the Vietnam veteran proceeds from a thorough evaluation which attempts to integrate pre-service levels of adjustment, a detailed military history (nature of his entry, response to basic training, how he came to go to Vietnam, nature of his assignment, extensions, post-Vietnam military service), and the quality of the veteran's readjustment to civilian life. The rationale for and skill involved in eliciting a detailed early history should not stop at the point of taking a military history. Because the veteran may deny, fear or exploit the impact of his Vietnam experience, we advise our trainees to take a step-by-step factual military history rather than an open-ended "tell me what it was like." A review of events will, hopefully, elicit the associated affects in those who need to deny or who are fearful, and will put into perspective the reactions of those who appear to exploit and use their Vietnam experience defensively.

Treatment of the Vietnam combat veteran is a challenging, painful, and, at times, frightening experience—challenging because the nature of the Vietnam war renders the traditional treatment model for traumatic war neurosis inadequate; painful because of its demands on the therapist to risk "being there," to share something of the overwhelming assault on the ego that the psychotic reality of combat involves; and frightening because of its imperative "physician, know thyself." In treating Vietnam veterans one is immediately involved with issues of countertransference as they relate to the Vietnam veteran specifically; perhaps, as clinicians, our countertransference difficulties extend to all those involved in catastrophic stress experiences.

In all of us our need to feel in control of our lives, our destinies, is strong and greatly threatened by our awareness of random or collective disruptions of or assaults on that control. How many times, when watching media accounts or interviews of the survivors of natural catastrophies such as floods and tornadoes, has one blunted one's response by the attitude, "well, I wouldn't live in those places," or noted a tendency to view the victims of rape or other violent crimes as somehow having "asked for it"?

We would like to see ourselves as self-determining. With Frankl (1959) we would share the view that what man becomes, within the limits of endowment and environment, he has made himself: ". . . we watched our comrades behave like swine while others behaved like saints. Man has both potentialities within himself; which one is actualized depends on decisions but not on conditions" (p. 212). But what of conditions so stressful that we come face to face with the reactions and choices we would make in order to survive? "We who have come back, we know: the best of us did not return" (p. 7).

Field, clinical and experimental evidence demonstrates that everyone is predisposed to severe, persistent traumatic disorder given sufficient stress. Massive stress has the capability of breaking up the balance between the ego and the environment by overwhelming the coping devices the ego has at its disposal (Kardiner, 1959), leading either to death or to strikingly similar disturbances in all who are exposed to it (Lifton, 1968). Whether we consider, like Frankl, that man is responsible for his "decisions" despite "conditions" or that stressful conditions have the potential to make a permanent intrusion into our ego functioning, who among us wants to contemplate his own response? Without this contemplation, however, treatment of patients with stress disorders, particularly Vietnam veterans, is greatly compromised if not impossible.

Theoretical Background

Horowitz (1974) states that "the state of stress imposed by a particular life event may impose a general regression in which developmentally primitive adaptive patterns will be noted, latent conflicts will be actuated and more apparent, and increased demand for parental objects will affect all interpersonal relationships" (p. 772). Ego regressions during combat are crucial to preserve psychic integrity. Return from combat to civilian life demands a realignment of psychic structures, with ego functions once again predominating.

On completion of their Vietnam tours of duty, most combat veterans reentered the United States alone, unnoticed and uncelebrated (Polner, 1971). Horowitz and Solomon (Chapter 13) have suggested that these men generally experienced a period of relief similar to that following any stressful event. Many enjoyed a lull period, a feeling of well-being and good functioning.

After this peaceful interlude, many veterans suddenly experienced recurrent intrusive dreams, nightmares, daytime images, and waves of painful memory, and denial, numbing and constriction. Such changes seemed independent of premorbid personality characteristics. The denial, numbing, alienation, and isolation of the experience from everyday life typically continued for a while. Paradoxically, with the relaxation of defenses and coping operations, combat veterans seemed to enter a phase of intrusive recollections of the experience. Such "breakthrough" has been noted to occur one to ten years after the experience. Horowitz and Soloman have suggested that stress disorders may have physiological contributants. They feel stress reactions may be triggered by a similar stress situation, but often there is simply a surfacing, possibly owing to endocrine changes.

Why sympton breakthrough follows a lull period is not entirely clear, but it is frequently precipitated by an event which echoes the original trauma. Delayed stress reactions may be triggered by almost anything, depending on the individual veteran, his Vietnam experience and the quality of his readjustment to civilian life. Such precipitants are often a clue to that aspect of his experience which remains most conflictual; they include, for example, media accounts of the murders at My Lai; the Calley trial; the return of the POWs; news accounts of the war; and sensory stimuli, such as an intensely hot, humid day or the smell of burning garbage.

In our clinic we have been particularly concerned with the pervasiveness of a seeming trade-off to passivity in order to counter fears of the past and potential aggressiveness in our veteran population. Although Vietnam veterans have been characterized in the public and clinical media as having explosive aggressive reactions, these episodes are often punctuation marks in a more stultifying passivity. Activity, initiation, assertion, aggression and murder have clearly become fused in a dynamic continuum for many. The reentry rituals and supportive social matrix so important for the returning combatant have been nearly absent for the Vietnam veteran.

The Marriage and Family Context

It has been this author's repeated observation that as the veterans' time away from Vietnam passes, precipitants tend to cluster around issues of intimacy, marriage, and child-rearing. Veterans who continue to mourn the death of close friends or suffer survivor guilt are often unable to involve themselves in close personal relationships (Haley, 1974; Figley, 1976a; Lifton, 1973a; Shatan, Chapter 3). One veteran described his wedding as "worse than a fire fight." As he swore to "love, honor and obey until death do us part," he remembered, in vivid detail, standing over the mutilated body of his best friend and swearing he would "never again let anyone matter to me, so I couldn't ever hurt that much again." Figley and Sprenkle (1977) have noted that the veteran's family may have an expectation that he reenter the family unchanged or may provoke and exploit his combat sequelae as an acting out of unrelated family difficulties. Optimally, however, it is the family which provides a supportive matrix for healing and reintegration.

Because of the guerrilla nature of the Vietnam war, the "enemy" could be anyone, including women and children. Thus, some stress responses are activated by closeness to women and the responsibility of marriage, a wife's pregnancy and the birth of a child. Veterans who have fought and killed women and children during combat often find it impossible to make a smooth transition to the roles of husband, protector and father (Haley, 1975). One veteran had warned his close friend, the squad medic, not to go near a crying baby lying in a village road until they had checked the area. In his haste to help the child, the medic raced forward and "was blown to bits" along with the child, who had been booby-trapped. The veteran came into treatment three years later, after a period of good adjustment, because he was made fearful and anxious by his eight-month-old daughter's crying. He had been unable to pick her up or hold her since her birth despite his conscious wish to "be a good father."

Thus, fatherhood may overtax the veteran's ability to resolve a trauma. Any point during the child's development can impinge upon the veteran's depression, withdrawal or conflicts with aggression. Intensification of these conflicts hampers the father's ability to provide an environment which facilitates the growth and development of ego autonomy and initiative in his preschool child. The activity and aggression of the "terrible two's" in the preschool child, particularly a son, may reawaken painful effects of combat aggression and guilt about sadism. Attempts to control aggressiveness in his child may lead to overreaction in the father (Haley, 1975, p. 3). This reaction may reflect his murderous anger at his child for stirring up painful conflicts, as well as a fear that he has somehow contaminated the child with his own aggression.

My work with combat veterans, especially those involved in atrocities (Haley, 1974), demonstrates clearly that shame, doubt, guilt, fear of violent impulses and reparation/atonement are central and conflictual issues in the lives of these men. The veterans' delayed stress response symptoms represent a breakdown of defenses, but are also defenses against repetition to completion of their violent impulses and ward off and numb the intolerable ideas and emotions. These veterans may have difficulty distinguishing between the sadistic aspects of combat aggressiveness and the age-appropriate competitiveness of their preschool child. The reason may lie in the veteran's perception that there is a thin line separating past violent acts and current and future violent fantasies. According to Horowitz and Soloman (Chapter 13), the veteran's fear of acting violently may be related to past experiences and not just fantasy. They are well aware that violence is a viable alternative which can be both pleasurable and guilt-provoking.

For certain veterans with ego regressions originally induced by combat, the experience of pleasurable, sadistic activities in the child mirrors the continuing struggle within the veteran himself (Haley, 1975, p. 9). These regressive signs will subside if the state of stress is reduced by working through the personal meanings of the previous life-threatening event (s). Horowitz (1976) suggests a strategem for treatment of stress response syndromes which aims to prevent either extreme denial or extreme intrusiveness. In contrast to the concepts of "abreaction" or "catharsis," the task of treatment is to bring stress-related information to a point of completion.

COUNTERTRANSFERENCE AND THE THERAPEUTIC TASK

Just as his child's aggression may trigger unbidden hate, guilt, depression and shame in the veteran, so may also the veteran-patient trigger unbearable negative affects and countertransference resistance in the therapist (Haley, 1974). A crucial element in the therapy program is a trustful therapist-client relationship. Such a therapeutic alliance enables the veteran to tolerate remembering, re-experiencing, understanding and working through stressful experiences. Psychotherapy with Vietnam combat veterans is difficult for the veteran, but sometimes equally difficult for the therapist. From my perspective it is difficult for the therapist for three reasons: (1) confrontation with one's own personal vulnerability to catastrophe; (2) the challenge to one's moral attitudes about aggression and killing; and (3) the fear of the intensity of the countertransference and the transference.

Confrontation of Vulnerability

Contemplation of and confrontation with one's anxiety and vulnerability to catastrophic stress are both expected and necessary when working with combatants. It is necessary in order for the full impact of the veteran's experience to be "alive" and accessible in the treatment. Intellectualization by the therapist, on the other hand, may send the therapist on a search for the "fatal flaw," that feature of premorbid experience and adaptation which makes understandable to the therapist the veteran's current difficulties, but bypasses the reality of combat. A parallel phenomenon has been noted with rape counselors who find themselves relieved at their discovery of the victim's "fatal flaw," a behavior by the victim that made her vulnerable to rape. The counselors, assured that they would have behaved differently, are thereby able to control for catastrophe and avoid confrontation with the possibility of rape.

Discomfort with a Combatant

Secondly, veterans express a wide range of responses to combat aggression and killing. Their reactions then and now can reflect acceptance, discomfort, disbelief, sadness, rage, guilt, and pride. As these reactions emerge in the treatment, they have the potential to overtax the therapist's management of his own aggression. Few therapists have treated people who have killed other human beings. Therefore, the therapist must continually monitor and confront his reactions to the patient's experiences. Although the patients who report atrocities (Haley, 1974) are a significant minority, they may be a factor in the therapist's resistance and avoidance of listening. ("Is this veteran going to confide in me information I cannot bear, tolerate or process?")

As therapists, we are familiar with the loss of romance that occurs during the gradual passage from adolescence to adulthood. We have been able to draw on our own experiences with loss and disappointment to empathize with our patients who struggle with what meaning their lives will have after the loss of a job, a loved one, or a cause. With many Vietnam veterans, the therapist is faced with men who, as adolescents, suffered the shattering of their ego ideal, who were abruptly stripped of their illusions and who now struggle to find life's meaning anew. In terms of countertransference, the therapist may be threatened by working with a patient during a critical reappraisal of the ideals and values that prior to combat gave life meaning. Since this country has undergone recent events which threatened a shared value system, the therapist may attempt to hamper the patient's exploration until the therapist's own illusions and meanings are restored.

Facing the Need for Absolution

The issue of sanction is critical for veteran and therapist. The legitimacy of a government to declare war, raise an army and assume the moral responsibility for the suspension of the man-made prohibition "Thou shalt not kill" must be credible to its citizens in order for repression and recovery to be achieved. In *Totem and Taboo,* Freud (1913) noted the elaborate rituals set up by primitive societies to provide psychological support for their warriors and to keep the "extraordinary" behavior of their warriors outside the realm of daily life and normal human conduct. Purification rites had to be undergone before the warrior killer could be accepted back into the tribe. This provided both a support for the warrior and the war deeds and clearly defined codes of conduct for the normal society. It then follows, unfortunately, that the traditional treatment model for the combat-related guilt and depression of traumatic war neurosis is to take the responsibility from the individual and place it on a higher authority. One was simply following orders. In addition to being expedient and simplistic, this treatment approach is generally insulting and insufferable to Vietnam combat veterans. Most Vietnam veterans have generally struggled alone without societal supports to integrate their combat experiences of five and ten years ago. Absolution is necessary, but must evolve over time and within the protective shield and containment of the therapeutic alliance.

CONCLUSION

In conclusion, the therapist, as a member of that society that did not provide rites of passage and purification to the returning Vietnam veteran, must accept the fact that he may be mistrusted and tested by the Vietnam veteran client. A therapeutic alliance becomes possible when the therapist endures his own discomfort and permits anger and blame by the veteran in the combatant's search for meaningful re-integration. Progress is inevitable when the therapist can be genuinely empathic and tolerate the affects aroused within his client. Within a protective therapeutic alliance, the original trauma can be re-experienced, re-examined, tolerated and finally assimilated. Under these circumstances, there is an opportunity for the resolution of the trauma and the resumption of living.

The occurrence of intense negative countertransference toward the Vietnam veteran brings the therapist face-to-face with his own murderousness and his vulnerability to being murdered. These issues appear to be a factor in the failure to recognize, diagnose and treat these disorders. Therapists and treatment facilities often avoid taking the military histories which would render the trauma available for therapeutic intervention. In treating Vietnam veterans the therapist must deal with his own attitudes toward vulnerability to catastrophic stress, aggression and sanction. Mental health professionals mirror the country's ambivalence toward the Vietnam war. In order to know how many need healing, they will have to risk "hearing" what these veterans have to tell us about themselves.

13

DELAYED STRESS RESPONSE SYNDROMES IN VIETNAM VETERANS

MARDI J. HOROWITZ, M.D.,
and GEORGE F. SOLOMON, M.D.

Military psychiatrists in Vietnam (Bourne, 1970b) did not encounter the frequency of major stress response syndromes noted during World War II (Grinker & Spiegel, 1945). But stress response syndromes often begin only after termination of real environmental stress events and after a latency period of apparent relief.

We expect that civilian mental health professionals will see stress response syndromes in Vietnam veterans over the next few years, will tend to overlook the etiological importance of their military history, and will encounter difficulties in establishing effective treatment for such persons. Because this topic is so important, we have attempted to formulate here our initial observations of psychopathology and treatment difficulties on the basis of case reports and in the absence of formal survey or research quantification and control. These assertions, therefore, must be regarded as preliminary and speculative.

COMBAT STRESS RESPONSES

In World War II, it was the custom to keep fighting personnel at the front line for long periods of time and psychiatric disability often increased in direct proportion to the length of time in combat. In air crews with repeated combat missions, 50 percent or more of those involved (Grinker & Spiegel, 1945) might eventually have severe symptoms of combat neuroses. Similar statistics were accumulated for those in

Reprinted with permission from *Journal of Social Issues*, Vol. 31, No. 4, 67-80, 1975.

ground forces (Lewis & Engel, 1954). In the Korean War, and again in the Vietnam War, military psychiatrists were prepared for numerous psychiatric casualties by the experiences of World War II. In the Vietnamese conflict fewer psychiatric casualties than expected were reported (Bourne, 1970b) and, of special note, there were fewer signs and symptoms of traumatic neuroses than anticipated.

Phases of Stress Response in Clinical and Field Studies

Important background to present considerations is found in the consistent data from clinical, field and experimental studies of stress response syndromes. Breuer and Freud (1895) in their study of hysterical neuroses, then felt to be a posttraumatic syndrome, documented the intrusion of warded off ideas, the compulsive repetition of trauma-related behavior and the recurrent attacks of trauma-related emotional sensations. They also documented the interrelated but seemingly opposite syndrome constellation of denial, repression and emotional avoidance. Subsequent psychoanalytic studies, as summarized by Furst (1967), indicated the generality of such tendencies after stress. Field studies, especially those which have investigated concentration camp victims, confirm these observations. Persons exposed to severe stress, perhaps not until after an extended period of relief or latency, will have (1) recurrent intrusive dreams, nightmares, daytime images and waves of painful emotional reexperience and (2) ideational denial, emotional numbing and behavioral constriction (Krystal, 1968; Lifton, 1970; Niederland, 1968; Oswald & Bittner, 1968). Such syndromes may continue for decades (Matussek & Mandell, 1971; Nefzger, 1970). Experimental studies also confirm the generality of these tendencies across persons who vary in predisposition (Horowitz, 1969, 1970; Horowitz & Becker, 1972).

Stated briefly, these coherent and convincing studies indicate two main aspects of stress response: an intrusive-repetitive tendency and a denial-numbing tendency. It is believed that the former tendency is an automatic property of mental information processing which serves the functions of assimilation and accommodation, a kind of "completion tendency" (Freud, 1920; Horowitz, 1976). The denial-numbing tendency is believed to be a defensive function that interrupts repetition-to-completion in order to ward off intolerable ideas and emotions. The intrusive-repetition symptoms usually lead to the diagnosis of stress response syndrome; the signs of denial and numbing may go unobserved.

Special Characteristics of the Vietnam Experience

The Vietnam experience, especially for those involved in combat, may differ from experiences in World War II. Combat experiences in Vietnam were shorter and relieved by rotations to relative safety. These rotations affected individuals rather than units. Fidelity to a small group or a leader was thus sometimes limited. Wide availability of drugs made withdrawal or self-treatment for fear or boredom possible. Variegated attitudes towards the Vietnam War prevailed and opposition among military and civilian populations was relatively frequent. The purposes of the war were unclear and often stated in terms of killing rather than liberation of territory as a goal.

In World War II, persons under great stress might initially go into a period of denial and numbing. They would be retained at the front line. Stress would mount. When it exceeded the person's ability to maintain denial and numbing, signs and experiences characteristic of intrusive and repetitive feelings, ideas and behaviors developed. In Vietnam, because of the repeated periods of safety, it would be relatively possible for the soldier to enter and remain in the denial and numbing phase of stress response syndromes because the lower pace of accumulating stressful perceptions allows maintenance of defense. This denial and numbing, as suggested by Lifton (1973a), would be fostered by the availability of drugs. The lack of group fidelity would also contribute to a state in which the person felt alienated, reacted with depersonalization, and isolated the experience from other events in the past and future.

Next, the veteran would return to the United States. At this time he would experience a period of relief, a latency period in which there was a feeling of well-being and relatively good functioning. The denial and numbing, the alienation, compartmentalization and isolation of the experience from everyday life would continue for awhile. Paradoxically, it might only be with the vision of continued safety, with the permissible relaxation of defensive and coping operations, that the person might then enter a phase in which intrusive recollections of the experience are reemergent.

For instance, a returning veteran might ostensibly adapt quite well, establish a marriage, engage in a satisfactory employment situation or return to school, only to experience the emergence of such symptoms as nightmares, daytime intrusive images or emotional attacks related to his Vietnam experience. This is paradoxical in that it would be opposite to what is commonly assumed in clinical practice. The common assumption is that compulsive repetitions of past traumas occur when they are related to or precipitated by more current stresses. The emergence of such symptoms might occur as late as a year or more after release from the stressful experience. This emergence, of course, could also be precipitated by arousal of new conflicts and damage to defensive-adaptive fantasies about (a) the patriotic purposiveness of his war work and (b) wonderful anticipations of what homecoming would be.

PRELIMINARY OBSERVATIONS

In 1969 a series of consultations was begun by the authors with staff members at two different Veterans Administration Hospitals. It turned out that one of the more typical patients seen, quite frustrating to all staff members, was a young veteran, who came in with a history of current and past usage of drugs such as LSD, speed and heroin. The overt reason for the contact was usually a request for drugs such as sleeping pills and tranquilizers. The veteran would be seen for only one or two visits and then would drop out, failing to establish or maintain a treatment contract. In one hospital, veterans identifying themselves as having served in Vietnam were seldom seen. At the other hospital, white Vietnam veterans were seen, but black Vietnam veterans rarely came for treatment. After a reaching out, at both hospitals, Vietnam veterans of various races entered the treatment program. The earlier "absence" of cases was due, we felt, to distrust on the part of Vietnam veterans of any facility attached to the government.

A second observation was then made, a negative one: According to the staff, stress response syndromes were not spontaneously reported by the population of Vietnam veterans. In spite of reports of a low incidence of such syndromes in the combat zone, we expected that delayed responses would occur in the population returned to civilian life. We suspect that these veterans not only wished to hold back their experiences in Vietnam but might not spontaneously report the relevant symptoms.

Correspondingly, an educational program was undertaken to review for the psychiatric staffs both the intrusive-repetitive and denial-numbness aspects of common stress response syndromes. This included theoretical discussions supplemented by bringing in a representative of a veterans' organization and showing the film "Winter Soldier" which evokes many of the psychodynamic issues as they are experienced subjectively by veterans.

As a result of these efforts, new cases of stress response syndromes in Vietnam veterans began to be reported in each subsequent case conference. It seemed that these patients were now being found in the existing case load because therapists were alert to the possible presenting symptoms and could ask for them in spite of the weakness of the therapeutic alliance and the tendency of the patients to present only details related to their immediate requests, as for sleeping pills.

As these new case vignettes were presented, classical stress response syndromes were noted. These are similar to those reported by other investigators (Borus, 1973a; Fox, 1972; Lifton, 1973a; Solomon *et al.*, 1971; Shatan, 1974).

A typical case can be composited as follows.

> The person has been back from Vietnam for about one and a half years. He has done ostensibly well, has been able to get a job and to marry. He feels somewhat estranged from his peers at work and does not discuss combat experiences with them. Recently he has begun to have difficulty sleeping, has intrusive daytime images and some nightmares of combat scenes although not necessarily one repetitive "story." These commonly involve atrocities whether or not he was involved in committing them himself.
>
> During the daytime he is often suspicious and, when frustrated or in fear-arousing situations, feels that he is in great danger of losing control over his hostile and aggressive impulses. With growing hostility and suspicion he may conceal firearms to protect himself. There is also fear of going crazy and guilt over his own pleasurable responses to his intrusive ideas of committing severe physical violence to others. There may be startle reactions, psychosomatic syndromes, anxiety attacks, loss of motivation and depression.
>
> The person often turns to drugs such as heroin or sedatives because they temporarily relieve the depressive, anxious, fearful and hostile mood states. Interpersonal difficulties may supervene because of the patient's continued and uncontrollable suspicions, moodiness, surly behavior or excessive dependency. Threats by the person are frequent and will also alienate interested friends and family members. The person wants to ward off any reminders that may create intrusive and repetitive experiences and will tend to be defensive in any inquiry by others as to his past experience.
>
> He thus becomes progressively more isolated and develops secondary syndromes ranging from neurosis to psychosis.

PREDICTIONS

On the basis of the above formulations and observations one may predict that, after a latency period characterized by relief and relatively good functioning, typical stress response symptoms may appear. These symptoms might include nightmares, painful moods and emotional storms, direct or symbolic behavioral repetitions and concomitant secondary signs such as impaired social relationships, aggresive and/or self-destructive behavior and fear of loss of control over hostile impulses. Many veterans will find it difficult to integrate the memory and associated fantasies of their Vietnam experiences with their life schemata of the past, present and future. This inability to assimilate a time of life into an ongoing schemata will lead to impaired self-concepts, tendencies to depersonalization, depression, shame, frustration and reactive rage and psychosocial disabilities.

Such veterans are unlikely to seek help from ordinary psychotherapeutic facilities, especially those associated with the government. If and when they do seek help, they may conceal their Vietnam experiences and reactive signs and symptoms. Even if patients develop trust in a treatment facility, perhaps due to the good reports of their peers, they may nonetheless experience unusual difficulties in establishing a therapeutic relationship.

Some Treatment Difficulties

As indicated above, establishment of a therapeutic relationship is difficult for these patients. They distrust any agency affiliated with the government and "the establishment." This difficulty is related to both their experiences with a war in which the issues were unclear, and, upon their return, feelings of estrangement from contemporary society. Their demeanor is suspicious, fearful or a defensive stance of hostility and arrogance or a combination of these characteristics.

They are fearful of their own mood states and hostile impulses. They fear they cannot control them, and do not believe that the therapist can help with this. They know that many of their experiences are beyond the realm of the experience of the therapist and may conflict with his value judgments.

Such veterans are afraid of authority figures. If they reveal their current impulses towards aggressive and destructive acts, they imagine they might be committed to hospitals or revealed to legal authorities. While this fear is usually a protective fantasy, in some cases it has rational components. The person may know he has acted illegally or violently or may be close to doing so. He may not know the infrequency of involuntary commitment or the ethics of confidentiality.

One of the great misfortunes and difficulties in the treatment of some of these patients is that their fear of committing violence is based on historical reality, not fantasy. Contrast their situation with that of obsessional neurotics. Obsessional neurotics may have similar recurrent intrusive thoughts of doing harm to other persons. In their past, however, they have not done the degree of physical harm that they imagine. In contrast, some Vietnam veterans will have witnessed such violence and may have participated in it. They know not only that such violence is really possible since they have committed it, but also that it may be pleasurable as well as guilt-provoking. The obsessional patient usually has available the reassurance that he has never acted on his fantasy. Some Vietnam veterans may have the damaging knowledge that they have acted violently in the past. This leads to a blurred distinction between what is current fantasy, past reality or current and future possibility. In other words, there has been a shortening of the conceptual distance between impulse and act, fantasy and reality, so that conditioned inhibitions to destructive behavior have been reduced and are difficult to reimpose.

The presence of reduction in inhibitory capacity and increased fears of loss of control does not mesh well with the existing technical procedures familiar to most psychotherapists. Many maneuvers in dynamic psychotherapies are designed to counteract defenses and reduce inhibition in general. Maneuvers designed to increase control capacities and to separate realms of fantasy and real action are less familiar. The therapist may add his own uncertainty to the equation. Further, the therapist may fear the patient's potential for violence, a fear that is readily transmitted to the patient through nonverbal communications. The unhappy synergy of patient and therapist fears impairs the therapeutic relationship.

Another treatment difficulty is related to the observation of impaired self-concept frequently found in such veterans. This may be due not only to the nature of this particular war but to the life phase in which many of the veterans find themselves afterwards. They have often gone into the military service from situations in which they were relatively dependent on their peer group or family (Morris, 1970). They have been separated relatively abruptly from the military service and catapulted back into adult civilian life. This happens at a time when cultural values are indistinct and blurred, when there are multiple routes to life, many of which are blocked because of their race, lack of skills or appropriate credentials (Borus, 1973).

The ready availability of drugs in Vietnam, and the possible adaptational use of such drugs (although self-administered) may lead them again into this route to a sense of well-being. The use of such drugs, especially those that induce daydreaming, fantasies or pleasantly altered states of consciousness, further blurs distinctions between reality and fantasy and promotes grandiose self-images. Such grandiose fantasies provide restitution for feelings of defect in self-esteem, self-values or self-peer and self-society commitments.

The compensatory grandiosity alluded to above is sensed by the person to be fantasy and not reality and hence is a secret. Were this secret revealed there is danger of appearing contemptible in the eyes of those who would not share the fantasy belief system. Such patients are generally shy or they isolate specific areas from communication because they fear that their grandiosity might be revealed to the therapist or to peers (Kaplan, 1972). The need to avoid shame intensifies the problems of balancing realistic self-appraisals with idealized hopes. To avoid shame, humiliation or identity diffusion, such patients often maintain a third attitude which is one of distance, arrogance, superiority, suspiciousness and disdain towards therapists. This defensive attitude may intermix with a realistic lack of rapport with some therapists who cannot fully empathize with the Vietnam experience.

These focal difficulties, when present, add to the everyday problems of beginning and continuing a useful therapeutic situation. Some strategies for surmounting such difficulties are considered below.

TREATMENT STRATEGIES

Shatan (1972a) and Lifton (1973a) emphasize the unique aspects of the problems of Vietnam veterans. While not in disagreement, we are predicting general and delayed stress response syndromes as are not uncommon in civilian populations. These syndromes, we expect, will be appropriately treated by the conventional techniques and arts of individual and group psychotherapy (Horowitz, 1973, 1976). Nonetheless, "special" features are expected to complicate these treatments. Discussion of the common practices of psychotherapy is beyond the scope of this paper but we can describe some approaches to the treatment difficulties described in the previous section. The combination of contempt, distrust and fear of authority figures, with impaired self-concept and fear of loss of self-control, makes the therapeutic relationship especially hard to establish and this becomes the first hurdle of treatment.

Ideally, the aim is to help the patient develop a very clear idea of what his current problems are and what can be done to help him with them. Towards this end, a pitfall must be sidestepped, the pitfall of assuming a kind of governmental commitment often implied by the organizational relationship between the veteran and an agency such as the Veterans Administration Hospitals. This pitfall is hard to skirt, however, because of the complex tangles of legality, reparations and financial aid to the disabled. In spite of these complex issues, the therapist must center with the patient on some focal concerns that cause current subjective pain. The issue of loss of control is of extreme importance, vital to the therapeutic alliance, and should be explored early.

Part of this exploration includes asking the patient about fears of loss of control in a direct, simple and calm manner. Any possible episodes of loss of control should be described in detail. It is especially important that the therapist ask what has helped the patient to regain control, however brittle or fragmentary this control may have been.

The conceptual labeling of experience that occurs during this process is already a step in the direction of gaining control. This step towards gaining of control by establishment of conceptual labels and explanations is sometimes called intellectualization and then, in an unclear manner, regarded as a defense mechanism to ward off emotional experience. But intellectualization and rationalization are high order adaptive maneuvers as well as defenses. One wants to help the patient to use these operations before emotional explorations in order to keep emotional recollections within tolerable limits. Premature interpretation of intellectualization and rationalization as defensive maneuvers is therefore an error.

Given the vulnerability of these patients to narcissistic injury, inquiring about their difficulties in self-control must be done in a tactful manner. Many of the controlling efforts introduced by patients into their lives will themselves appear to be symptoms of psychopathology and thus patients will also be reluctant to discuss them. For example, one patient moved from one chair to another during therapeutic interviews, a procedure which was also followed at home while talking with friends. This maneuver had become a ritual which he used to terminate intrusive thoughts of an aggressive nature. The moving from one chair to another appeared to be a compulsion and the patient had to disguise it with some excuse such as "going to the bathroom" or "looking for an ashtray." When this behavior was noted in therapy the patient was quite embarrassed but, with a tactful approach and intellectual scaffolding provided by the therapist, was able to discuss the purpose of the movements, intrusive thoughts and his fear of loss of control over violent impulses.

The distrust and withdrawal of some Vietnam veterans from therapists are not to be attributed only to internal psychological conflicts. Many of these patients have been through a different order of experience from that of most therapists. This may give both participants a continued aura which one therapist aptly called "spooky." When this problem occurs a professional, paraprofessional or lay co-therapist with Vietnam experience may be useful in firming a tenuous therapeutic relationship, as suggested by Shatan (1972a) and Lifton (1973a) in their attempts to explain the effectiveness of self-help groups organized by veterans organizations.

Dealing with Impairments in Control of Violent Impulses

As described above, the establishment of a therapeutic relationship including inquiry into the patient's own methods of control is in and of itself a step towards improving control capacity. This first step can be called conceptual labeling; it increases the power of problem-solving thought as a tool for conflict reduction. This process is continued in attempts to find routes that the patient may take when he is in danger of being triggered into explosive aggressive actions. The relationship with the therapist is already one such route since patients commonly use an introject of the therapist as a quasi-presence during a potentially explosive situation. That is, the patient talks to himself "as if" he were the therapist or else he tells himself during the tense moment that he will tell the therapist about this episode later. This possibility of discourse with the therapist provides one route out of a dangerous interpersonal situation because there is a sense that something can be done about it.

Even in a phase of therapy focused on control of violent impulses there is an interrelationship between at least three factors: (1) the felt commitments that compose the therapeutic relationship, (2) the internalizations and externalizations that flow into and around the relationship, and (3) the cognitive and emotional processing of ideas and feelings. Ordinarily there will be gradual exposure of warded off components of real memories and fantasies of the past, present and future. The therapist will help the patient preserve a sense of safety and tolerable exposure by interpretation, clarification, suggestion, "presence" or direction.

Psychotherapists are most familiar, as noted earlier, with interventions designed to unfreeze responsivity. They try to promote the cognitive and emotional processes that lead to assimilation of the implications of stressful events and accommodation of the self to a changed situational configuration. Part of this process involves what has been called "abreaction" and "catharsis." At times, in efforts to subvert defensive functions and evoke abreactions, forced role-playing, hypnosis or chemical hypnosis have been used. A potential error is premature use of such procedures. The recollections and emotional storms are often beyond the current capacity of the patient to assimilate. The therapist may gain information about stressful events and associations to these events but the patient may, in effect, receive an "overdose" of his own repressed memories and fantasies. A gradual procedure of cognitive and emotional working-through with repair of impaired control capacities is, in our opinion, preferable.

Problems of control over violent impulses are complicated whenever real violence has occurred, whenever human beings are dehumanized or devalued, and whenever reality and fantasy images are fused. In some instances, the patterns of impulsive violent behavior are so marked that experimental approaches to treatment are indicated. One such approach is described below. It has been tried in only two cases and was found to be useful in both. It can only be presented as a speculation for the consideration of other therapists.

Let us presume a patient who is preoccupied with impulses and fears of conducting a murderous physical attack on another human. When the patient is in a state of discontrol, he may be unable to prevent himself from doing some violent physical act. Unfortunately, insight into the sources of frustration, fear and aggression do not always provide adequate mitigation of impulses or increases of controls. One approach to such patients is what could be called the establishment of hierarchical routes of behavior. The act of physical bodily assault is placed as number one on this hierarchy.

The hierarchy thus starts from the "worst possible outcome" and reduces the severity of behavior patterns progressively. The next place on the hierarchy is developed in further discussions with the patient. He is asked this type of question: If he is in a period of explosive arousal, one in which control is not possible for him, what could he do which would be almost equivalent to the physical assault on another but, in his own mind, not quite as destructive to another? The patient may offer the idea that he thinks he could slam his fist into a wall instead of into a face.

The third place on the hierarchy of actions is developed by discussing what might be almost as "good" a discharge as slamming his fist into the wall but would be somewhat less destructive to him. The answer might be to walk away from the argument or upsetting confrontation. The dangerous action, murderous assault, is thus gradually worked down until it is of lesser order. In the patients on whom this method was tried, the incremental steps seem possible even during the explosive state. That is, it was at first possible to avoid physical assault by wall striking but not by retreat. Later it was possible to move from wall striking to retreat. Finally it was possible to move to verbal but not physical aggression.

This type of talk with patients also accomplishes the steps described earlier as approaches to problems of control including: (1) increases in the hope and trust of a therapeutic relationship, (2) development of conceptual labels which allow rationalization and intellectualization as adaptive maneuvers, (3) establishment and practice of new routes of behavioral expression and (4) reestablishment of controls that have been deconditioned by warfare.

Dealing with Guilt

Another special feature germane to the treatment of stress response syndromes in Vietnam veterans is the nature of their guilt and shame responses. As discussed for problems concerning control of violent impulses, the unusual feature may be the reality and indelibility of the relevant memories. Unlike guilt from childhood neuroses, revolving around the fantasies of oedipal and proedipal configurations, realistic shame and guilt cannot be relieved simply by clear expression and rational working-through.

Lifton (1973a) has dealt at length with these issues and we agree with his principle of the need to convert static guilt to animated guilt. That is, maneuvers in addition to insight are necessary to balance the stress related memories (and fantasies) with enduring self-images and values. What is helpful is not novel. It can be briefly summarized as clarification, atonement or penance and restitution.

Clarification consists of the usual psychotherapeutic maneuvers for clear expression. The therapist may route the patient with questions: Who is he now? How powerful or how weak is he now? How responsible was he and is he now? How responsible were others and society in general? How much atonement and penance are necessary and sufficient to relieve his sense of guilt? Atonement and penance are of course the classical maneuvers of the Catholic church for the reduction of guilt. The maneuvers are classical because they work comparatively well. Confession, a period of emotional pain, and self-accusation are included in this concept. Unfortunately, self-destructive behavior is also included. Again, clarification with the patient of how much self-impairment he must inflict on himself is important. Otherwise there will be endless and repetitive episodes of self-destructive behavior such as job loss, object loss or self-lacerations. In some instances, plans for symbolic restitution provide a route away from self-destructive patterns and towards life-affirming strategies. By symbolic restitutions we mean actions which heal people or the environment.

SUMMARY

The Vietnam situation led to the kinds of events that predispose participants to a denial-numbing type of stress response while in military service. Discharge may be associated with relief and ostensible readaptation to civilian life. Unresolved stress will, however, lead to intrusive-repetitive type responses even months or years after situational exits. We therefore predict delayed stress response syndromes in Vietnam veterans that may surface during the coming years. In addition, all the usual therapy problems and solutions relevant to the treatment of stress response syndromes are expected to prevail. Special treatment consideration should be given to problems in the establishment of the therapeutic relationship, in imposing controls over violent impulses, and in reducing the effects of shame and guilt.

14

TREATING THE VIETNAM VETERAN WITHIN THE FAMILY SYSTEM

M. DUNCAN STANTON, Ph.D.,
and CHARLES R. FIGLEY, Ph.D.

The purpose of this chapter is twofold: First, to present information about the Vietnam veteran which may help the family-oriented therapist work with Vietnam veterans and their families; second, to set forth some guidelines for marital and family treatment when service in Vietnam becomes an issue for veteran clients. Before proceeding, however, it is important to place the Vietnam veteran in perspective.

Most of the Vietnam-era veterans have their share of individual and family problems. Their specific difficulties, however, are not significantly more severe than those of nonveterans when compared *as a group*. Further, recent reviews of veteran research (DeFazio, 1975; Figley, 1976a) suggest that most veterans have adjusted very well following their military tours of duty, and a significant number are better adjusted after service than before, which is discussed in some detail in Chapter 8. Unfortunately, the popular media, including television, have consistently presented a stereotype of the Vietnam veteran which includes, but is certainly not limited to, the characteristics identified by Robert Brewin, a disabled Vietnam veteran:

> . . . if I acted according to what I have seen on television in the last six months or so, I would be harboring extreme psychopathic tendencies that prompt me to shoot up heroin with one hand while fashioning explosives with the other as my war-and-drug crazed mind flashes back to the rice paddy where I fragged my lieutenant (1975, p. 4).

Collectively, the press has been imprudent in citing individual case histories of veterans and implying that these illustrations represent *all* veterans. Even we scholars and practitioners who have worked with the Vietnam veteran have wittingly or unwittingly perpetuated the "sick veteran" stereotype. When our observations are picked up by the popular media, our warnings not to overgeneralize are omitted along with the other cautionary statements for the sake of "readability," or more often, for the sake of sensationalism to increase circulation or viewer ratings.

This "bad press" has had a number of unfortunate consequences for the veteran. One consequence, perhaps, is the common finding that many Vietnam veterans have attempted to disown their veteran status. Most veterans, for example, did not wear their uniform home from the war, and the large veterans' organizations have had great difficulty recruiting Vietnam veterans (Starr, 1973). Figley and Eisenhart (1976) found that almost half of the Vietnam veterans were not proud to be veterans, and among the *combat veterans*, over 60 percent felt that way.

Perhaps the most disturbing consequence of this disownment process, however, is the reluctance of veterans who *are* troubled about their military experiences to seek professional assistance. This problem is especially acute among veterans who are suffering from stress disorders related to their combat experiences in Vietnam. For some time a significant minority of mental health specialists have attempted to alert their colleagues to the unmet needs of Vietnam veterans who suffer from some form of combat-related distress (Bourne, 1970; DeFazio, 1975; Figley, 1975; 1976a; Figley & Sprenkle, 1977; Lifton, 1973a; Shatan, 1973a; 1974; Stanton, 1970a). Certainly this volume is dedicated not only to alerting professionals to the problem, but also to providing specific information to enable them both to understand and help the veteran.

COMBAT STRESS DISORDER MODELS

The vast majority of mental health service agencies both inside and outside the Veterans Administration rarely ask clients about military experience in general and combat experience in particular (Figley, 1976a). Further, as Haley (Chapter 12) points out, even if a presenting problem is Vietnam-related, the American Psychiatric Association DSM II does not have a category for combat-related stress disorders. Thus, less complete diagnoses have been routinely substituted. Haley's findings, in concert with others reported in this volume, appear to validate some of the theoretical and clinical observations of a number of mental health professionals, particularly DeFazio, Figley, Neff, Shatan, Horowitz and Solomon.

TREATMENT

Individually Oriented Treatment

Most of the clinical writing in the area of combat-related stress disorders has been individually oriented (e.g., Archibald & Tuddenham, 1965; Grinker & Spiegel, 1945; Horowitz, 1976; Horowitz & Solomon, Chapter 13; Hall & Malone, 1975; Kardiner, 1959; Shatan, 1973a, 1974) with few exceptions (Figley, 1976a, 1976b; Figley & Sprenkle, 1977). Horowitz and Solomon, for example, describe a treatment strategy which attempts to help the veteran "gain control over his violent impulses."

On the other hand, a number of other clinicians have attempted to ameliorate Vietnam veteran problems through the use of "rap" groups composed entirely of Vietnam veterans (see Chapter 10).

Family Treatment

The interpersonal context of stress reactions. Individually oriented treatment may have been indicated for most veterans, during or immediately following military service. Years into the post-Vietnam era, however, we believe that most presenting problems are enmeshed in the veteran's interpersonal network (Figley, 1976a). Thus, the network should be the context of therapy. This view is in direct contrast to the contention of others that combat stress reactions can occur at any time independent of the veteran's social milieu. Certainly the veterans may have gotten used to the combat-related stress reactions (i.e., nightmares, flashbacks). Also, the disorder may have limited the veteran's coping abilities, interpersonal competence and social effectiveness. We believe, however, that war-related problems (physical as well as psychological) are not only linked to the veteran's interpersonal life, but also often serve a key function in the interpersonal system (Stanton, 1976b). Thus, to treat the war-related problem independently of this system may do more harm than good.

It is our contention that the family system has potential for both maintaining and eliminating the disorder. The tasks of the therapist are (1) to assess accurately the degree of severity of the disorder, the ways and means by which the veteran's interpersonal network tends to maintain or complicate the disorder, and the specific relationship dysfunctions within which the disorder is enmeshed, and (2) to develop an effective therapy program to deal with both the stress disorder and the associated dysfunctions within the system.

Some basic concepts. Later in this section we will consider the process by which combat-related stress may be entwined with family dynamics and effective methods of treating it within the family system. First, we wish to set forth some basic concepts. Although we use the term "family," it is often more helpful to think in terms of interpersonal systems, especially where treatment is concerned. Since the family is usually the primary interpersonal system, it is often the focus of intervention programs. However, other systems, such as the co-worker system or the neighborhood, could also be used as effective leverages for change and are thus appropriate for inclusion in the therapy program.

Second, family life is an important source of stress (Croog, 1970; Figley, 1977). Families go through stages of development, including, for example, marriage, the birth of the first child, children entering school, the "empty nest" and the death of a member. At each of these points, the family has to change in order to adapt to the new situation (Haley, 1976; Minuchin, 1974). This also applies to external events which it may face, such as change in employment or residence. The family adjusts and, if external events return it to the original condition, it must readjust again. Both internal and external events, then, change the family structure in terms of, for example, power, responsibility, interfamily coalitions, economics. Excellent examples of this process have been shown in the work of McCubbin and his colleagues (McCubbin, Dahl, Metres & Plag, 1975; McCubbin, Dahl & Hunter, 1976; Hunter, Chapter 3) with families of American prisoners of war and missing in action. When husbands were gone, wives assumed many of their functions within the family and, upon their return, the wives were not always ready to relinquish the family throne—a situation leading to overt power struggles. The point is that some families adjust readily to such occurrences and others get "stuck." They cannot make the appropriate shift and they become dysfunctional. The likelihood of symptoms of combat stress arising is increased at these times.

The third basic concept related to the family system concerns *family patterns*. If one observes a family for any length of time, one will note that certain of its interactional behaviors are predictable. Some members may interrupt when others talk but will be selective, i.e., they will interrupt only certain dyads or triads. When A and B talk, for example, C interrupts, but C does not interrupt when A and D or B and D talk. Other patterns will revolve around mood. For instance, when A is happy, B is sad or depressed, but when B becomes happy, the roles are reversed and A grows sad; the two are complementary. These and similar phenomena are generic, but in dysfunctional families, they tend to rigidify. Further, even when blatant, they are not the kinds of events which most people working with Vietnam veterans either look for or recognize. They also have implications for treatment, as will be discussed later in this chapter.

Finally, it should be remembered—as Jay Haley (1971) has pointed out—that individual therapy is actually *one* way of intervening in a family, whether the therapist views it that way or not. To bring about change in one member, i.e., the veteran, is also to affect those within his intimate relations network. If the individually oriented therapist helps the veteran to improve or change, he is also altering the rules and roles of his family. This can lead to undercutting of the treatment by relatives or spouse, perhaps for no other reason than that they are frightened of any kind of change, no matter how "beneficial." The therapist who ignores this may be placing himself at considerable disadvantage. For example, when a veteran who has been drug-dependent for four years since he left the military attempts to become drug-free, his family will often throw up roadblocks. His drug problem serves a key function in the family; if he changes, perhaps his parents' marriage may start to break up or the family may start to fall apart. This puts pressure on the veteran to return to his drug use; such pressure is not alleviated efficiently without including the family in treatment.

The discussion below is divided into treatment which includes the veteran's family of origin (parents, siblings) and that which centers on his family of procreation (wife, children). This distinction between family units can be misleading. There may be times when both family units (and non-family members as well) should be dealt with simultaneously).

Family of Origin. Based on our experience in working with Vietnam veterans in a clinical setting, the extent to which the veteran is in contact with his family of origin—quantitatively and qualitatively—is extremely important. To what degree has the veteran successfully moved away from his family—psychologically as well as physically (i.e., differentiation of self from family)? If, for example, the family of origin or any member thereof exerts any appreciable influence over the veteran now, those members should be included in the therapy program at some point. Support for this notion has emerged from some recent research (Stanton, 1977a, 1977b; Stanton & Todd, in press) with drug addicted veterans aged 25 to 35 (some of whom first became addicted in Vietnam). Survey of their family contact showed that 82 percent of them saw their parents at least weekly and 67 percent either lived with their parents or stopped by daily. In such cases, family therapy was clearly indicated and has proven very effective.

In situations where the family of origin is involved it is important to know what events have recently occurred which may be associated with the diagnosed problem. For example, one of the veteran's parents may be quite ill or may have died, leaving the other parent in a state of acute or prolonged bereavement. At such times it is not uncommon for the surviving parent to exert a strong pull on the offspring to return home—perhaps even at the expense of the veteran's family of procreation. The problem may be further exacerbated by the awakening in the veteran of memories of combat experiences—deaths of buddies, for example. The combination of all these could overwhelm him. Treatment would have to deal with stabilization of the new, depleted family structure, perhaps by working to gain other natural supports (friends, relatives, employment) for the bereaved parent.

Other possibilities must also be considered. Does the veteran's problem—be it stress reaction or other—serve a purpose within the family? Does it incapacitate him so he is too handicapped to leave the family by moving out or getting a job? Does it interfere with his marriage so that he cannot get too close to his wife, thus guaranteeing his family of origin that they will not lose him totally to an outsider Is he acting out for his father the guilt and terror the "old man" was unable to work through from his own experiences in World War II? Or is the veteran, because of his combat skills, his explosiveness and his potential loss of control, used within the family as a weapon to cow other members in a battle between family coalitions? These and other possibilities must be explored in order for the therapist to determine the direction of the therapy program and which family patterns must be altered to effect improvement. Haley (1976) and Minuchin (1974) provide some strategies for going about this.

Family of Procreation. While our primary focus in this section is on the marital dyad, the veteran's children can also be included in the therapy unit. It is important that the children be aware of the nature of the problem and the major factors associated with the problem. When parents have problems, often the children feel that *they* are the cause because of something they have done. On the other hand, the children may well be one source of strain, particularly older children. In both cases, including the children in some or all of the sessions provides additional insights into the nature of the family system.

In dealing with the veteran and his wife it is important to know the history of the relationship and its current state. If the union is recent, it is appropriate to speculate that the veteran's existent symptoms arise from a fear of closeness, perhaps because of the close friends he lost in combat. On the other hand, combat-related experiences may be less important than factors inherent in the interpersonal relationship.

In both old and new relationships, often the veteran is reluctant to show his mate his weaker side. He may feel guilty about his war experiences and not want her to know what he has done, fearing that she will be shocked and will respect him less if he tells her. Sometimes the therapist cannot effectively deal with this issue by meeting with the couple conjointly and may need to see each partner separately during the session. Then the therapist can have a better feel as to how to help the couple change their communication and interaction (Haley, 1976). At some point the therapist must evaluate the degree to which the mate can understand what the veteran has gone through and can accept it, while at the same time helping the veteran to be able to share at least a little of his pain with her. Alternatively, the therapist may encourage the couple to disclose their feelings in some other area with hopes that it will generalize. Indeed, the content may not be as important as the process of disclosure. Once the pattern changes and a sense of safety and acceptance is gained, the fear of openness may dissipate and along with it the specifics and some of the affect associated with Vietnam.

If the partners were joined prior to the veteran's Vietnam tour, certain information must be gleaned. Wives often report that their husbands were different after return and the counselor will want to know in what way (Figley, 1975). After his tour was he more impulsive? Demanding? Moody? The usual answer is "yes." The therapist then wants to know if he is still this way after all these years. Is it still affecting their lives? If so, why is the problem being confronted *now*? At this point issues may arise which indicate that the marriage is being stressed by problems other than the husband's Vietnam experience. These other events may have put pressure on him, perhaps because they place him in a position of impotence, anger or guilt similar to what he felt overseas. Alternatively, his symptoms may serve the function of taking pressure off him or off his family in general. They may also serve to keep the marriage together, as his wife might leave him if he were "well." In addition, he may feel trapped and be using his combat-related problem as a threat or weapon which she is unable to counter. A different pattern is one of post-Vietnam depression, anomie or a "what does it matter" attitude (see Nace *et al.*, Chapter 5). The veteran's values may have been shaken to the extent that he doesn't care anymore—as a husband, as a man. Whatever the case, the therapist should try to ascertain the pattern into which the stress symptoms fit, and, if they are recurrent, what common conditions apply across all instances.

Infidelity is a problem which can relate to stress reactions. Either partner or both could have been unfaithful during the Vietnam tour. Once again, individual interviews with each spouse may be necessary to delineate past and present "transgressions." This step might also help to determine to what extent these have been forgiven and whether the unfaithful partner can (or should) "tell all" at this point. Perhaps the wife can be helped to understand that her husband needed to be "close to someone" while away for so long a period, or the husband can be assisted in tuning into her longing and sense of desertion. It may also be that a recent affair by the wife reawakened old memories of the impotence and guilt her husband felt when he was overseas and unable to help with the problems at home. Another possibility is that his symptoms could be a way of trying to keep her in the marriage after she discovered a recent affair he had engaged in. Conversely, the symptoms could serve to drive her away so he would be free to obtain a divorce and/or indulge in further cavorting. In any event, the counselor must be aware of the many possible reasons for symptom appearance so that his attempts at exploration and elimination can effect the most change in the least amount of time.

CONCLUSION

It has not been our purpose here to present a detailed outline of treatment techniques for performing family therapy with veterans. That would require more exposition than could be encompassed by a single chapter. Instead, we have attempted to provide an overview aimed at (a) alerting our colleagues to the interpersonal systems aspects of veteran stress responses and (b) highlighting those aspects of veteran experience which should be kept in mind by therapists who normally take a family systems approach in their work.

It helps for the family-oriented counselor or therapist who deals with

Vietnam veterans to be aware of the kinds of problems and syndromes such men present. Since most Vietnam veterans have been away from the war for a number of years, it makes sense to view their difficulties as being precipitated or perpetuated by events occurring within their present lives. Frequently the problems arise from changes in their family/ marital systems. The counselor must be sensitive to the pain, agony, guilt, and rage with which veterans have had to cope. However, he should not lose sight of the fact that the symptoms may serve a function within the family. His interventions should be tailored accordingly.

EPILOGUE: SOCIAL AND HISTORICAL PERSPECTIVES ON THE VIETNAM VETERAN

SEYMOUR LEVENTMAN, Ph.D.

The rationalization of suffering is that it is a process allowing persons to withstand, overcome, even glorify pain, providing there is sufficient social support to render it meaningful and relevant for goals understood to be constructive. Philosophers, social scientists and writers have long been intrigued by this process. The German philosopher Friedrich Nietzsche wrote that "What makes people rebel against suffering is not really suffering itself but the senselessness of suffering. . . . Man . . . does not deny suffering *per se;* he wants it, he seeks it out, provided that it can be given a meaning" (Nietzsche, 1956, pp. 200 and 298). Following Nietzsche, Max Weber noted that suffering can be transformed into religion when made meaningful through social and cultural means (Weber, 1946). And in his study of "anomic suicide," Emile Durkheim argued that not misery but lack of group support in time of stress led to the anomie of self-destruction (Durkheim, 1951).

That wars are hell and that participation in them may breed stress disorders are hardly novel observations. What is unique in American history is a war fought in a "technological blizzard" and a "moral vacuum" (Starr, 1973, p. 12). Vietnam was the longest war in American history (almost 15 years) and the only one in which the U.S. did not emerge as clear-cut victor. It was a war inherited from the French and fought against an agrarian society whose combatants were nevertheless unified by high morale and strong ideological commitment. On the other hand, American troops seemed to lack any particular ideological commitments and American goals seemed ambiguous at best (Moskos, 1970). For the U.S., the Vietnam War was ostensibly waged to "contain Chinese communism." Yet while American troops were still being killed for this purpose, leaders were drinking champagne toasts with Chinese leaders in a spirit of "thawed relations." Falsified intelligence reports and "body counts," an invisible enemy, high civilian involvement, breakdown or ineffectiveness of sophisticated weaponry, stalemated battles fought under confusing restrictions, casualties often due more to booby traps and anti-personnel devices than to conventional weapons, in addition to an awareness of divided political support at home, contributed to a prevailing mood of futility, despair and senselessness among American troops in Vietnam.

While most men fought as their duty, some opposed the war while still in the service and others returned home to form organizations opposed to the very war in which they had just fought. Many veterans came to feel they had been used as human pawns in a complex struggle that was essentially political. The uniqueness of Vietnam and American responses to the war requires, therefore, placing the issues of stress disorders within broader social and historical contexts. While other wars in American history have been unpopular and controversial (see Friedel et al., 1970), few have so eroded homefront morale as to produce reactions of fear, suspicion and downright hostility toward Vietnam veterans. In a film about a Vietnam veteran especially popular with psychiatrists, *Taxi Driver*, it is difficult to say whether past combat or presently experienced hypocrisy at home is most stressful for him.

Americans have always been somewhat uneasy about their returning warriors, even though America has won virtually all of its major wars. Returning American war veterans have often been greeted as heroes but they have also been seen as social problems, potentially threatening to the "domestic tranquility" (see Wecter, 1944). This response goes back to the American Revolution. George Washington hesitated to inform his troops of the war's end, fearing his "bedraggled and drunken" riff-raff might harm the peaceful countryside (Waller, 1944, p. 7). At the close of World War II, America's last great heroic war, sociologist Willard Waller wrote that returning veterans were a potentially "revolutionary class" unless quickly reincorporated into civilian society (Waller, 1944, pp. 183-191). Indeed, the usual societal reaction to returning American war veterans has been their co-optation through various pension and benefit programs, usually issued by the U.S. Congress in response to post-war political and moral pressure, as if granting "payoffs" for services rendered (see Ross, 1967).

But American society has also been ambivalent toward veterans' benefits. The problem is that in a society committed to guaranteeing the priority of civilian over military rule, the warrior is recognized as performing vital wartime functions but has no clear-cut or permanent role during peacetime. While according its war veterans short-run compensatory payments, Americans remain attached to norms of competitive democracy stressing a heritage of individual merit and achievement. Preferential treatment as public policy is anathema. As President Franklin D. Roosevelt remarked to an American Legion convention in 1933, ". . . no person, because he wore a uniform, must thereafter be placed in a special class of beneficiaries over and above all other citizens" (Starr, 1973, p. 44). So, in their treatment of war veterans, the traditional generosity and compassion of Americans have often been tempered by pressures for self-improvement in a highly competitive environment. And the special character of the Vietnam era (1963-1973) even further exacerbated these problems.

The Vietnam War occurred during a period of great change and tension in the world while American society itself experienced stress disorders of considerable magnitude and intensity. In fact, one might say that Vietnam was America with many of the latter's problems projected onto the world scene for all to witness and its fighting men to suffer and endure. Bureaucratic formalism and inefficiency, inept and ill-informed policy-making, political and military gamesmanship, all capped by revelations of high level executive misconduct, produced an unprecedented crisis of faith and confidence in American institutions. Entry into the post-Vietnam era was marked by a pervasive anxiety, generalized "resentment" (Scheler, 1972) and disillusionment that was disconcerting and even uprooting for many Americans. Writings appeared suggesting that the Vietnam War was fought for no tangible cause whatsoever but represented a symbolic effort by the U.S. to reinforce the illusion of omnipotence (Schell, 1976).

Part of this scenario was the victimization of Vietnam veterans. First there were bad discharge numbers. According to a discreet coding system, numbers were entered on discharge papers which identified veterans who had been seen as "troublemakers" while still in the service (ACLU, 1975). This code was distributed to employers and personnel counselors who, under general economic pressure of their own, could make "judicious" choices on job selection. This form of discrimination and stigmatization was furthered by the portrayal of Vietnam veterans in the media, especially television, as dangerous and psychotic freaks, murderers and rapists. This portrayal is summed up in a "Kojak" program in which, after a murder has been committed, Kojak instructs his staff to roundup suspects by obtaining a list of "recently discharged Vietnam veterans."

In other circles, however, Vietnam veterans were presented more pathetically as clinical cases (e.g., Lifton, 1973a). This image emerged as veterans with problems sought psychiatric help which led eventually to a literature such as that contained in the present volume. Studies of stress and other types of psychiatric disorders obviously are intended to demonstrate and explain in symptomatic ways problems experienced by Vietnam veterans, especially those who were in combat. But the result often substantiates the more popular "Kojak" image of veterans as deranged and morbid persons. Even when veterans are viewed as "victims," the focus tends to be on their behavior rather than on broader causative conditions and they become victims blamed for their own plight (Ryan, 1971). At least this is the way they eventually emerge in the popular view, regardless of original intentions. The "blaming the victim" pattern is not unique in its application to Vietnam veterans. It is simply one instance of a broader American tendency which blames all indigent groups for their plights—the poor, the mentally ill and minorities. The noted American writer, Richard Wright, has written, "Perhaps it would be possible for the Negro (read 'Vietnam veteran') to become reconciled to his plight if he could be made to believe his sufferings were for some remote, high, sacrificial end; but sharing the culture that condemns him, and seeing that a lust for trash is what blinds the nation to his claims, is what sets storms rolling in his soul" (in Howe, 1977).

Indeed psychologists and psychiatrists may themselves become victims of their clinical and diagnostic tools. These may so predispose them to see only symptoms of psychopathology that the veterans they treat tend to become just another collection of sick types ultimately separated from the conditions that produced them. In the quest for theoretical (and bureaucratic) parsimony, for example, combat stress becomes just stress and veterans become just sick patients.

On the other hand, in focusing largely on combat stress other important questions remain unexplored. How did combat veterans not suffering from disorders manage to cope with the stresses unique in Vietnam? How did noncombat veterans stationed mainly in rear echelons deal with stresses unique to those areas of duty? And in diagnosing disorders, how is the "fatal flaw" fallacy avoided, that is, the tendency to search for some prior existing emotional weakness to make combat breakdown appear likely and inevitable? One might even argue that for Vietnam, combat-related disorders were a "normal" response, more so than repressing or coping in other ways.

Many veterans understandably recoil at the "heartbreaking" type of psychiatric accounts of the tragic details of combat in Vietnam, especially if they involve stories of burning villages, babies, women and old people, hospitals and other innocent targets. Veterans feel that they are the only people in American history who became viewed as deviants by those at home even though they did what they thought American society expected of them. An alternative view in veterans studies might heed their claims that research should be focused on the problems of the "good civilians" whose policies created the war and then recruited as "dirty workers" young men from working class and minority group backgrounds to fight it. This is a case where professional, theoretical and scientific orientations may become or support prevailing culture ideologies which seek to divert responsibility for an unpopular war from the policy-makers to the policy-doers.

In the war's aftermath of recrimination and bitterness on the one hand and official unconcern on the other, veterans clearly do not relish being blamed for "losing" the kind of war Vietnam was. In 1975 I wrote that nothing "reflects so much of what is wrong with American society" as its treatment of Vietnam veterans (Leventman, 1975). Since then one can only reiterate that the negative legacy of Vietnam lies more in civilian society than in the psyches of veterans.

FIGLEY, C. R. & SOUTHERLY, W. T. Residue of war: The Vietnam veteran in mainstream America. Paper presented at the annual meeting of the American Psychological Association, San Francisco, August 1977.

FIGLEY, C. R. & SPRENKLE, D. W. Delayed stress response syndrome: Family therapy implications. *Journal of Marriage and Family Counseling*, 1978, 4:175-184.

FIMAN, B. G., BORUS, J. F., & STANTON, M. D. Black-white and American-Vietnamese relations among soldiers in Vietnam. *Journal of Social Issues*, 1975, 31:39-48.

FITTS, W. H. *Tennessee Self Concept Scale*. Nashville: Counselor Recordings and Tests, 1964.

FOX, R. P. Post-combat adaptational problems. *Comprehensive Psychiatry*, 1972, 13: 435-443.

FOX, R. P. Narcissistic rage and the problem of combat aggression. *Archives of General Psychiatry*, 1974, 31:807-811.

FRANKL, V. E. *Man's Search for Meaning*. Boston: Beacon Press, 1959.

FREEDMAN, A. M., KAPLAN, H. I., & SADOCK, B. J. (Eds.). *Comprehensive Textbook of Psychiatry*. Baltimore: Williams & Wilkins, 1975.

Free Fire Zone: Stories by Vietnam Veterans. Brooklyn: First Casualty Press, 1975.

FREUD, S. Identification with the aggressor. In *The Ego and Mechanisms of Defense*. New York: International Universities Press, 1946.

FREUD, S. *Beyond the Pleasure Principle*. Standard Edition 18. London: Hogarth Press, 1955. (Originally published in 1920.)

FREUD, S. *Introductory Lectures on Psychoanalysis*. Standard Edition 16. London: Hogarth Press, 1955. (Originally published in 1917.)

FREUD, S. *Psychoanalysis and the War Neurosis*. Standard Edition 17. London: Hogarth Press, 1955. (Originally published in 1919.)

FREUD, S. *Inhibitions, Symptoms and Anxiety*. Standard Edition 20. London: Hogarth Press, 1955. (Originally published in 1926.)

FREUD, S. *Moses and Monotheism*. Standard Edition 23. London: Hogarth Press, 1955. (Originally published in 1939.)

FREUD, S. *Mourning and Melancholia*. Standard Edition 14. London: Hogarth Press, 1957. (Originally published in 1912.)

FREUD, S. *On the History of the Psycho-analytic Movement*. Standard Edition 14. London: Hogarth Press, 1957.

FREUD, S. *Totem and Taboo*. Standard Edition 14. London: Hogarth Press, 1957. (Originally published in 1913.)

FREUD, S. Reflections upon war and death. In P. Rieff (Ed.), *Character and Culture*. New York: Macmillan, 1963.

FREUD, S. Psychoanalysis and war neuroses. In P. Rieff (Ed.), *Character and Culture*. New York: Macmillan, 1963.

FRIEDEL, F., MORRISON, S., & MERK, F. *Dissent in Three American Wars*. Cambridge, Mass.: Harvard University Press, 1970.

FURST, S. (Ed.). *Psychic Trauma*. New York: Basic Books, 1967.

FUTTERMAN, S. & PUMPIAN-MINDLIN, E. Traumatic war neuroses for five years later. *American Journal of Psychiatry*, 1951, 108:401.

GAULT, B. W. Some remarks on slaughter. *American Journal of Psychiatry*, 1971, 128: 450-454.

GILLOOLY, D. & BOND, T. C. The why of fragging. *Military Medicine*, 1976, 141:700-703.

GLASS, A. J. Effectiveness of forward treatment. *Bulletin of the U.S. Army Medical Department*, 1947, 7:1034-1041.

GLASS, A. J. Psychotherapy in the combat zone. *American Journal of Psychiatry*, 1954, 110:725-731.

GLASS, A. J. Paper presented at the Symposium on Prevention and Social Psychiatry,

Walter Reed Army Institute of Research, Walter Reed Army Medical Center, April 1957. Available through the U.S. Government Printing Office, Washington, D.C., 185-197.

GLASS, A. J. Introduction. In P. G. Bourne (Ed.), *The Psychology and Physiology of Stress*. New York: Academic Press, 1969, xiv-xxx.

GLASSER, R. J. *365 Days*. New York: Bantam Books, 1971.

GLICK, I. O., WEISS, R. S., & PARKES, C. M. *The First Year of Bereavement*. New York: Wiley, 1974.

GOODWIN, D. W. Is alcoholism hereditary? A review and critique. *Archives of General Psychiatry*, 1971, 25:545-549.

GOODWIN, D. W., DAVIS, D. H., & ROBINS, L. N. Drinking amid abundant illicit drugs. *Archives of General Psychiatry*, 1975, 32:230-233.

GOUGH, H. G. *California Psychological Inventory*. Palo Alto, Calif.: Consulting Psychologists Press, 1956.

GRINKER, R. R., WILLERMAN, B., BRADLEY, A. D., & FASTOVSKY, A. A study of psychological predisposition to the development of operational fatigue. *American Journal of Orthopsychiatry*, 1946, 16:191-214.

GRINKER, R. R. & SPIEGEL, J. P. *Men Under Stress*. Philadelphia: Blakiston, 1945.

GUNDERSON, E. K. E. & ARTHUR, R. J. Demographic factors in the incidence of mental illness. *Military Medicine*, 1966, 131:429-433.

HALBERSTAM, D. *The Best and the Brightest*. New York: Random House, 1973.

HALEY, J. A review of the family therapy field. In J. Haley (Ed.), *Changing Families*. New York: Grune & Stratton, 1971.

HALEY, J. *Problem-Solving Therapy*. San Francisco: Jossey-Bass, 1976.

HALEY, S. A. When the patient reports atrocities. *Archives of General Psychiatry*, 1974, 30:191-196.

HALEY, S. A. The Vietnam veteran and his preschool child: Child rearing as a delayed stress in combat veterans. Read at the American Orthopsychiatric Association, Washington, D.C., March 1975.

HALEY, S. A. Implications of post-combat stress response syndromes for mental health professionals. Paper presented at the American Psychological Association, Washington, D.C., September 1976.

HALL, R. C. W. & MALONE, P. T. Psychiatric residuals of prolonged captivity experience. In H. I. McCubbin, B. B. Dahl, P. J. Metres, & Plag, J. A. (Eds.), *Family Separation and Reunion: Families of Prisoners of War and Servicemen Missing in Action*. Washington, D.C.: U.S. Government Printing Office, 1975.

HAMMOND, W. A. *A Treatise on Insanity in Its Medical Relations*. London: H. K. Lewis, 1883.

HANSON, F. R. The factor of fatigue in the neuroses of combat. *Army Medical Bulletin* (Supplement 9), 1949, 147-150.

HASSENER, P. W. & McCARY, P. W. A comparative study of the attitudes of veterans and non-veterans at the University of Northern Colorado. *Colorado Journal of Educational Research*, 1974, 14:11-18.

HEINL, COL. The disintegration of the armed forces. *Journal of the Armed Forces*, 1971.

HELMER, J. *Bringing the War Home*. New York: Free Press, 1973.

HELZER, J., ROBINS, L., & DAVIS, D. Depressive disorders in Vietnam returnees. Unpublished manuscript, Washington University, 1974.

HELZER, J. E., ROBINS, L. N., & DAVIS, D. H. Antecedents of narcotic use and addiction. *Drug and Alcohol Dependence*, 1975/76, 1:183-190.

HERBERT, A. *Soldier*. New York: Holt, Rinehart & Winston, 1973.

HERSH, S. My Lai 4—A report on the massacre and its aftermath. *Harper's Magazine*, March 1970.

HILL, R. *Families Under Stress, Adjustment to the Crisis of War Separation and Reunion.* New York: Harper, 1949.

HOCKING, F. Extreme environmental stress and its significance for psychopathology. *American Journal of Psychotherapy*, 1970, 24:4-26.

HOOPER, T. & SPILKA, B. Some meanings and correlates of future time and death among college students. *Omega*, 1970, 1:49-56.

HORNEY, K. The value of vindictiveness. *American Journal of Psychoanalysis*, 1949, 8:3-12.

HOROWITZ, M. J. Psychic trauma: Return of images after a stress film. *Archives of General Psychiatry*, 1969, 20:552-559.

HOROWITZ, M. J. *Image Formation and Cognition*. New York: Appleton-Century-Crofts, 1970.

HOROWITZ, M. J. Stress response syndromes. *Archives of General Psychiatry*, 1974, 31: 768-781.

HOROWITZ, M. J. *Stress Response Syndromes*. New York: Aronson, Inc., 1976.

HOROWITZ, M. J. Phase oriented treatment of stress response syndromes. *American Journal of Psychotherapy*, 1977, 31:38-42.

HOROWITZ, M. J. & BECKER, S. S. Cognitive response to stress: Experimental studies of a "compulsion to repeat trauma." *Psychoanalysis and Contemporary Science*, 1972, 1:258-305.

HOROWITZ, M. J. & SOLOMON, G. F. A prediction of delayed stress response syndromes in Vietnam veterans. In D. M. Mantell & M. Pilisuk (Eds.), *Journal of Social Issues: Soldiers In and After Vietnam*, 1973, 31 (4):67-80.

HOWE, I. Black boy, black man. Review of Richard Wright, *American Hunger*. New York: Harper & Row, 1977, in the *New York Times Book Review*, June 26, 1977, 34.

HUGETT, W. T. *Body Count*. New York: Putnam, 1973.

HUNTER, E. A comparative analysis of family adjustment of returned POWs and Vietnam veterans. Paper presented at the fourth annual DoD Health Care Task Force meeting on POW/MIA Matters, San Antonio, Texas, November 1976.

HUNTER, E. The prisoners of war: Coping with the stress of isolation. In Moos, R. (Ed.), *Human Adaptations Coping with Life Crises*. Lexington, Mass.: D. C. Heath & Co., 1976.

HUNTER, E. POW resistance posture in captivity in relation to subsequent career and family adjustment. *Naval Health Research Publication No. 76-65*, 1976.

HUNTER, E., PLAG, J., PHELAN, J., & MOWERY, E. Resistance posture and the Vietnam prisoner of war. *Journal of Political and Military Sociology*, 1976, 4 (4):295-308.

HUNTER, E. & PHELAN, J. Resistance posture in the POW in relation to personality, in press.

JENNINGS, M. K. & MARKUS, G. B. The effects of military service on political attitudes. *American Political Science Review*, 1975.

JOHNSON, A. Psychiatric treatment in the combat situation. *United States Army Republic Vietnam Medical Bulletin*, 1975, 32:14-20.

JONES, E. D. & JOHNSON, A. Medical and psychiatric treatment policy and practice in Vietnam. *Journal of Social Issues*, 1975, 31 (4):49-65.

KAISER, L. *The Traumatic Neurosis*. Philadelphia: Lippincott, 1968.

KALINOWSKI, L. B. Problems of war neuroses in the light of experiences in other countries. *American Journal of Psychiatry*, 1950, 107:340-346.

KAPLAN, D. M. *On shyness. International Journal of Psychoanalysis*, 1972, 53:439-453.

KARDINER, A. *War Stress and Neurotic Illness*. New York: Hoeber, 1947.

KARDINER, A. Traumatic neurosis of war. In S. Arieti (Ed.), *American Handbook of Psychiatry*, Vol. 1, 1st ed. New York: Basic Books, 1959.

Kastenbaum, R. & Aisenberg, R. *The Psychology of Death.* New York: Springer, 1972.

Kernberg, O. *Borderline Conditions and Pathological Narcissism.* New York: Aronson, 1975.

Kingry. Personal communication. October, 1972.

Klonoff, H., McDougall, G., Clark, C., Kramer, P., & Horgan, J. The neuropsychological, psychiatric, and physical effects of prolonged and severe stress: 30 years later. *Journal of Nervous and Mental Disease,* 1976, 163:246-252.

Kovic, R. *Born on the Fourth of July.* New York: Simon & Schuster, 1976.

Kris, E. The recovery of childhood memories in psychoanalysis. *Psychoanalytic Study of the Child,* 1956, 11:54-88.

Krystal, H. (Ed.). *Massive Psychic Trauma.* New York: International Universities Press, 1968.

Kubler-Ross, E. *On Death and Dying.* New York: Macmillan, 1969.

Kuhn, T. *The Structure of Scientific Revolution.* Chicago: University of Chicago Press, 1962.

Kushner, F. To live or die. *AMEDD Spectrum:* U.S. Army Medical Department, Vol. 1, No. 1, 1974, 16-21.

Laing, R. *The Divided Self.* London: Penguin, 1960.

Laing, R. *The Politics of Experience.* London: Penguin, 1967.

Langer, S. *Philosophy in a New Key.* Cambridge: Harvard University Press, 1942.

Langer, S. *Feeling and Form.* New York: Scribners, 1953.

Langer, S. *Philosophical Sketches.* Baltimore: Johns Hopkins Press, 1962.

Langer, S. *Mind: An Essay on Human Feeling* (two volumes). Baltimore: Johns Hopkins Press, 1967-72.

Lester, D. Experimental and correlational studies of the fear of death. *Psychological Bulletin,* 1967, 67:27-36.

Lester, D. Religious behaviors and attitudes toward death. In A. Godin (Ed.), *Death and Presence.* Brussels, Belgium: International Center for Studies in Religious Education, 1972, 107-124.

Leventman, S. Official neglect of Vietnam veterans. *Journal of Social Issues,* 1975, 31:171-179.

Leventman, S. & Camacho, P. The gook syndrome: The Vietnam war as a racial encounter. Paper presented at the annual meeting of the American Sociological Association, Montreal, August 1974.

Levy, C. J. *Spoils of War.* Boston: Houghton Mifflin, 1971 (a).

Levy, C. J. ARVN as faggots: Inverted warfare in Vietnam. *Transaction,* October 1971, 18-27 (b).

Lewis, N. D. C. & Engel, B. (Eds.). *Wartime Psychiatry: A Compendium of the International Literature.* New York: Oxford University Press, 1954.

Lidz, T. Nightmares and the combat neurosis. *Psychiatry,* 1946, 3:37-49.

Lieberman, E. J. War and the family: The psychology of antigrief. *Modern Medicine,* 1971, 179-183, 191.

Lifton, R. J. *Thought Reform and the Psychology of Totalism.* New York: Norton, 1961.

Lifton, R. J. *Death in Life: Survivors of Hiroshima.* New York: Random House, 1968.

Lifton, R. J. *Death in Life.* New York: Vintage Books, 1969 (a).

Lifton, R. J. Vietnam: Betrayal and self-betrayal. *Transaction,* 1969, 6:6-9 (b).

Lifton, R. J. The scars of Vietnam. *Commonweal,* 1970, 91:554-556 (a).

Lifton, R. J. On psychohistory. *Partisan Review,* 1970, 37:11-32 (b).

Lifton, R. J. Introduction. In *History and Human Survival.* New York: Random House, 1970 (c).

Lifton, R. J. Questions of guilt. *Partisan Review,* 1972, 39:514-530.

LIFTON, R. J. *Home from the War.* New York: Simon & Schuster, 1973 (a).

LIFTON, R. J. The sense of immortality: On death and the continuity of life. *American Journal of Psychoanalysis,* 1973, 33:3-15 (b).

LIFTON, R. J. The struggle for cultural rebirth. *Harpers,* 1973, 84-90 (c).

LIFTON, R. J. The postwar war. In D. M. Mantell & M. Milisuk (Eds.), *Journal of Social Issues: Soldiers In and After Vietnam,* 1975, 31:181-195.

LINDEN, E. Fragging and other withdrawal symptoms. *Saturday Review,* January 1972.

LIVINGSTON, G. Quoted in the *Saturday Review,* September 20, 1969.

LORR, M., PECK, C. P., & STENGER, C. A. Interpersonal styles of Vietnam-era veterans. *Journal of Personality Assessment,* 1975, 39:507-510.

LUMRY, G. K., CEDARLEAF, C. B., WRIGHT, M. S., & BRAATZ, G. A. A further look at the Vietnam-era veteran. Paper presented at the Fifteenth Annual Conference of the Veterans Administration Cooperative Studies in Psychiatry, Houston, Texas, April 1970.

LUMRY, G. K. & BRAATZ, G. A. The Vietnam-era veteran and psychiatric implications. Paper presented at the Workshop on the Unique Problems of the Vietnam Era Veteran, V. A. Hospital, New Orleans, October 1970.

MANTELL, D. M. *True Americanism: Green Berets and War Resistors.* New York: Teachers College Press, 1974.

MANTELL, D. M. & PILISUK, M. (Eds.). Soldiers in and after Vietnam. *Journal of Social Issues,* 1975, 31:4.

MATUSSEK, P. & MANTELL, D. *Die Konzentrationslagerhaft und ihre Folgen.* Berlin: Springer Verlag, 1971.

McCUBBIN, H. The returned prisoner of war and his children: Evidence for the origin of second generational effects of captivity. In R. Spaulding (Ed.), *Proceedings of the Third Annual Joint Medical Meeting Concerning POW/MIA Matters,* San Diego, November 1975, 1976, 40-50.

McCUBBIN, H. I., DAHL, B. B., METRES, P. J., HUNTER, E. J., & PLAG, J. A. (Eds.). *Family Separation and Reunion.* Washington, D.C.: U.S. Government Printing Office, 1975.

McCUBBIN, H., DAHL, B., LESTER, G., & ROSS, B. The returned prisoner of war: Factors in family reintegration. *Journal of Marriage and the Family,* August 1975, 471-478.

McCUBBIN, H., HUNTER, E., & DAHL, B. Residuals of war: Families of prisoners of war and servicemen missing in action. *Journal of Social Issues,* 1975, 31 (4):95-109.

McCUBBIN, H. I., DAHL, B. B., & HUNTER, E. J. *Families in the Military System.* Beverly Hills, Calif.: Sage, 1976.

McCUBBIN, H., DAHL, B., LESTER, G., BENSON, D., & ROBERTSON, M. Coping repertoires of families adapting to prolonged war-induced separations. *Journal of Marriage and the Family,* 1976, 461-471.

MENNINGER, W. C. Psychiatric experience in the war, 1941-1946. *American Journal of Psychiatry,* 1947, 103:587-593.

MENNINGER, W. C. *Psychiatry In a Troubled World.* New York: Macmillan, 1948.

MILGRAM, S. Behavioral study of obedience. *Journal of Abnormal and Social Psychology,* 1963, 67:371-380.

MILGRAM, S. Some conditions of obedience and disobedience to authority. *Human Relations,* 1965, 18:57-65.

MILGRAM, S. The compulsion to do evil. *Patterns of Prejudice,* 1967, 1.

MILGRAM, S. *Obedience to Authority.* New York: Harper & Row, 1974.

MINTON, B. & SPILKA, B. Perspectives on death in relation to powerlessness and form of personal religion. *Omega,* 1976, 7:261-267.

MINUCHIN, S. *Families and Family Therapy*. Cambridge, Mass.: Harvard, 1974.

MORRIER, E. Passivity as a response to psychic trauma. Unpublished manuscript 1977.

MORRIS, L. E. "Over the hump" in Vietnam: Adjustment patterns in a time-limited stress situation. *Bulletin of the Menninger Clinic,* 1970, 34:352-363.

MOSKOS, C. *The American Enlisted Man*. New York: Russell Sage, 1970, 148-149.

MOTIS, G. & NEAL, R. D. Freud in the boonies. *USARV Medical Bulletin,* 1968, 40-47.

MULLINS, W. S. (Ed.). *Neuropsychiatry in World War II,* Volume II. Washington, D.C.: Office of the Surgeon General, 1973.

MUSSER, M. J. & STENGER, C. A. A medical and social perception of the Vietnam veteran. *Bulletin of the New York Academy of Medicine,* 1972, 48:859-869.

NACE, E. P. & MEYERS, A. L. The prognosis for addicted Vietnam returnees: A comparison with civilian addicts. *Comprehensive Psychiatry,* 1974, 15 (1):49-56.

NACE, E., MEYERS, A., ROTHBERG, J. M., & MALESON, F. Addicted and non-addicted drug users: A comparison of drug usage patterns. *Archives of General Psychiatry,* 1975, 32:77-80.

NACE, E. P., MEYERS, A. L., O'BRIEN, C. P., REAM, N., & MINTZ, J. Depression in veterans two years after Vietnam. *American Journal of Psychiatry,* 1977, 134 (2): 167-170.

NACE, E. P., O'BRIEN, C. P., MINTZ, J., REAM, N., MEYERS, A. L. Drinking problems among Vietnam veterans. *Currents in Alcoholism,* 1977, 2.

NAUGHTON, R. Motivational factors of American prisoners of war held by the Democratic Republic of Vietnam. *Naval War College Review,* 1975, 27 (4):2-14.

NEFF, L. Personal communication, 1975.

NEFF, L. Traumatic neurosis. Paper presented at the annual meeting of the American Psychological Association, California, May 1975 (b).

NEFF, L. Traumatic neuroses: A syndrome seen in Vietnam war veterans. Read at the American Orthopsychiatric Association meeting, Atlanta, Georgia, March 1976.

NEFZGER, M. D. Follow-up studies of World War II and Korean War prisoners. 1. Study plan and mortality findings. *American Journal of Epidemiology,* 1970, 91: 123-128.

NICHOLSON, L. Military Chaplaincy Section, Lutheran Church of America. Personal communication, 1971.

NIEDERLAND, W. G. Clinical observations on the "survivor syndrome." *International Journal of Psychoanalysis,* 1968.

NIEDERLAND, W. Workshop presentation on the guilt and grief of Vietnam veterans and concentration camp survivors. IV International Psychoanalytic Forum, New York, 1972.

NIETZSCHE, F. *The Genealogy of Morals*. New York: Doubleday, 1956.

NORDHEIMER, J. *New York Times,* May 26, 1971.

O'BRIEN, C. P., NACE, E. P., & MEYERS, A. L. *Alcohol and Drug Abuse in the Vietnam Veteran* (DAMD 17-14C-4015). Washington, D.C.: U.S. Army Medical and Development Command, 1976.

O'BRIEN, T. *If I Die in a Combat Zone . . .* New York: Delacorte Press, 1973.

O'CONNELL, P. Trends in psychological adjustment: Observations made during successive psychiatric follow-up interviews of returned Navy-Marine Corps POWs. In R. Spaulding (Ed.), *Proceedings of the Third Annual Joint Medical Meeting Concerning POW/MIA Matters, San Diego, California, November 1975,* 1976, 16-22.

O'DONNEL, J. A. Young men and drugs—A nationwide survey. National Institute on Drug Abuse. Research Monograph No. 5, February 1976.

O'NEILL, D. J. & FONTAINE, G. D. Counseling for the Vietnam veteran. *Journal of College Student Personnel,* 1973, 14:153-155.

OPTON, E. M., JR. It never happened and besides they deserved it. In N. Sanford & C. Comstock (Eds.), *Sanctions for Evil.* San Francisco: Jossey-Bass, 1971.

ORWELL, G. *1984.* London: Praeger, 1948.

OSMOND, H. The medical model in psychiatry: Love it or leave it. *Medical Annals of the District of Columbia,* 1971, 41:171-175.

OSWALD, P. & BITTNER, E. Life adjustment after severe persecution. *American Journal of Psychiatry,* 1968, 124:1393-1400.

PARKS, D. *A G. I.'s Diary.* New York: Harper, 1968.

PAYNE, E. Psychic Trauma. Manuscript in preparation.

PLAG, J. A. & GOFFMAN, J. M. The prediction of four year military effectiveness from characteristics of Naval recruits. *Military Medicine,* 1966, 131:729-735.

POLLOCK, J. C., WHITE, D., & GOLD, F. When soldiers return: Combat and political alienation among white Vietnam veterans. In D. Schwartz & S. Schwartz (Eds.), *New Directions in Political Socialization.* New York: Free Press, 1975, 317-333.

POLNER, M. *No Victory Parades.* New York: Holt, Rinehart & Winston, 1971.

RANGELL, L. The metapsychology of psychic trauma. In S. Furst (Ed.), *Psychic Trauma.* New York: Basic Books, 1967.

REDL, F. The superego in uniform. In N. Sanford & C. Comstock (Eds.), *Sanctions for Evil.* San Francisco: Jossey-Bass, 1971.

REDLICH, F. G. & FREEDMAN, D. X. (Eds.). *The Theory and Practice of Psychiatry.* New York: Basic Books, 1966.

RENNIE, T. A. National planning for psychiatric rehabilitation. *American Journal of Orthopsychiatry,* 1944, 14:386-399.

ROBINS, L. N. *The Vietnam Drug User Returns.* Special Action Office Monograph, Series A, No. 2, 1974. Washington, D.C.: U.S. Government Printing Office (a).

ROBINS, L. N. *Veterans' Drug Use Three Years after Vietnam.* St. Louis: Department of Psychiatry, Washington University School of Medicine, 1974 (b).

ROBINS, L. N., BATES, W. M., & O'NEAL, P. Adult drinking problems of former problem children. In D. T. Pittman & C. R. Snyder (Eds.), *Society, Culture and Drinking Patterns.* New York: John Wiley & Sons, Inc., 1962.

ROBINS, L. N., MURPHY, G. C., & BRECHENRIDGE, M. B. Drinking behavior of young urban Negro men. *Q. J. Stud. Alcohol,* 1968, 19:657-684.

ROBINS, L. N., DAVID, D. H., & GOODWIN, D. W. Drug use by U.S. Army enlisted men in Vietnam: A follow-up on their return home. *American Journal of Epidemiology,* 1974, 99:235-249.

ROSS, D. *Preparing for Ulysses.* New York: Columbia University Press, 1967.

ROWLAND, B. An overview of free-world personnel captured in South Vietnam. Paper presented at CPWS-SERE Conference, San Diego, California, 1975.

ROWLAND, B. An overview of Americans captured in North Vietnam. Paper presented at CPWS-SERE Conference, San Diego, California, 1975.

RUTLEDGE, H., HUNTER, E., & DAHL, B. Human values and the prisoner of war. *Environment and Behavior,* in press.

RYAN, W. *Blaming the Victim.* New York: Random House, 1971.

S., J. American Orthopsychiatric Association: The Vietnam experience—Its impact on the individual American serviceman. Special panel, 48th annual meeting, Washington, D.C., March 1971. (Unpublished remarks by an ex-Marine on the panel. Transcript available.)

SACKS, J. In *Smiling Through the Apocalypse,* an *Esquire Magazine* anthology. New York: Esquire, 1970.

SANFORD, N. & COMSTOCK, C. (Eds.). *Sanctions of Evil: Sources of Social Destructiveness.* San Francisco: Jossey-Bass, 1971.

SAUNA, V. D. War, stress and bereavement. Paper presented at the annual meeting of the American Psychological Association, Chicago, September 1975.

SCHELER, M. *Resentment*. New York: Schocken Books, 1972.

SCHELL, J. *The Time of Illusion*. New York: Knopf, 1976.

SEARLES, H. The psychodynamics of vengefulness. *Psychiatry*, 1956, 19:31-39.

SEGAL, D. R. & SEGAL, M. W. The impact of military service on trust in government, international atitudes and social status. In N. L. Goldman & D. R. Segal (Eds.), *The Social Psychology of Military Service*. Beverly Hills: Sage Press, 1976, 201-211.

SEGAL, J. Correlates of collaboration and resistance behavior among U.S. Army POWs in Korea. *Journal of Social Issues*, 1957, 13 (3):31-40.

SEGAL, J. Long-term psychological and physical effects of the POW experience: A review of the literature. *Naval Health Research Center Publication No. 74-2*, 1974.

SEGAL, J., HUNTER, E., & SEGAL, Z. Universal consequences of captivity: Stress reactions among divergent populations of prisoners of war and their families. *International Journal of Social Science*, 1976, XXVIII (3):593-609.

SHAPIRO, E. (Ed.). Combat effectiveness. In *PsychoSources: A Psychology Resource Catalog*. New York: Bantam Books, 1973.

SHATAN, C. F. Congressional Record (House). Testimony on relationship of counter-guerrilla training to Vietnam war crimes, March 1, 1971.

SHATAN, C. F. The grief of soldiers. *American Report*, 1972, 2:1-3.

SHATAN, C. F. Post-Vietnam syndrome. *The New York Times*, May 6, 1972, 35.

SHATAN, C. F. The grief of soldiers—Vietnam combat veterans' self-help movement. *American Journal of Orthopsychiatry*, 1973, 43:640-653 (a).

SHATAN, C. F. Inside the Vietnam veteran. *Behavior*, 1973, 56-61 (b).

SHATAN, C. F. Through the membrane of reality: Impacted grief and perceptual dissonance in Vietnam combat veterans. *Psychiatric Opinion*, 1974, 11 (6):6-15.

SHATAN, C. F. Bogus manhood, bogus honor: Surrender and transfiguration in the U.S. Marine Corps. *Psychoanalytic Review*, 1977, 25:335-349.

SHATAN, C. F. Genocide and bereavement. In R. Arens (Ed.), *Genocide in Paraguay*. Philadelphia: Temple University Press, 1977.

SHATAN, C., SMITH, J. R., & HALEY, S. Preliminary draft of formulation on post-traumatic stress reactions for DSM-III. (Unpublished draft, private circulation. Updated versions available from the first author).

SHATAN, C. F., HALEY, S., & SMITH, J. Johnny comes marching home: Combat stress and DSM III. Paper presented at the annual meeting of the American Psychiatric Association, Toronto, May 1977.

SHORT, L. O. & STANKUS, J. C. The symptom checklist: A brief questionnaire for psychological screening. *Proceedings, 1974 Psychology in the Air Force Symposium*. U.S.A.F. Academy, 1974, 133-136.

SHUR, M. *The Id and the Regulatory Principles of Mental Functioning*. New York: International Universities Press, 1966.

SIGAL, J. Second generation effects of massive psychiatric trauma. *International Psychiatry Clinic*, 1971, 8:55-65.

SMITH, J. R. The lonely veterans: Sanction, atonement and the Vietnam veteran. Manuscript in preparation.

SOLNIT, A. J. & KRIS, M. Trauma and infantile experiences. In S. Furst (Ed.), *Psychic Trauma*. New York: Basic Books, 1967.

SOLNIT, A. J. & PRIEL, B. Psychological reactions to facial and hand burns in young men. *Psychoanalytic Study of the Child*, 1975, 30:549-566.

SOLOMON, G. F. Psychiatric casualties of the Vietnam conflict with particular reference to the problem of heroin addiction. *Modern Medicine*, 1971, 38:199-201, 211, 215.

SOLOMON, G. F., ZARCONE, V. P., YOERG, R., SCOTT, N. R., & MAURER, R. G. Three psychiatric casualties from Vietnam. *Archives of General Psychiatry*, 1971, 25:522-524.

SPAULDING, R. (Ed.). Proceedings of the Third Annual Joint Medical Meeting Concerning POW/MIA Matters, San Diego, California, November 1975. 1976.

SPILKA, B., PELLEGRINI, R. J., & DAILEY, K. Religion, American values and death perspectives. *Sociological Symposium*, 1968, 1:57-66.

SPILKA, B., STOUT, L., MINTON, B., & SIZEMORE, D. Death and personal faith: A psychometric investigation. *Journal for the Scientific Study of Religion*, 1977, 16:168-178.

STANTON, M. D. Some psychological factors in the Vietnam experience. In L. Houghton (Ed.), *The Unique Problems of the Vietnam-era Veterans*. New Orleans: Veterans Administration Hospital, 1970 (a).

STANTON, M. D. Understanding the Vietnam veteran: Some social-psychological considerations. Paper presented at the meeting of the Veterans Administration's Cooperative Studies in Mental Health and Behavioral Sciences, St. Louis, Missouri, March 1970 (b).

STANTON, M. D. The military family: Its future in the all volunteer context. In N. Oldman & D. Segal (Eds.), *Social Psychology of Military Service*. Beverly Hills: Sage, 1976 (a).

STANTON, M. D. Drugs, Vietnam and the Vietnam veteran: An overview. *American Journal of Drug and Alcohol Abuse*, 1976, 3:556-670 (b).

STANTON, M. D. Family treatment of the drug addicted veteran. In C. J. Hunter (Ed.), *Changing Families in a Changing Military System*. San Diego: NHRC, 1977 (a).

STANTON, M. D. Some outcome results and aspects of structural family therapy with drug addicts. Paper presented at the National Drug Abuse Conference, San Francisco, May 1977 (b).

STANTON, M. D. & TODD, T. C. Family therapy with heroin addicts. In E. Kaufman & P. Kaufman (Eds.), *From Enmeshed Enemy to Ally: The Family Therapy of Drug and Alcohol Abusers*. New York: Gardner, 1978.

STARR, P. *The Discarded Army: Veterans after Vietnam*. New York: Charterhouse, 1973.

STENGER, C. A. Perspectives on the post-Vietnam syndrome. VA Paper, Veterans Administration Central Office (111F2), July 1974.

STONE, R. *Dog Soldiers*. Boston: Houghton Mifflin, 1973.

STOUFFER, S. *The American Soldier: Combat and Its Aftermath*. Princeton, N.J.: Princeton University Press, 1949.

STRANGE, R. E. & ARTHUR, R. J. Hospital ship psychiatry in a war zone. *American Journal of Psychiatry*, 1967, 124:281-286.

STRAYER, R. & ELLENHORN, L. Vietnam veterans: A study exploring adjustment patterns and attitudes. *Journal of Social Issues*, 1975, 31:81-94.

STUEN, M. R. & SOLBERG, K. B. The Vietnam veteran: Characteristics and needs. In L. J. Sherman & E. M. Caffey (Eds.), *The Vietnam Veteran in Contemporary Society*. Washington, D.C.: Veterans Administration, 1972, 106-112.

SZASZ, T. *The Myth of Mental Illness*. New York: Harper & Row, 1961.

TANAY, E. Initiation of psychotherapy with survivors of Nazi persecution. In H. Krystal (Ed.), *Massive Psychic Trauma*. New York: International Universities Press, 1968.

TANAY, E. The dear John syndrome during the Vietnam war. *Diseases of the Nervous System*, 1976, 37:165-167.

TASK FORCE ON NOMENCLATURE AND STATISTICS OF THE AMERICAN PSYCHIATRIC ASSOCIATION. *Progress Report on the Preparation of DSM III*. Washington, D.C.: American Psychiatric Association, 1976.

TEMPLER, D. I. The construction and validation of a death anxiety scale. *Journal of General Psychology,* 1970, 82:165-177.

TIFFANY, N. J. Mental health of army troops in Vietnam. *American Journal of Psychiatry,* 1967, 123:1585-1586.

TIMMERMAN, F. W., JR. Prediction of enlisted soldier discipline problems in line combat units of the United States Army. *Proceedings, 1974 Psychology in the Air Force Symposium.* U.S.A.F. Academy, 1974, 117-121.

TISCHLER, G. L. Patterns of psychiatric attrition and of behavior in a combat zone. In P. Bourne (Ed.), *The Psychology and Physiology of Stress: With Special Reference to Studies on the Vietnam War.* New York: Academic Press, 1969.

TROSSMAN, B. Adolescent children of concentration camp survivors. *Canadian Psychiatric Association Journal,* 1969, 13:12.

VAN PUTTEN, T. & EMORY, W. H. Traumatic neurosis in Vietnam returnees. *Archives of General Psychiatry,* 1973, 29:695-698.

VERNON, G. M. A study of attitudes toward death. Unpublished manuscript, 1968, cited in G. M. Vernon, *Sociology of Death.* New York: Ronald Press, 1970, 110.

VETERANS ADMINISTRATION. *The Vietnam Veteran in Contemporary Society: Collected Materials Pertaining to the Young Veterans.* Washington, D.C., 1972.

VIETNAM VETERANS AGAINST THE WAR. *Winter Soldier Investigation.* Boston: Beacon Press, 1972.

VOHDEN, R. *Stress and the Vietnam POW.* Industrial College of the Armed Forces, Washington, D.C., Student Research Report No. 091, 1974.

WALLER, W. *The Veteran Comes Back.* New York: Dryden Press, 1944.

WARNER, W. L., MEEKER, M., & EELS, K. *Social Class in America.* New York: Harper & Row, 1960.

WEBER, M. The social psychology of the world religions. In *From Max Weber,* translated by Hans Gerth and C. Wright Mills. New York: Oxford University Press, 1946, 267-301.

WECTER, D. *When Johnny Comes Marching Home.* Cambridge, Mass.: Houghton Mifflin, 1944.

WEINBERG, S. K. Social psychological aspects of neurotic anxiety. In S. K. Weinberg (Ed.), *The Sociology of Mental Disorders.* Chicago: Aldine, 1967.

WEINSTEIN, E. The function of interpersonal relations in the neurosis of combat. *Psychiatry,* 1947, 10:307-314.

WEXLER, H. The life master: A case of severe ego regression induced by combat experience in World War II. *Psychoanalytic Study of the Child,* 1972, 27:568-597.

WHITEHEAD, A. N. *Science and the Modern World.* New York: Mentor, 1948.

WHITEHEAD, A. N. *Modes of Thought.* New York: Capricorn (Macmillan), 1958.

WHYTE, L. L. *The Next Development in Man.* London: Cresset Press, 1944.

WIKLER, N. J. Vietnam and the veterans' consciousness. Paper presented at the annual meeting of the Pacific Sociological Association, San Jose, California, March 1974.

WILNER, N. & HOROWITZ, M. J. Intrusive and repetitive thought after a depressing film: A pilot study. *Psychological Reports,* 1975, 37:135-138.

WILSON, J. P. & DOYLE, C. Identity, ideology and crisis: The Vietnam veterans in transition. Paper presented at the American Psychological Association Conference, San Francisco, August, 1977.

WILSON, J. P. *Identity, Ideology, and Crisis: The Vietnam Veteran in Transition, Part I.* A partial preliminary report submitted to the Disabled American Veterans Association, Forgotten Warrior Project. Mimeographed, Cleveland State University, 1977.

WINNICOTT, D. *The Maturational Process and the Facilitating Environment.* New York: International Universities Press, Inc., 1956.

WINNICOTT, D. The use of an object. *International Journal of Psychoanalysis,* 1969, 50:711-716.

WINNIK, H. Z. Psychiatric disturbances of holocaust ("shoa") survivors. *Israel Annuals of Psychiatry and Related Disciplines,* 1967, 5:91-100.

Winning Hearts and Minds: Poems by Vietnam Veterans. Brooklyn, New York: First Casualty Press, 1972.

WORTHINGTON, E. R. *The Vietnam-era Veterans Adjustment and Anomie.* Unpublished doctoral dissertation, University of Utah, 1973.

WORTHINGTON, E. R. Post-service adjustment and Vietnam-era veterans. Paper presented at the 83rd annual convention, American Psychological Association, August 1975.

WORTHINGTON, E. R. The Vietnam era veteran, anomie and adjustment. *Military Medicine,* 1976, 141:169-170 (a).

WORTHINGTON, E. R. Human factors evaluation of training methods. *Symposium Proceedings, 5th Symposium on Psychology in the Air Force.* U.S.A.F. Academy, 1976, 181-183 (b).

WORTHINGTON, E. R. The American soldier: Those who make it and those who do not. Regional Conference, Inter-University Seminar of Armed Forces and Society, Arizona State University, Tempe, Arizona, February 1976. (ERIC Document Reproduction Service, in press.)

WORTHINGTON, E. R. The Vietnam-era veteran, anomie and adjustment. *Military Medicine,* 1977, 142.

YANKELOVICH, D. *A Study of American Youth.* New York: McGraw-Hill, 1974.

YANKELOVICH, E. & BARRETT, W. *Ego and Instinct.* New York: Random House, 1970.

YEZZO, D. *A G. I.'s Diary.* New York: Franklin-Watts, 1974.

ZARCONE, V. P., SCOTT, N. R., & KAUVER, K. B. Psychiatric problems of Vietnam veterans. *Comprehensive Psychiatry,* 1977, 18:41-53.

NAME INDEX

SUBJECT INDEX